W9-BGY-599

Freedom, Power and Political Morality

Felix E. Oppenheim

Freedom, Power and Political Morality

Essays for Felix Oppenheim

Edited by

Ian Carter
Research Fellow
University of Pavia
Italy

and

Mario Ricciardi
Research Fellow
University of Milan
Italy

palgrave

Editorial matter and selection © Ian Carter and Mario Ricciardi 2001
Chapter 3 © Mario Ricciardi 2001
Chapter 6 © Ian Carter 2001
Chapters 1, 2, 4, 5, 7–14 © Palgrave Publishers Ltd 2001

All rights reserved. No reproduction, copy or transmission of
this publication may be made without written permission.

No paragraph of this publication may be reproduced, copied or
transmitted save with written permission or in accordance with
the provisions of the Copyright, Designs and Patents Act 1988,
or under the terms of any licence permitting limited copying
issued by the Copyright Licensing Agency, 90 Tottenham Court
Road, London W1P 0LP.

Any person who does any unauthorised act in relation to this
publication may be liable to criminal prosecution and civil
claims for damages.

The authors have asserted their rights to be identified
as the authors of this work in accordance with the
Copyright, Designs and Patents Act 1988.

First published 2001 by
PALGRAVE
Houndmills, Basingstoke, Hampshire RG21 6XS and
175 Fifth Avenue, New York, N.Y. 10010
Companies and representatives throughout the world

PALGRAVE is the new global academic imprint of
St. Martin's Press LLC Scholarly and Reference Division and
Palgrave Publishers Ltd (formerly Macmillan Press Ltd).

ISBN 0–333–76332–7

This book is printed on paper suitable for recycling and
made from fully managed and sustained forest sources.

A catalogue record for this book is available
from the British Library.

Library of Congress Cataloging-in-Publication Data
Freedom, power, and political morality : essays for Felix
Oppenheim / edited by Ian Carter and Mario Ricciardi.
        p. cm.
    Includes bibliographical references and index.
    ISBN 0–333–76332–7
    1. Liberty. 2. Power (Social sciences) 3. Political ethics.
    4. International relations—Moral and ethical aspects.
    I. Oppenheim, Felix E., 1913– II. Carter, Ian, 1964–
    III. Ricciardi, Mario, 1967–
    JC585 .F743 2000
    172—dc21
                                                        00–066574

10   9   8   7   6   5   4   3   2   1
10   09   08   07   06   05   04   03   02   01

Printed in Great Britain by Antony Rowe Ltd, Chippenham, Wiltshire

Contents

Notes on the Contributors

Terence Ball is Professor of Political Science at Arizona State University. He is the author of *Rousseau's Ghost: a Novel* (1998), *Reappraising Political Theory* (1995) and *Transforming Political Discourse* (1988), and co-editor of the forthcoming *Cambridge History of Twentieth-Century Political Thought*.

Hugo Adam Bedau is Austin Fletcher Professor of Philosophy Emeritus at Tufts University. An honorary fellow with the Bentham Project at University College London, he is also the author or editor of several books, including *The Death Penalty in America* (1964, 1982, 1997) and *Making Mortal Choices* (1997).

Norberto Bobbio is Emeritus Professor of Political Philosophy at the University of Turin, Italy, and has written extensively on legal and political philosophy. English translations of his works include *Democracy and Dictatorship* (1989), *Thomas Hobbes and the Natural Law Tradition* (1993), *The Age of Rights* (1996) and *Left and Right* (1996).

Luigi Bonanate is Professor of International Relations at the University of Turin, Italy, and has written on strategy, nuclear deterrence, international terrorism and the general theory of international relations. He is the author of *Ethics and International Politics* (1995).

Ian Carter is a Research Fellow in Political Philosophy at the University of Pavia, Italy. He has written on the concepts of freedom and equality, and is the author of *A Measure of Freedom* (1999).

Amedeo G. Conte is Professor of Philosophy of Law at the University of Pavia, Italy. He is the author of *Filosofia del linguaggio normativo*, volume I (*studi 1965–81*) and volume II (*studi 1982–94*), both published in 1995, and of *Filosofia dell'ordinamento normativo. Studi 1957–1968*, published in 1997.

Paolo Di Lucia is Professor of Philosophy of Law at the University of Camerino, Italy. He is the author of *Deontica in von Wright* (1992) and

L'Universale della promessa (1997). He is currently working on a book on legal ontology and the philosophy of action.

Jean Bethke Elshtain is the Laura Spelman Rockefeller Professor of Social and Political Ethics at the University of Chicago. Her books include *Public Man, Private Woman: Women in Social and Political Thought* (1981), *Democracy on Trial* (1995) and *Real Politics: at the Centre of Everyday Life* (1997).

George Kateb is William Nelson Cromwell Professor of Politics at Princeton University. His most recent book is *Emerson and Self-Reliance* (1995).

Thomas Pogge is Professor of Philosophy at Columbia University and has written extensively in moral and political philosophy and on Kant. He is currently at the Princeton Institute for Advanced Study, completing a book entitled *Real World Justice*.

Mario Ricciardi is a Research Fellow in Jurisprudence at the University of Milan and Lecturer in Jurisprudence at the 'C. Cattaneo' University, Castellanza, Italy. He has written on collective rights, the philosophy of action and causation in the criminal law. He is currently working on a book on responsibility.

Hillel Steiner is Professor of Political Philosophy at the University of Manchester. He is the author of *An Essay on Rights* (1994) and (with Matthew Kramer and Nigel Simmonds) *A Debate Over Rights: Philosophical Enquiries* (1998), and editor (with Peter Vallentyne) of a two-volume anthology on left-libertarianism (2000).

Mark R. Weaver is Professor of Political Science at the College of Wooster. His most recent written work has focused on Machiavelli's conception of political leadership, civic republicanism as a model of political reform, and Weber's formulation of the proper role of the social scientist.

Introduction

Ian Carter and Mario Ricciardi

Felix Oppenheim began his long intellectual career as one of the most forceful representatives of a new philosophical movement which used the sharp instruments of logical analysis and semantic reconstruction to model new ways of thinking about politics and law. His first main work, published in 1944, is one of the earliest examples of the application of Carnap's logical analysis to the field of law. More than fifty years of subsequent research have seen the publication of numerous articles and four books devoted to the analysis of fundamental political concepts like freedom, equality, power and interests, to metaethics applied to political issues, and to international relations. Much time has passed, but Felix has continued to work with patience and intellectual honesty *per metter ordine al gran disordine.*

Commentators in earlier years rightly considered Oppenheim's approach a revolutionary one, while many now see it as outdated and of purely antiquarian interest. Logical analysis and conceptual reconstruction are today often perceived as the annoying fixations of pipe-smoking philosophers interested only in preliminary or purely academic questions. All too often we hear it said that conceptual analysis is too abstract, that all forms of rationality are 'context-dependent', and that the most we can do is struggle to bring about change (if change happens to be what we desire).

The idea of dedicating a collection of essays to Felix Oppenheim is certainly no tribute to these recent tendencies. Its realization is testimony to an intellectual debt felt by many colleagues and former students both to Oppenheim's work and, no less, to the dedication and generosity with which he has contributed to their philosophical development – commenting, dissenting, suggesting alternative hypotheses and exposing confusions or lapses into rhetoric. Fashions pass, but the ideas behind them remain. It may be true that those who once seemed revolutionary tend today to appear the conservative opponents of methodological change. But is it not right to ask those who would have us abandon the rigours of conceptual analysis and follow some alternative methodological course to provide us with a coherent account of where, exactly, they wish to take us? Oppenheim's work continues to remind us of the importance of asking questions like this. It reminds us of the importance of providing reasons and arguments for our theses, of being clear and precise about the questions we are posing, and of not being in too much of a hurry to arrive at particular answers.

We should conclude our brief introduction to this volume with a note about the subject matter of the individual essays. Our original proposal for the volume consisted in an invitation to contribute essays on themes related to the work of Felix Oppenheim. We expected, and received, contributions on fundamental political and legal concepts and on the nature and scope of political morality. Reading the essays, however, we were pleased to see that many of the authors had gone further and had taken up issues on which they disagreed with their old friend and colleague, directly criticizing particular aspects of his work. For this reason, we asked Oppenheim to conclude the volume with a reply. We mention this by way of apology to those of our authors who, because they simply followed our original instructions, have been denied the privilege of having their arguments rebutted.

Part I
Normative Analysis and Political Concepts

1

Felix Oppenheim's Deontics

Paolo Di Lucia

> All questions of law are no more than questions concerning the import of words. Questions the solution of which depends upon skill in metaphysics.
>
> Jeremy Bentham

Introduction

The German noun 'Deontik' (*Deontics*) and adjective 'deontisch' (*deontic*) were both invented in 1926. Both are due to the Austrian philosopher and logician Ernst Mally, author of *Grundgesetze des Sollens*.[1]

Mally uses the noun 'deontics' to refer to a counterpart of logic (*Gegenstück der Logik*). In Mally's words:

> Alongside the logic of thought should be placed a discipline that can be called the logic of the will. But this is not a part of logic, as in the case of the logic of concepts or the logic of judgement; rather, it has to do with the essential laws governing the way we relate to objects, which is not itself thought. Therefore it is better to give this counterpart of logic its own name: something like 'deontics'.[2]

Independently of Mally, the adjective 'deontic' reappeared in 1951 in the article 'Deontic Logic' by Georg Henrik von Wright. Unlike Mally, von Wright uses this adjective to qualify that part of modal logic dealing with 'deontic modes or modes of obligation. These are concepts such as the obligatory (that which we ought to do), the permitted (that which we are allowed to do), and the forbidden (that which we must not do).'[3]

Neither the noun 'deontics' nor the adjective 'deontic' occur in Felix Oppenheim's pioneering 1942 essay, 'Outline of a Logical Analysis of Law'. However, that essay does anticipate a number of theses now taken for granted in deontics. In particular, Oppenheim's essay marks the birth of semiotics as applied to legal language, and anticipates theses found in two major research areas of deontics – two research areas which Georg Henrik von Wright (the most important of the founders of deontic logic) describes as the *semantics of deontic language* on the one hand, and *deontic logic* on the other.[4]

This chapter concentrates on Felix Oppenheim's place in the history of deontics.[5] Section 1 is devoted to the semiotic construction of law in Oppenheim's work, while sections 2 and 3 are devoted respectively to his analysis of the semantico-pragmatical properties and syntactical properties of sentences-of-law.

1. Felix Oppenheim's semiotic construction of law

1.1. Law and language: a comparison of Oppenheim and Bobbio

In the history of the study of the relation between law and language, the idea of a *comparison* between law and language goes back a long way. We find this idea, for example, in the work of Hume, according to whom this comparison is one of those that can be made between three variables: law, language and exchange value. Hume compares law with natural languages on the one hand, and with money on the other:

> In like manner are languages gradually establish'd by human conventions without any promise. In like manner do gold and silver become the common measures of exchanges, and are esteem'd sufficient payment for what is of a hundred times their value.[6]

A much more recent idea is that of the *equation* of law with language: the *linguistic* conception of law. The equation of law with language has been affirmed twice during the last century, independently, and in works loosely inspired by the methodology of logical positivism. It was first affirmed by Felix Oppenheim in 'Outline of a Logical Analysis of Law' (1942)[7] and was then to appear eight years later in Norberto Bobbio's 'Scienza del diritto e analisi del linguaggio' (1950).[8]

Both Oppenheim and Bobbio, then, affirm the linguistic nature of law. They both equate law with language. Moreover, both Oppenheim and Bobbio affirm a natural corollary of this equation: the *metalinguistic* nature of the science of law. Let us begin by comparing the approaches of these two authors.

1.2. A similarity in Oppenheim's and Bobbio's law-as-language theses

Oppenheim's law-as-language thesis

The main aim of Oppenheim's work was to demonstrate the possibility of applying logical analysis to the field of jurisprudence, and the '*usefulness* of this method for exhibiting some essential features of the law'.[9] In Oppenheim's words:

> Logical analysis has been applied until now chiefly in mathematics, logic, and some of the natural sciences. In order to show that logical analysis can be applied in the field of jurisprudence as well, we must first point out that law may be viewed as language.[10]

Oppenheim's fundamental presupposition, then, is that we see the law of any given community as a class of *sentences* constituting a *language*.[11]

> Legal rules, decisions, commands, are generally expressed by words and expressions of a natural language, like English. If non-linguistic signs are used – e.g., the whistle of the policeman, stoplights, gestures – it is always possible to translate them into the word-language. We may therefore consider the law of any given community at any given moment as a class of *sentences*, constituting a *language* which expresses the legal rules, decisions, commands of that community at that moment.[12]

Bobbio's law-as-language thesis

Eight years later, Bobbio developed a thesis along similar lines. As in the case of Oppenheim, Bobbio begins by examining the epistemological and gnoseological foundations of the science of law.

> My first move will consist in tackling the problem which has become a traditional starting point for all research on legal methodology, namely the extent to which jurisprudence can be considered a science.[13]

Bobbio believes an affirmative answer can be given to this question, but only on condition that the law be conceived as a set of sentences: the set of normative propositions of the legislator:

We shall focus our attention on what constitutes the real work of the jurist proper. Rules are expressed in propositions which may be described as normative, since they have ideal rather than actual validity. The object of the jurist's research is a set of normative propositions.[14]

Bobbio ascribes the same value to the propositions of the legislator that the scientist ascribes to protocol sentences (*Protokollsätze*). In this way, legislative language becomes the *Protokollsprache* (protocol language) of the science of law. According to Bobbio, for the jurist, legislative sentences constitute the protocols (*Protokolle*) of juridical experience.

Oppenheim and Bobbio on the science of law as the analysis of the language of law

Oppenheim's and Bobbio's conceptions of law as language (or, more precisely, the idea that every example of law is a text) therefore has immediate consequences for the way in which the science of law is conceived: this science, as a science *of* law, is the metalanguage[15] of the object-language[16] which is law. Let us see, more analytically, how Oppenheim and Bobbio arrive at this conclusion.

According to Oppenheim, 'since any kind of legal system constitutes a group of sentences (of law), it follows that any kind of science of law must consist of sentences *about* sentences (of law), thus of sentences of the second category.'[17] The task of jurisprudence is to apply 'logical analysis' to law: 'the logical analysis of a language expressing the law of a certain country at a certain time. This task consists, as we have seen, in constructing a "corresponding" language-system and in establishing its syntactical, semantical and pragmatical properties.'[18]

The same thesis (that the science of law is the metalanguage of the object-language which is law) can be found in the work of Italian analytic legal philosophers such as Norberto Bobbio and Uberto Scarpelli.[19] According to Bobbio, the founder of the Italian analytic school, the 'science of law is thus essentially an analysis of language, more precisely of the language through which the legislator expresses himself through normative propositions.'[20] In other words, and to use an expression common among logical positivists, 'the jurist is concerned with defining the grammar of the particular language which is the language of that particular legislator'.[21]

1.3. A dissimilarity between Oppenheim's and Bobbio's law-as-language theses

How are the theses of Oppenheim and Bobbio (and their respective corollaries) related? Are the two theses semantically equivalent? At first glance, it would seem so. In fact, however, this is not the case.

Bobbio's redefinition of the science of law

In Bobbio's work, the thesis according to which the science of law is the analysis of legal language is equivalent to a *redefinition* of the science of law in terms of the logic and semantics of legislative texts. Bobbio's concern is above all to deny that the science of law has any object other than the text of the legislator and any method other than that of the logico-semantic interpretation of a text. As Bobbio writes:

> The core of operations, in the case of jurisprudence, is but the *inter-pretation of law*, the job, by long standing tradition, of the jurist. And what is the interpretation of law if not the analysis of legisla-tive language, of the language in which legal rules are expressed? But if the analysis of legal language and legal interpretation are one and the same thing, and if the analysis of language is indeed the scientific part of the work of the jurist, we would have to conclude that the jurist in the traditional sense, by doing his job of interpret-ing the law, in fact constructs the science of law. In other words, there is no such thing as a science of law outside the activity of the interpreting jurist. Precisely in his role of interpreter he will perform that very linguistic analysis which no science can forsake and will construct that rigorous language which forms the essence of any research claiming scientific status. This he will do in full accordance with the modern conception of science which shifted the criterion of what is scientific from truth to rigour.[22]

In claiming that the science of law is the logical analysis of law, then, Bobbio limits himself to *redefining* the science of law as the logico-semantic analysis of legislative texts.

Oppenheim's foundation of legal semiotics

This is not so in the case of Oppenheim, whose essay specifies, *ex novo*, the confines of what can only be described as a new discipline: the semiotic analysis of sentences-of-law.

The novelty of Oppenheim's approach to the science of law, regarding both its object and its method, was clearly emphasized by the Polish philosopher Georges Kalinowski in his 1980 preface to the Spanish translation of Oppenheim's essay:

> F. E. Oppenheim thus initiated a new legal discipline: semiotics. His essay marks a new epoch, because it marks the birth of the legal semiotics, conceived as pure semiotics composed of pure syntactics, semantics and pragmatics. By this means, Oppenheim distanced himself slightly from R. Carnap for whom pragmatics was in itself empirical or, to put it another way, *a posteriori*; he thus anticipated R. M. Martin who, only in 1958, was to construct a pure *a priori* pragmatics in *Towards a Systematic Pragmatics*.[23]

On this very idea of the specificity of the pragmatic dimension of the language of law, Oppenheim had himself written:

> One of the particularities of any language of law consists in the fact that the validity – in the sense of correctness – of its sentences depends not only upon syntactical and semantical, but also upon pragmatical conditions.[24]

2.   Oppenheim's legal semiotics

2.1.   What are sentences-of-law?

According to Oppenheim, legal semiotics deals with semiotic (syntactic, semantic, pragmatic) *properties of sentences* constituting the *language of law*:

> It is convenient for the purpose of exhibiting the syntactical, semantical and pragmatical features of a certain language, to establish syntactical, semantical, pragmatical rules for a purified form of this language. This purified language must, of course, constitute an exact model of the language as it stands.[25]

But what, exactly, are *sentences-of-law*? Oppenheim's answer can be usefully interpreted as consisting of *two* theses.

The *first* is a *methodological* thesis: according to Oppenheim, in order to know which sentences are sentences-of-law, we must investigate the whole to which sentences-of-law belong: the legal system.

The *second* is an *ontological* thesis: according to Oppenheim, the whole just referred to (the legal system) is not the totality of sentences-of-law, but the totality of relationships between sentences-of-law. As Louis Hjelmslev says, '[a] totality does not consist of *things* but of relationships'.[26]

2.2.   Oppenheim's methodological and ontological theses on sentences-of-law

The methodological thesis

According to Oppenheim, in order to investigate which sentences are sentences-of-law we must investigate the whole to which sentences-of-law belong: the legal system.

The strategy Oppenheim adopts for investigating the juridicity of *sentences-of-law* anticipates (by a few years) that adopted by Bobbio for investigating the juridicity of *norms*. As Bobbio writes in *Teoria dell'ordinamento giuridico*, juridicity is not a property of single norms, but of systems – that is, of sets of norms:

> What we call law is usually more a feature of certain normative systems than a feature of certain norms. ... Given this, in order to define a juridical norm it is sufficient to say that the juridical norm belongs to a juridical system, thus clearly shifting the problem of determining what 'juridical' means from the level of norm to that of system.[27]

The ontological thesis

Oppenheim's second thesis in answer to the question 'what are sentences-of-law?' is, as I have said, an *ontological* thesis: according to Oppenheim, the legal system to which the sentences-of-law belong, is not a totality of *sentences* (sentences of a single kind) but a totality of *relationships* (between sentences of different kinds).

My interpretation of Oppenheim's thesis seems to be confirmed by the fact that the members of the set of sentences constituting the language of law are not homogeneous sentences-of-law. Oppenheim enumerates four heterogeneous kinds of sentence-of-law:

(i)   sentences capable of being either true or false (expressing *decisions* like 'John is guilty of larceny');

(ii) sentences not capable of being either true or false (expressing *rules* like 'If x is guilty of larceny, x is punishable by imprisonment');

(iii)   sentences that have an *imperative* meaning (expressing *rules* like 'If x is guilty of larceny, x is punishable by imprisonment');

(iv)   sentences that have *declarative* meaning (expressing *definitions* like 'x is guilty of homicide if and only if x is guilty of murder, or manslaughter').

Under what conditions do sentences of different kinds share the property of being sentences-of-law? Or, to put the question another way, what are the necessary and/or sufficient conditions for sentences of different kinds to be parts of that whole, constituted not by *things* but by *relationships*, which is a legal system?

2.3.   Three semiotic validity-conditions of sentences-of-law

The language of law as a three-dimensional whole

According to the methodological thesis, in order to know which sentences are sentences-of-law we must investigate the whole to which sentences-of-law belong: the legal system. According to the ontological thesis, the legal system is not a totality of things (sentences), but a totality of relationships (between sentences). What kinds of relationships? According to Oppenheim, the whole just referred is not a totality of *sentences*, but a totality of *semiotic relationships* – that is, of *syntactical* relationships between sentences, of *semantical* relationships between sentences and their *designata*, and of *pragmatical* relationships between sentences and their interpreters. The language of law is, in Oppenheim's view, a *three-dimensional* whole.

Oppenheim's three negative theses

That the whole of which a sentence-of-law is a part is, for Oppenheim, a three-dimensional whole, is confirmed by three negative theses sustained by Oppenheim: being-a-sentence-of-law is *neither* a syntactical property, *nor* a semantical property, *nor* a pragmatical property.

   (i) *First negative thesis.* A sentence-of-law has syntactic validity-conditions, but its being-a-sentence-of-law is not itself a syntactical property. It is true that the satisfaction of a syntactical validity-condition (being valid or non-valid) is a necessary condition for sentences expressing *rules* (for example, 'If x is guilty of larceny, x is punishable by imprisonment'), for sentences expressing *definitions* (for example, 'x is guilty of homicide if and only if x is guilty of murder, or manslaughter') and for sentences expressing *decisions* (for example, 'John is guilty of larceny') to be sentences-of-law.[28]

But it is nevertheless false that being-a-sentence-of-law is a syntactical property (the syntactical property of being valid or non-valid), either in the case of apophantic sentences (i.e. sentences which are true-or-false), such as those expressing *decisions* (for example, 'John is guilty of larceny'), or in the case of non-apophantic sentences (i.e. sentences which are not true-or-false), such as those expressing *rules* (for example, 'If x is guilty of larceny, x is punishable by imprisonment') or expressing *definitions* (for example, 'x is guilty of homicide if and only if x is guilty of murder, or manslaughter').

(ii) *Second negative thesis*. A sentence-of-law has semantic validity-conditions, but its being-a-sentence-of-law is not itself a semantical property. It is true that the satisfaction of a semantic validity-condition (being true or false) is a necessary condition for sentences expressing *decisions* (for example, 'John is guilty of larceny') to be sentences-of-law.[29] But it is nevertheless false that being-a-sentence-of-law is a semantical property (the semantical property of being true or false) in the case of apophantic sentences such as those expressing *decisions* (for example, 'John is guilty of larceny').

(iii) *Third negative thesis*. A sentence-of-law has pragmatical validity-conditions, but its being-a-sentence-of-law is not itself a pragmatical property. It is true that the satisfaction of a pragmatical validity-condition (having or lacking 'official quality'), is a necessary condition for sentences expressing *rules* (for example, 'If x is guilty of larceny, x is punishable by imprisonment'), for sentences expressing *definitions* (for example, 'x is guilty of homicide if and only if x is guilty of murder, or manslaughter') and for sentences expressing *decisions* (for example, 'John is guilty of larceny') to be sentences-of-law.[30] But it is nevertheless false that being-a-sentence-of-law is therefore a pragmatical property (the pragmatical property of having or lacking 'official quality'), either in the case of apophantic sentences such as those expressing *decisions* (for example, 'John is guilty of larceny') or in the case of non-apophantic sentences such as those expressing *rules* (for example, 'If x is guilty of larceny, x is punishable by imprisonment') or expressing *definitions* (for example, 'x is guilty of homicide if and only if x is guilty of murder, or manslaughter').

I have enumerated three validity-conditions of sentences of law: a *syntactical* validity-condition, a *semantical* validity-condition, and a *pragmatical* validity-condition. These validity-conditions are disjunctively (disjointly) necessary and conjunctively (jointly) sufficient conditions. According to Oppenheim, then, to qualify as a sentence-of-law it is sufficient that a sentence jointly statisfy three validity-conditions: a syntactical validity-condition (validity in the language of law), a semantical validity-condition (truth in the language of law), and a pragmatical validity-condition (officiality in the language of law).

Apophantic and non-apophantic sentences of law do not have the same necessary validity-conditions.

(i) Syntactic validity and pragmatic validity are disjunctively (disjointly) necessary and conjunctively (jointly) sufficient conditions for sentences expressing *rules* (sentences not capable of being true or false) and for sentences expressing *definitions* (sentences capable of being true or false) to qualify as sentences-of-law.

(ii) Syntactic validity, semantic validity and pragmatic validity are disjunctively necessary and conjunctively sufficient conditions for sentences expressing *decisions* (sentences capable of being true or false) to qualify as sentences-of-law.

Emphasizing the importance of the pragmatic dimension of the language of law and of the metalanguage of the science of law, Oppenheim concludes:

> These considerations demonstrate the fundamental difference between the language of *science* and the language of *law*. Science is interested merely in the validity or truth of its statements. Sentences of law, however, may not only have the syntactical property of being valid or non-valid and the semantical property of being true or false, but also the pragmatical property of having or lacking official quality.[31]

2.4.   Graphic representations of Oppenheim's two classes of sentences-of-law

The set of *sentences-of-law* is not homogeneous, but comprises two subsets: a set of non-apophantic sentences-of-law, that is, *rules and definitions* not capable of being true or false (respective examples being 'If x is guilty of larceny, x is punishable by imprisonment', and 'x is guilty of homicide if and only if x is guilty of murder, or manslaughter') and a set of apophantic sentences-of-law, that is, *decisions* capable of being true or false (for example: 'John is guilty of larceny').

(i) The first subset (the class of sentences of law *not capable of being true or false*) is the intersection (represented by the shaded area in figure 1) of *two* different classes of sentences: a class of syntactically valid sentences-of-law, and a class of pragmatically valid sentences-of-law.

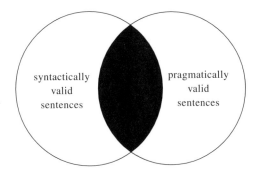

Figure 1   The shaded area represents sentences-of-law not capable of being true or false (*rules and definitions*).

(ii) The second subset (the class of sentences of law *capable of being true or false*) corresponds, on the other hand, to the intersection (represented by the shaded area in figure 2) of *three* different classes of sentence: a class of syntactically valid sentences-of-law, a class of pragmatically valid sentences-of-law, and a class of semantically valid sentences-of-law.

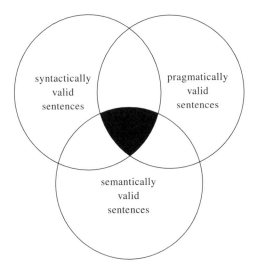

Figure 2   The shaded area represents sentences-of-law capable of being true or false (*decisions*).

3.   Oppenheim's deontics

3.1.   Deontic logic vs. Oppenheim's syntax of sentences-of-law

Oppenheim's 1942 essay not only marked the birth of a new discipline (the semiotics of legal language), but can also be seen as an original contribution to a discipline that was only to come fully into being at the beginning of the 1950s: *deontic logic*.[32]

Within deontic logic there are (as Amedeo G. Conte has stressed), two logically independent questions.[33]

The *first question* concerns *deontic truths*. Are there *deontic formulas* which are logically true in virtue of the meaning of the deontic terms occurring in them? (In other words: Are there *deontic-logical* truths?)

The *second question* concerns not deontic truths but the logical behaviour of *deontic sentences*. Can deontic sentences be terms of logical *entailment-relationships*? (In other words: Are there *logical entailment-relationships* between deontic sentences?)

As Conte says, the answer to the second question will necessarily be negative if we make the following assumptions:

(i)   Logical entailment-relationships can only exist between *apophantic* sentences (i.e. between sentences which are true-or-false);
(ii) Deontic sentences are *anapophantic* (i.e. non-apophantic) sentences.

Oppenheim does not address the first question, but he does address the second. And the answer he gives to this second question is still of considerable relevance to contemporary deontics.

3.2.   Oppenheim's hypothesis about the possibility of deduction-relationships between sentences-of-law

In his 1942 essay, Oppenheim raises the question whether there are logical relations between sentences-of-law (in particular, whether there can be a logical relation of deduction between sentences belonging to the same legal system). In Oppenheim's words:

> We do not intend to force logic into law, but to investigate what kind of logical relations exist between the sentences of a given system of law. To carry out this program of logical analysis of law, we should choose a certain legal system: the whole law or a certain part of the law of a certain community at a certain time.[34]

According to Oppenheim, we may state, within the language of law, a certain number of primitive sentences. By applying certain transformation rules (i.e. rules of logic), we may deduce from these *primitive sentences* other sentences which are called *derived sentences*. Oppenheim provides two examples:

(i) *First example.* From the two *basic* sentences:
'If x is guilty of larceny, x is punishable by imprisonment'
and
'John is guilty of larceny'
we can deduce the *derived* sentence:
'John is punishable by imprisonment'.[35]

(ii) *Second example.* From the two *basic* sentences:
'X is guilty of murder if and only if x is guilty of killing ... etc.'
and
'Jack is guilty of killing ... etc.'
we can deduce the *derived* sentence:
'Jack is guilty of murder'.[36]

According to Oppenheim, these logical relations of *deduction* between sentences are valid solely in virtue of the form of the sentences themselves, *without referring either to the meaning or to the truth-value* of the sentences-of-law.

3.3. A comparison between Oppenheim's contribution and Stzykgold's fragment of deontics.

Oppenheim's thesis that one sentence-of-law can be deduced from another was anticipated six years earlier by Jerzy Stzykgold, an author not named by Oppenheim. But there is a great difference between the two theses.

Sztykgold defends the possibility of deductive relations between norms by attributing to them a semantic property analogous to truth: that of 'rightness' (*słuszność*). In Stzykgold's view, it is in virtue of the analogy between rightness and truth that deontic sentences can be terms of logical entailment-relationships.[37] Invoking a deontic analogue of truth, he presupposes therefore the traditional view according to which only apophantic sentences (i.e. sentences which are true-or-false) can be terms of logical-entailment relationships.

Oppenheim's thesis, on the contrary, does not invoke any deontic analogue of truth (for instance rightness or validity or fulfilment). In Oppenheim's view, the logical relations between sentences-of-law hold *without referring to any semantic value* – either to *truth-value* or to any other semantic value, like *rightness-value.*

Notes

1. However, the English noun 'deontics', used in the sense of 'deontology', occurs as early as the nineteenth century – for example, in John Grote, *A Treatise on the Moral Ideas* (Cambridge: Bell, 1876).
2. 'Der Logik des Denkens soll etwas an die Seite gestellt werden, das eine Logik des Willens heißen kann; aber da es nicht um ein Teilgebiet der Logik – wie z.b. die Logik des Begriffs, die Logik des Urteils – handelt, sondern um die Wesensgesetze eines Verhaltens zu Gegenständen, das kein Denken ist, mag diese Gegenstück der Logik besser einen selbständigen Namen, etwa den der Deontik haben.' Ernst Mally, *Grundgesetze des Sollens. Elemente der Logik des Willens* (Graz: Leuschner und Lubensky, 1926), reprinted in Ernst Mally, *Logische Schriften* (Dordrecht: Reidel, 1971, pp. 227–324), p. 232. The same year saw the appearance of another important contribution to deontics: Jean Ray, *Essai sur la structure logique du code civil français* (Paris: Alcan, 1926).
3. Georg Henrik von Wright, 'Deontic Logic', *Mind*, 60 (1951), pp. 1–15. At note 1 von Wright says that he is indebted for the term 'deontic' to professor Charlie Dunbar Broad (1887–1971). Broad had introduced 'deontic' in his essay 'Imperatives, Categorical and Hypothetical', *The Philosopher*, 2 (1950), pp. 62–75. As Amedeo G. Conte has pointed out, in the German form 'deontisch', the term 'deontic' also appeared in a posthumous work by Oskar Fechner: *Das System der ontischen Kategorien. Grundlegung der Allgemeinen Ontologie oder Metaphysik*, 1961. On deontic modes the most up-to-date work is Andrea Rossetti, *Modi deontici nell'ordinamento giuridico* (Padova: CEDAM, forthcoming).
4. 'By deontics should be understood the general theory of duty, that is, of normative concepts and of normative systems. The analysis of normative concepts (of deontic concepts) and of their relations to concepts belonging to the sphere of being (ontic concepts) constitute the object of the semantics of normative language. Deontic logic consists in the application of the methods of exact, modern logic (axiomatization, formalization, and so on) to the problems of deontics.'
   'Unter *Deontik* versteht man die allgemeine Theorie des Sollens, also der normativen Begriffe und der Normensysteme. Die Analyse der normativen Begriffe (der deontische Begriffe) und ihr Verhalten zu den Seinsbegriffen (zu den ontischen Begriffe) ist Gegenstand der *Semantik der normativen Sprache*. *Deontische Logik* wiederum besteht in der Anwendung der Methoden der modernen exakten Logik (Axiomatisierung, Formalisierung u. dgl.) auf die Probleme der Deontik.' Cf. Georg Henrik von Wright, *Zur*

Einführung, in Amedeo G. Conte, Risto Hilpinen and Georg Henrik von Wright (eds), *Deontische Logik und Semantik* (Wiesbaden: Athenaion, 1977), p. 1.

5. On the history of deontics see the works collected in Giuseppe Lorini, *Il valore logico e la logica delle norme* (Pavia, Ms. forthcoming).
6. David Hume, *A Treatise of Human Nature* (Oxford: Clarendon Press, 1978), p. 490.
7. Felix E. Oppenheim, 'Outline of a Logical Analysis of Law.' PhD Dissertation, Princeton University, November 1942. An abridged version appeared in *Philosophy of Science*, 11 (1944), pp. 142–60. Cf. Nelson Goodman's review of Oppenheim, 'Outline of a Logical Analysis of Law', *Journal of Symbolic Logic*, 9 (1944), pp. 105–6, and Everett W. Hall, *What is Value? An Essay in Philosophical Analysis* (New York: Humanities Press, 1952), pp. 120–3.
   The published version of Oppenheim's essay has been translated into two foreign languages. A first translation in Spanish by Carlos Santiago Nino, *Lineamientos de un análisis lógico del derecho* (Valencia, Venezuela: Oficina Latinoamericana de Investigaciones Jurídicas y Sociales, 1980), was published with a preface (pp. 11–12) by Georges Kalinowski, one of the founders of deontic logic. A second translation into Italian by Mario Ricciardi, *Lineamenti di analisi logica del diritto*, appeared in U. Scarpelli and P. Di Lucia (eds), *Il linguaggio del diritto* (Milano: LED, 1994), pp. 59–85.
8. Norberto Bobbio, 'Scienza del diritto e analisi del linguaggio', in *Saggi di critica delle scienze* (Turin: Silva, 1950), pp. 21–66. Reprinted in *Rivista trimestrale di diritto e procedura civile*, 4 (1950), pp. 342–67, trans. Zenon Bankowski, 'The Science of Law and the Analysis of Language', in A. Pintore and M. Jori (eds), *Law and Language. The Italian Analytical School* (Liverpool: Deborah Charles Publications, 1997). ('Scienza del diritto e analisi del linguaggio' had been the title of a short note by Uberto Scarpelli which appeared in *Rivista del diritto commerciale*, 46 (1948), pp. 212–16. Scarpelli defended the reducibility of legal language to a Carnapian thing-language. Cf. 'Elementi di analisi della proposizione giuridica', *Jus*, 4 (1953), pp. 42–51.)
9. Oppenheim, 'Outline of a Logical Analysis of Law', 1942, p. 2.
10. Oppenheim, 'Outline of a Logical Analysis of Law', 1942, p. 8.
11. Oppenheim makes an important addition. 'A certain class of sentences may constitute a language. We use this term in a broad sense; thus, we may speak not only of the English language, but also of a language of arithmetic, of physics, of law.' Oppenheim, 'Outline of a Logical Analysis of Law', 1942, p. 6.
12. Oppenheim, 'Outline of a Logical Analysis of Law', 1942, p. 8.
13. Bobbio, 'The Science of Law and the Analysis of Language', p. 21.
14. Bobbio, 'The Science of Law and the Analysis of Language', p. 34. Bobbio does not here distinguish sentences from propositions.
15. The term 'metalanguage' (*métalangage*, *Metasprache*, *metajęzyk*) seems to have been invented by Alfred Tarski, who, however, attributes the intuition behind the concept of a metalanguage to the Polish logician Stanisław Leśniewski.

16. The distinction between *object-language* and *metalanguage* seems to be antic-
     ipated by Hans Kelsen's distinction between *Sollnormen* and *Sollsätze*. On
     the one-to-one correspondence between *Sollnormen* and *Sollsätze* cf. Amedeo
     G. Conte, 'Hans Kelsen's Deontics', in Stanley L. Paulson and Bonnie
     Litschewski Paulson (eds), *Normativity and Norms. Critical Perspectives on
     Kelsenian Themes* (Oxford: Clarendon Press, 1998), pp. 331–41.
17. Oppenheim, 'Outline of a Logical Analysis of Law', 1942, p. 9.
18. Oppenheim, 'Outline of a Logical Analysis of Law', 1942, p. 11.
19. See the works collected in A. Pintore and M. Jori (eds), *Law and Language.
     The Italian Analytical School*.
20. Bobbio, 'The Science of Law and the Analysis of Language', 1997,
     pp. 21–50, p. 35. From the *linguistic conception of law* we must distinguish
     the *linguistic conception of a norm*. On the latter cf. Georg Henrik von Wright,
     Norm and Action. A Logical Enquiry (London: Routledge and Kegan Paul,
     1963).
21. Bobbio, 'The Science of Law and the Analysis of Language', p. 41.
22. Bobbio, 'The Science of Law and the Analysis of Language', pp. 21–50,
     p. 36.
23. 'F. E. Oppenheim ha iniciado así una nueva disciplina jurídica: la semiótica.
     [...] El artículo de F. E. Oppenheim marca una época porque con él nace la
     semiótica del lenguaje del derecho, concebida come semiótica pura, es decir
     compuesta de una sinctáctica, una semántica, y una pragmática puras, con
     lo cual F. E. Oppenheim se separa un poco de R. Carnap para quien la prag-
     mática era, por su naturaleza, empirica, o, dicho de otro modo, *a posteriori*;
     adelantándose así a R. M. Martin quien solamente en 1958 se dedicó a con-
     struir una pragmática pura, *a priori*, en *Towards a systematic pragmatics*.'
     Georges Kalinowski, *Prefacio de* F. E. Oppenheim, *Lineamentos de análisis
     lógico del derecho*, 1980, pp. 11–12. A detailed analysis of Oppenheim's con-
     tribution can be found in G. Kalinowski, *Introduction à la logique juridique*
     (Paris: R. Pichon & R. Durand-Auzias, 1965).
24. Oppenheim, 'Outline of a Logical Analysis of Law', 1942, p. 11.
25. Oppenheim, 'Outline of a Logical Analysis of Law', 1942, p. 6.
26. 'En totalitet bestaar ikke af ting men af sammenhaenge.' Cfr. Louis
     Hjelmslev, *Omkring sprogteoriens grundlaeggelse* (København: E. Munksgaard,
     1943, København, Akademisk Forlag, 1966), p. 22, trans. Francis
     J. Whitfield, *Prolegomena to a Theory of Language* (Madison: University of
     Wisconsin Press, 1961).
27. 'Ciò che noi chiamiamo diritto è di solito un carattere di certi ordinamenti
     normativi più che di certe norme. [...] In questo caso, per definire la
     norma giuridica basterà dire che norma giuridica è quella che appartiene a
     un ordinamento giuridico, rinviando manifestamente il problema di deter-
     minare che cosa significa "giuridico" dalla norma all'ordinamento.'
     N. Bobbio, *Teoria dell'ordinamento giuridico* (Turin: Giappichelli, 1960), p. 15.
28. According to Oppenheim ('Outline of a Logical Analysis of Law', 1942,
     p. 27), 'any sentence occurring within a certain language is valid in that
     language, if and only if it is a primitive or derived sentence in that lan-
     guage'. Oppenheim here traces a useful analogy between *validity* in the lan-
     guage of law and *validity* in the language of arithmetics. 'Thus the following
     sentences are valid within this language of arithmetic: "0 is a number";

"1 is the successor of 0"; "2+2=4"; but "2+2=5" is a non-valid sentence of this language; and " +2=" is not a sentence of arithmetic at all'.

29. As Oppenheim writes ('Outline of a Logical Analysis of Law', 1942 p. 52): 'Many expressions of everyday language, when taken in the legal sense, acquire a different or a more specific meaning, which it is the function of the semantical rules to exhibit, e.g. "guilty of murder" designates the fact of having been adjudged to have killed a human being with the design to effect the death of the person killed. ... This shows that the semantical rules of those predicates in A which designate facts fulfil another purpose besides explaining their meaning; they state the truth-conditions of sentences on which those predicates occur.'

30. 'In order to know if a sentence belonging to a legal system has official quality within that system, it is necessary to make a pragmatical inquiry, namely to ask *who* has stated the sentence in question.' Oppenheim, 'Outline of a Logical Analyisis of Law', 1942, pp. 56–7.

31. Oppenheim, 'Outline of a Logical Analysis of Law', 1942, p. 59.

32. G. H. von Wright, 'Deontic Logic'.

33. Amedeo G. Conte, 'Three Levels of Deontics', in R. Egidi (ed.), *In Search of a New Humanism: the Philosophy of Georg Henrik von Wright* (Dordrecht: Kluwer, 1999), pp. 205–14, at p. 205.

34. Oppenheim, 'Outline of a Logical Analyisis of Law', 1942, p. 15.

35. Oppenheim, 'Outline of a Logical Analyisis of Law', 1942, p. 37.

36. Oppenheim, 'Outline of a Logical Analyisis of Law', 1942, p. 35.

37. Here are the relevant passages (in English) from Jerzy Stzykgold's 'Negacja normy', in *Przeglad filozoficzny*, 39 (1936), pp. 492–4:

(i)   To norms apply the criteria of rightness [*słuszność*] and unrightness [*niesłuszność*]. These criteria (rightness and unrightness) correspond to the criteria of truth [*prawda*] and falsity [*falsz*].

(ii) Therefore, all theses of propositional calculus [*rachunek zdań*] also apply to norms.

On Stzykgold's fragment of deontics, see A. G. Conte, 'Three Levels of Deontics', p. 210.

2
From Hobbes to Oppenheim: Conceptual Reconstruction as Political Engagement*

Terence Ball

> In the right Definition of Names, lyes the first use of Speech;
> which is the Acquisition of Science: And in wrong, or no
> Definitions, lyes the first abuse; from which proceed all false
> and senseless tenets.
>
> Thomas Hobbes, *Leviathan* (1651)

In my study are two large file cabinets. One of them holds copies of correspondence accumulated over thirty-odd years. Among the thickest file folders is one labelled 'Felix O.' From time to time I clean out this file cabinet, filled with the flotsam and jetsam of years past. But the Felix file has survived all the annual purges, and for good reason. I reread its contents every year or so, and always with appreciation and profit. For it is full to overflowing with carefully typed letters gently chiding and correcting me for my attempts to analyse 'power' and other political concepts from an 'ordinary language' perspective, for relying too readily on claims about the 'essential contestability' of political concepts, and various other errors of my youth. Those letters also thank me – more generously than justly, I now think – for my critical comments on his work.

Something of the spirit of the man resides in that thick file. His defining qualities – kindness, courtesy and respectful but unrelenting criticism – are amply evident in this voluminous correspondence with a young upstart of an assistant professor. Most of our disagreements remained private; only once did we air our differences in public.[1] But whatever the venue, the experience was, for me, both exhilarating and educative. I now describe my exchanges with Professor Oppenheim as my postgraduate education in analytical political philosophy. And a demanding education it was. On some points – the place of 'ordinary language' and the thesis of the 'essential contestability' of political concepts – I have come round to views very like his own, albeit often by different routes or for different reasons. On other points, however, our disagreements have persisted.

I propose to proceed in the following way. First, I shall say something about our deep and substantial agreement on several issues in analytical political philosophy. Second, I want to offer a conjecture to explain why Felix Oppenheim takes the approach he does, and why, historically and autobiographically, it was and is rationally understandable that he has done so. I then attempt to reflect (though I hope not refract unduly) his view of his enterprise through the distant mirror supplied by Thomas Hobbes. Hobbes, like his latter-day kinsman, attempted to clean the Augean stable of political philosophy by sanitizing and scientizing the language of politics – and the concepts of 'liberty' and 'power' in particular. My fourth move is to show why this stratagem did not work for Hobbes and will not work for Felix Oppenheim or anyone else who wishes to employ it. Fifth and finally, I shall conclude on a less critical and more agreeable note by reconsidering the essential contestability thesis which Felix Oppenheim has consistently and quite rightly contested.

1.   Meaningful (dis)agreements

I want to begin by saying something about our substantive agreements. We agree, I believe, about the following. First, politics is, in important and ineliminable ways, a linguistically or conceptually constituted activity. We agree with Bertrand de Jouvenel that 'The elementary political process is the action of mind upon mind through speech. Communication by speech completely depends upon ... both parties [having] a common stock of words to which they attach much the same meanings.' From this it follows that deep-seated, persistent and irreconcilable differences of meaning interfere with communication or make it altogether impossible: 'people belong ... to the same society by the understanding of the same moral language. As this common moral language extends, so does society; as it breaks up, so does society.'[2] Second, clarity is a virtue, and avoidable imprecision a vice. Our thoughts can be no clearer than the language in which they are conceived and communicated; muddy prose produces muddled thinking, and vice versa. The purpose and point of analytical political philosophy or 'conceptual analysis' is, insofar as possible, to clear up muddles and misunderstandings that are brought about by the use of unnecessarily vague or imprecise concepts. This involves exposing internal inconsistencies or contradictions, tracing out implications of conventional usage or proposed definitions, and – not least – proposing better alternative analyses and descriptive definitions in which emotive elements have been minimized if not eliminated entirely.

In sum, if our disagreements are to be at all meaningful – and perchance rationally resolvable – then we must be clear what exactly we disagree over or about. 'Meaningful disagreement,' Oppenheim observes, 'presupposes agreement on what it is one disagrees about; and that in turn requires an agreed system of descriptive definitions of the concepts involved. Effective reconstruction of basic political concepts is a prerequisite for effective political inquiry in all its aspects.'[3]

Thus the work of Felix Oppenheim proceeds from a premise that, to many modern (or perhaps postmodern) eyes, appears peculiar. That premise is that the analysis of political concepts – freedom, power, equality, etc. – is (or can, and should) be a matter of making these concepts fit for precise social-scientific use. 'Ordinary' language is too imprecise, confused and even contradictory to be of much (if any) use by political scientists in particular. The point and purpose of conceptual analysis of the sort that he advocates is two-fold: first, to expose the inadequacies of previous analyses (including those advanced by ordinary-language philosophers); and second, to replace confused conceptions or definitions with clearer and more concise descriptive ones. The role of the analytical political philosopher is that of handmaiden or, in Locke's term, 'underlabourer' to the social sciences, thereby 'clearing the ground a little, and removing some of the rubbish that lies in the way to knowledge'.[4] Thus unlike ordinary-language analysis – which as Wittgenstein rather cryptically remarked 'leaves everything as it is' – Oppenheimian analysis aims to reconstruct and thus improve upon our ordinary, vague and imprecise understandings of 'freedom', 'power' and other political concepts.

Felix Oppenheim has had no truck with trendy developments since mid-century – not only ordinary language analysis, but also semiotics, Derridean deconstruction, Foucauldian genealogy, and other (mainly French) approaches. Nor does he agree with the claim that the concepts typically deployed in political argument are essentially contested – that is, that their meaning is necessarily or 'essentially' open to contestation, debate and disagreement (about which I shall say more in my conclusion). To make this concession would be to give up the game before playing it or – to employ a more military metaphor – to surrender without a fight. And in political philosophy, Felix Oppenheim has always been a fighter.

But in whose cause and under which philosophical banner does he fight? Although he eschews all labels, his critics have been quick to tar him with the brush of philosophical positivism. He heatedly denies this.[5] And in the setting supplied by the modern (or perhaps postmodern) academy his disclaimer is entirely understandable. 'Positivist' has approximately the same valence in today's academic culture that 'heretic' had in the middle ages or 'witch' had in seventeenth-century Salem: it's not a nice thing to be, or to be called. And yet there is a sense in which the label fits Felix Oppenheim, and reasons why it should be worn proudly. Chief among these reasons is that the Logical Positivists prized precision, conceptual clarity and cogency of argument. I agree entirely with G. A. Cohen, himself no positivist, who in criticizing the late Louis Althusser wrote: 'It is perhaps a matter for regret that logical positivism, with its insistence on precision ... never caught on in Paris. Anglophone philosophy left logical positivism behind long ago, but it is lastingly the better for having engaged with it ... [L]ucidity is a precious heritage ...'[6] It is this small but significant residue of positivism that remains in Felix Oppenheim's philosophy. And any philosophy that prizes clarity of expression and cogency of argument cannot be all bad.

So much for our agreements, which are substantial. I turn now to a discussion of some of our differences, not in order to retread old and oft-trod ground but to try to reach some sort of *modus vivendi*. For I now think that, after many years of reading and reflecting upon his work, I am finally beginning to understand where Felix Oppenheim is 'coming from', and why he insists on taking a rigorously 'reconstructivist' approach to the language of politics.

2. Situating Oppenheim

What follows is decidedly *not* an attempt to psychoanalyse the man to whom the present volume is offered as a tribute. I want, rather, to exhibit his reconstructivist programme as one that we can now with the wisdom of hindsight see as a *rational response* to the situation that he faced as a young man. Or, to borrow Karl Popper's distinction, my proposed explanation-sketch is not 'psychologistic' but is instead concerned with the *logic of the situation* in which young Felix found himself.[7] The following is of course a bare-bones and greatly simplified reconstruction of some elements of that historical context.

Felix Oppenheim came of age in and emigrated from a Europe in which (some rough approximation of) a common moral language had broken down and civil society had broken up – a real-world condition not unlike Hobbes's imaginary but no less horrifying state of nature. As a young Jewish man he barely escaped detection and deportation to the death camps where life was especially 'nasty, poore, brutish, and short'. It is therefore not entirely surprising that he has often expressed his admiration for Hobbes, and in particular for Hobbes's value non-cognitivism and his attempt to reconstruct the language of politics along suitably 'scientific' lines.[8] But the affinities are more than merely methodological. There are deep and, I believe, profoundly political similarities between Thomas Hobbes's and Felix Oppenheim's reconstructivist programmes – or so I shall suggest in the following section. Here it is enough to note that Hobbes's idea of the state of nature had its immediate source in the run-up to the English Civil War and its more distant source in the Corcyrean Revolution described by Thucydides (whose first English translator was none other than Thomas Hobbes):[9]

> Words had to change their ordinary meaning and to take that which was now given them. Reckless audacity came to be considered the courage of a loyal ally; prudent hesitation, specious cowardice; moderation was held to be a cloak for unmanliness; ability to see all sides of a question inaptness to act on any. Frantic violence became the attribute of manliness; cautious plotting, a justifiable means of self-defense ... To succeed in a plot was to have a shrewd head, to divine a plot a still shrewder [one] ... Oaths of reconciliation, being only proffered on either side to meet an immediate difficulty, only held good so long as no other weapon was at hand; but when opportunity offered, he who first ventured to seize it and to take his enemy off his guard, thought this perfidious vengeance sweeter than an open one, since ... success by treachery won him the palm of superior intelligence ... The cause of all these evils was the lust for power arising from greed and ambition; and from these passions proceeded the violence of the parties ... [T]he use of fair phrases to arrive at guilty ends was in high reputation ... The ancient simplicity into which honor so largely entered was laughed down and disappeared; and society became divided into camps in which no man trusted his fellow. To put an end to this, there was neither promise to be depended upon, nor oath that could command respect; but all parties dwelling rather in their calculation upon the hopelessness of a permanent state of things, were more intent upon self-defense than capable of confidence.[10]

As we shall see, this and other passages from Thucydides's *History* held more than arcane or antiquarian interest for his translator. Hobbes held that linguistic distortion and upheaval preceded, and helped prepare the way for, political upheaval and civil war. Commmunicative breakdown presages political breakdown.

Like Hobbes, Felix Oppenheim came of age in a world turned upside down and gone mad. But whilst Hobbes knew only of civil war, Oppenheim knew and lived through a world war and the Holocaust. His version of conceptual analysis and reconstruction may well have as much to do with autobiography as with the real or imagined requirements of social science. Just as 'words lost their meaning' in the Corcyrean revolution described by Thucydides (and in the English Civil War described by Hobbes), so did conceptual chaos and confusion overtake Europe: this is the deeper historical background against which Oppenheim's programme of conceptual revision (and political pacification) comes into clearer view and can be readily understood as a rational response to systematic and collective irrationality.

Oppenheim's much older fellow emigré, the great German neo-Kantian philosopher Ernst Cassirer, noted that the wildly irrational legitimating myths used by the Nazis – the 'myth of the blood', the myth of the 'Zionist world conspiracy', and the like – were made possible in part by downplaying the descriptive use of language and emphasizing its emotional or 'magical' dimension:

> The first step that had to be taken [by the Nazis] was a change in the function of language. If we study the development of human speech we find that in the history of civilization the word fulfils two entirely different functions ... [–] the semantic and the magical ... Even among the so-called primitive languages the semantic function is never missing; without it there could be no human speech. But in primitive societies the magic word has a predominant and overwhelming influence. It does not describe things or relations of things; it tries to produce effects and to change the course of nature.

But, Cassirer continues, the horatory or magical aspects of language are with us still, and never more markedly than in Hitler's Third Reich in which there was a veritable

> transformation of human speech. The magic word takes precedence over the semantic word. If nowadays I happen to read a German

book, published in these last ten years [1934–44], not a political but
a theoretical book ... I find to my amazement that I no longer
understand the German language. New words have been coined;
and even the old ones are used in a new sense; they have undergone
a deep change of meaning. This change of meaning depends upon
the fact that those words which formerly were used in a descriptive,
logical, or semantic sense, are now used as magic words that are des-
tined to produce certain effects and stir up certain emotions ... and
violent passions.[11]

As one who lived through this era and witnessed first-hand the phe-
nomenon Cassirer describes, Oppenheim quite rightly and rationally
fears the magical and lauds the logical-semantic uses of speech. In this
light his reconstructivist programme – with its aspiration to de-magify
and magnify the descriptive function of the language of politics – is
not only understandable but quite commendable. It is also highly
problematic and probably unworkable, as we can see by turning once
again to Felix Oppenheim's fellow reconstructivist, Thomas Hobbes.

3.   Situating Hobbes

Thomas Hobbes began his long career as a classical humanist,
immersed in the tradition of the *studia humanitatis*. In the first phase
of his adult life he was not only the translator of Thucydides, but the
latter-day pupil of Aristotle and Cicero, amongst many other contributors to the older humanist tradition. But in the early 1640s, he began
to doubt the value of his own education. He, like Plato long before
him, began to distrust rhetoric, with its clever ploys and persuasive
appeals to the emotions and prejudices of this or that audience, painting falsehoods in lovely hues and putting truth to rout. Hobbes saw
all round him the radicals, the Presbyterians and other dissenters, who
preached sedition under the simulacrum of reason and the authority
of the ancients.[12] England was being divided and subdivided into
sects, each of which spoke in its own idiom or private language that
other sectarians could not or would not understand. Some sects held
that monarchs were mere men, and common men kings and sover-
eigns; that private property was a pernicious fiction and common
ownership a fact ordained by God; that the end of the world was nigh
and that with the second coming of Christ the haughty would be
brought low and the lowly raised up to replace them. The world was
indeed, in the words of a popular ballad of the time, 'turn'd upside

down'.[13] In this Heraclitian world where 'Whirl was king' Hobbes – quite understandably – sought stability and permanence in a world in which words do not change their meanings. Conceptual relativism, referential opacity, or chaos – the 'free play of signifiers', in a more postmodern idiom – was not something to be celebrated or welcomed, but a problem of monumental proportions that required a solution, and soon.

It was at this feverish juncture that Hobbes discovered the calm and unfevered world of Euclidean geometry. According to his friend and biographer John Aubrey,

> He was ... 40 yeares old before he looked on geometry; which happened accidently. Being in a gentleman's library ... Euclid's Elements lay open, and 'twas the 47 *El libri* I. He read the proposition. 'By G–', sayd he (He would now and then sweare, by way of emphasis), 'this is impossible!' So he reads the demonstration of it, which referred him back to such a proposition; which proposition he read. That referred him back to another, which he also read. *Et sic deinceps*, that at last was demonstrably convinced of that trueth. This made him in love with geometry.[14]

Geometers sometimes disagree; but they don't come to blows, because they speak a language that is dry and devoid of even the possibility of emotional appeals. Key concepts – 'line', 'point', 'angle', and the like – are defined precisely and in advance. Some possible states of affairs are ruled out by definition or by deductions from definitions. Thus one has rock-solid guarantees that straight lines will never curve, that parallel lines will never intersect, that the sum of the three angles of a triangle will never exceed 180 degrees. If only (Hobbes reasoned) the language of politics could be as calm, cool and precise as that of geometry, the world could be turned rightside up. Most if not indeed all disputes could be rationally, calmly – and peacefully – resolved.

It is just this aspiration that animated the reconstructivist programme to be found in *The Elements of Law* and *De Cive*. 'What hath hitherto been written by moral philosophers, hath not made any progress in the knowledge of the truth,' says Hobbes, because they have not defined their terms precisely and deduced their conclusions accordingly. 'For were the nature of human actions as distinctly known, as the nature of quantity in geometrical figures, the strength of avarice and ambition, which is sustained by the erroneous opinions of the vulgar, as touching the nature of right and wrong, would presently faint and languish; and mankind should enjoy such an immortal peace, that ... there would hardly be left any pretence for war.'[15]

But the pretence for civil war stems less from the crude views of the vulgar than from the pretentious and ostensibly learned opinions of the philosophers. And it is their failure to be 'scientific' that is, in Hobbes's view, the root of almost all political evils. Loose concepts, imprecisely defined terms, metaphors, tropes, and figurative speech of all sorts are the sources of sedition. And these are all the more pernicious because they purportedly derive their authority from philosophy itself. It is high time, Hobbes avers, to clean that Augean stable.

Hobbes's attempt to sanitize and scientize the concepts constitutive of political discourse had the very practical *political* purpose of promoting peace by minimizing or even eliminating conceptual contestation. However, Hobbes, for reasons recently retraced in meticulous detail by Quentin Skinner, came to believe that such a reconstructivist programme would not and perhaps indeed could not work.[16] In the world of politics – a world of passions and interests – science was but 'small power' in comparison with rhetoric. A language whose terms were tightly and precisely defined, shorn of metaphors and other tropes, and devoid of all appeals to the passions was, he concluded, no match for the greater power of rhetoric or 'eloquence'. Hobbes accordingly set out to write a work in which rhetoric was to be put in the service of science and thence of peace. That book was of course *Leviathan* (1651).

Leviathan is a rhetorical *tour de force*. It abounds in stunning and memorable metaphors and images (the state of nature as an intractable and bloody *bellum omnium contra omnes*, of course, but also of birds belimed in lime twigs, scholars fluttering bird-like over their books, etc.). Moreover, Hobbes purports to take the politically neutral high road of science even as he employs various rhetorical devices for turning the tables on political opponents and holding them up to ridicule. The words they use, Hobbes charges, do not refer to actual states of the world but to their own fevered mental states. Consider the king's critics who charge him with tyranny. What, Hobbes asks, does 'tyranny' really refer to? Monarchy is a descriptive term meaning rule by one; but tyranny is an emotionally charged term. Ever since Aristotle it has been the 'corrupt' or 'perverted' form of monarchy. These adjectives are intended to incite, not to inform; thus 'tyranny', far from describing any actual state of affairs, is purely emotive – is, indeed, merely 'monarchy misliked'.[17] If you call the king a tyrant you say nothing about the king or his policies but, on the contrary, a great deal about yourself and more especially your (unfavourable) attitude towards the king. 'Monarchy' is a descriptive term, 'tyranny' an expressive or emotive one. The former has a place in a truly scientific 'civil science'; the latter does not. Likewise 'liberty' is redefined in ostensibly descriptive terms as the absence of opposition or of impediments to material bodies in motion.[18] Hobbes, in short, purports to be a descriptivist, and portrays his opponents as emotivists who use words that are un- or ill-defined, imprecise and emotionally charged.[19] But to consider the intellectual and political context in which he offers his own reconstructions or definitions makes it clear that they are anything but purely descriptive. His claim that liberty signifies simply and only the absence of opposition is a profoundly partisan, and more particularly anti-republican, redefinition of liberty.[20] Hobbes's 'negative' view of liberty, like Oppenheim's,[21] can be located in a liberal-individualist and anti-republican tradition of political discourse.[22]

The moral of this Hobbesian tale and analogue is that all definitions, however descriptive they purport to be, are, because of the political contexts in which they are proffered, 'persuasive definitions' in something like C. L. Stevenson's sense.[23] Or, to borrow a phrase from Charles Taylor, every descriptive statement (except perhaps the most brutely 'empirical'), is to some degree dependent on some theory or other and thus inevitably and invariably has its own built-in 'value-slope'.[24]

The upshot is that Hobbes's rather boastful self-description cannot be accepted at face value. His own views are very clear, and they are far from normatively neutral. But neither are they partisan in any narrow or sectarian sense. If his masterpiece were merely a polemical *pièce d'occasion*, however brilliant, we would not require our students to read *Leviathan* three and a half centuries after its publication. It is, to borrow a phrase from Thucydides, 'a possession for all time'.[25] And at least part of its timelessness is due to the regularly recurring hope – expressed in both Hobbes's and Oppenheim's reconstructivist programmes – of purifying the language of politics by purging it of ambiguity, of tropes, metaphors, and all emotive appeals and thus rendering its constitutive concepts almost crystalline in their clarity.

4. Hobbes and Oppenheim

Oppenheim, like Hobbes, claims to offer normatively neutral redefinitions of problematic and hotly contested political concepts. The differences between them are, firstly, that Felix Oppenheim is not at all boastful and, secondly, that he is quite sincere when he says that his reconstructions of political concepts are purely descriptive and normatively neutral. Against this sincerely held self-understanding I want to suggest that Oppenheim's philosophical programme – positivist or not – is at odds with his practice, and very suggestively so.

Consider first Oppenheim's claim that his definitions are purely descriptive and normatively neutral. I would argue, by contrast, that they are thoughtful and ofttimes powerful interventions whose very point and purpose is to *change* the way we think about some concept X (say 'power' or 'equality' or 'freedom'). And since what and how we think about X has a direct bearing on our attitudes towards X and how we use X to act with or against others, the change in our thinking about X is not and cannot be normatively neutral. One need only think, for example, of the debate between 'positive' and 'negative' libertarians, or (what is largely an extension of the former) between civic-republican 'communitarians' and their liberal-individualist critics. The communitarians (and earlier republicans) claim that the enjoyment of liberty entails service to the community.[26] This assertion Oppenheim dismisses as confused, incoherent and 'not relate[d] to freedom in any sense'.[27] But what is confused and incoherent within the framework of liberal-individualist discourse is eminently clear and quite coherent within civic republican discourse. Oppenheim's reconstructed conception of freedom underpins and puts him squarely in the camp of 'negative' libertarian anti-communitarians.

And here, once again, autobiography both intrudes and informs: 'communitarian' discourse, with its 'positive' view of freedom as requiring the performance of public service, smacks of collectivist (dare one say it?) tyranny – of Orwellian Newsspeak in which slavery is freedom, of the stultifying and all-embracing *Gemeinschaft* (or worse, *Volksgemeinschaft*), of being 'forced to be free', and the cruelly cynical lie that *Arbeit macht frei*. 'And so,' says Oppenheim, 'freedom becomes its opposite.'[28] This is more than abstract conceptual analysis; it is political judgement of a particularly profound sort. It is not that the latter is cloaked or concealed or masked by the former; it is, rather, that the former has just the sort of 'value-slope' that supports the latter, and vice versa.

From this it follows that Oppenheim's analyses and reconstructions of freedom and other concepts can be seen as a form of political engagement that can contribute to *conceptual change* – that is, the alteration in the meaning of key concepts that constitute the discourse of politics (and, likewise, of political theory and political science). As the German practitioners of *Begriffsgeschichte* and their Anglo-American cousins, students of 'conceptual history', have noted, concepts have histories; their meanings change over time and in the course of political argument and debate.[29] A philosophical programme whose point is to bring about conceptual innovation can hardly be normatively neutral – especially insofar as politics is in important ways a conceptually and communicatively constituted activity. To bring about changes in the meaning of freedom and equality is to alter how we think about, and use – and act with – these concepts.

Reinhart Koselleck, perhaps the leading advocate and practitioner of *Begriffsgeschichte*, observes that 'Without common concepts there is no society, and above all, no political field of action.' But which concepts are to be the common coin of discourse – and what they mean – becomes, at crucial historical junctures, a veritable field of battle. 'The struggle over the "correct" concepts,' says Koselleck, 'becomes socially and politically explosive.'[30] In these battles the theorists and philosophers are the sappers who set the charges. What Alasdair MacIntyre says of the role of philosophy in changing moral concepts is no less true of its role in changing political ones:

> philosophical inquiry itself plays a part in changing moral concepts. It is not that we have first a straightforward history of moral concepts and then a separate and secondary history of philosophical comment. For to analyse a concept philosophically may often be to assist in its transformation by suggesting that it needs revision, or that it is discredited in some way. Philosophy leaves everything as it is – except concepts. And since to possess a concept involves behaving or being able to behave in certain ways in certain circumstances, to alter concepts, whether by modifying existing concepts or by making new concepts available or by destroying old ones, is to alter behavior. A history which takes this point seriously, which is concerned with the role of philosophy in relation to actual conduct, cannot be philosophically neutral.[31]

Nor, of course, and by the same token, can the critical reconstruction of political concepts be purely descriptive and normatively neutral.

Conceptual analysis and reconstruction, as Oppenheim conceives of it, therefore cannot be *wertfrei* or 'outside' politics; it is necessarily *engagé*. Oppenheim's analyses and proposed definition of (for example) 'power' are every bit as politically engaged as Hobbes's or Foucault's, and for much the same reason: to alter the way we understand power is to alter the way we think about power relationships and the ways in which they might be used, altered, subverted, sustained or legitimized.

To paraphrase what Marx once said about the ahistorical attitude of the political economists: Felix Oppenheim recognizes that there has been a history of conceptual contestation and change, but apparently believes that – if others would only follow his example – this long and unhappy history could conceivably come to a happy end. There would be an end to conceptual contestation, widespread agreement about the meanings of key concepts, a peaceful atmosphere in which people of different ideological perspectives would either find common ground or at least be clear about the precise nature of their differences, and perhaps even positivist lions would lie down with ordinary-language lambs.

But however attractive it may be, this peaceful prospect is illusory, not to say profoundly apolitical (or perhaps even anti-political). Hobbes, as we saw, claimed to be doing 'science', and Oppenheim to be engaging in descriptive analysis and normatively neutral reconstruction; both are mistaken. The difference is that Hobbes recognized that his kind of scientific redefinition was politically engaged, while Oppenheim apparently does not. To say this is to take nothing away from Felix Oppenheim's programme of conceptual criticism and reconstruction; on the contrary, it is to place his programme within a long and honourable tradition of politically engaged philosophical inquiry.

5.   Conclusion: essential vs. contingent contestability

If the foregoing has seemed unduly critical, I do not mean it to be. Or rather – let me be clear – it is intended to be critical in exactly the sense that Felix Oppenheim prizes and has himself long practised. It is intended, that is, to be appreciative and constructive criticism that clarifies the nature and sources of our disagreements as a prelude to their possible resolution. But I should like to close on an even more harmonious note by saying something about a still-controversial view over which we once differed but now largely agree – the thesis of 'essential contestability'.

As Mario Ricciardi has noted elsewhere in the present volume, Felix Oppenheim was an early and staunch critic of the 'essential contestability' thesis initially advanced by W. B. Gallie.[32] According to Gallie, a concept is 'essentially contested' if its meaning and criteria of application are forever open to dispute and disagreement. Such disputes are less apt to arise in the natural sciences than in social and political philosophy, the social sciences and the humanities. Indeed, almost all the concepts constitutive of ethical, political and aesthetic discourse are 'essentially contested'. Such disputes cannot be definitively and finally resolved, Gallie claimed, because there not only *are* but *can be* no commonly shared criteria for deciding definitively what is to count in aesthetics as 'art' or in politics as 'democracy' or 'equality'.

Consider again and by way of example the concept of power. Following what they took to be Gallie's lead, Steven Lukes and William Connolly contended that 'power' is an essentially contested concept characterized by unresolved – and in principle unresolvable – disputes over its meaning and proper application.[33] Just as art critics can never agree in all possible cases whether some object is indeed a work of art, so political actors and analysts will never agree in all instances that some particular action is an exercise of power. Applied to 'power' (and other political concepts), the thesis of essential contestability proved to be both bold and provocative. And, too, it purported to explain the persistence and intractability of conceptual disagreements: if competent speakers continue to disagree over the definition and meaning of 'power' or any other concept, that must be because its very 'contestability' is an 'essential' feature of its use or application. Moreover, the thesis of essential contestability was claimed to be admirably non-partisan, normatively neutral, and non-judgemental: does it not, after all, claim that no one conception of power (or freedom, equality, etc.) is clearly and demonstrably superior to any other? Felix Oppenheim has his understanding of power (etc.); Lukes and Connolly have theirs; and none is in any knockdown or decisive way superior to any other. Or so it might appear.

But here, as so often, appearances are apt to be misleading. For on closer examination the thesis of essential contestability suffers from several significant shortcomings. The first of these is that if the thesis is true, then all disputes about 'power' (and other concepts constitutive of political discourse) are unresolvable *a priori* and *in principle*. Anyone attempting to construct a conception of power in hopes that others might agree is on a misbegotten and completely misguided mission. One cannot expect or even *hope* to construct a conception of power upon which everyone might conceivably agree, since 'power' belongs to the class of essentially contested concepts. All arguments for or against any particular conception of power would therefore appear to be beside the point, if the point is not merely to express one's views but to participate in a meaningful conversation which could conceivably conclude with some sort of agreement.

Anyone who subscribes to different views of what constitutes or counts as 'power' (or 'freedom', 'justice', etc.) would thus appear to be left with only two ways of dealing with one another: coercion or conversion. And presumably those who cannot be converted must be coerced (excluded, silenced, ridiculed, ignored, etc.). Connolly puts the point succinctly: 'Disputes about the proper concept and interpretation of power, then, are part of larger ideological debates. To convert others to my idea of power is to implicate them to some degree in my political ideology.'[34] But this, if true, has deeply disturbing implications. To speak of 'converting' others to one's own view may be good theology; but it is very dangerous politics (if indeed it is politics at all). It is dangerous because political argument – which is to say, politics itself – is about the public airing of differences, not as an end in itself but as a prelude to resolving those differences through argument and persuasion. And this requires, as a precondition, a shared language or lexicon. As John Dewey famously observed:

> Society not only continues to exist ... by communication, but it may be fairly said to exist in ... communication. There is more than a verbal tie between the words common, community, and communication. Men [sic] live in a community in virtue of the things which they have in common; and communication is the way in which they come to possess things in common.[35]

But if the concepts constitutive of political discourse, and therefore of political life, are indeed *essentially* contested, then there can of course be no common moral language or civic lexicon; hence no communication; hence no community.

If the thesis of essential contestability were true, then political discourse – and therefore political life itself – would be well-nigh impossible, and for exactly the same reasons that civility and the civic life are impossible in Hobbes's imaginary and solipsistic state of nature: each individual is a monad, radically disconnected from all other individuals insofar as each speaks, as it were, a private language of his own devising. Because the concepts comprising these individual languages cannot be translated or otherwise understood, each speaker is perforce a stranger and an enemy to every other. The result, as Hobbes rightly recognizes, would be 'a state of warre' in which everyone's life is 'nasty, poore, solitary, brutish, and short'. Hobbes's imaginary state of nature is nothing less than a condition in which the thesis of essential contestability holds true: the inability to communicate is, as it were, the essential or defining characteristic of that state.[36]

Hence claims about the essential contestability of political concepts are not merely assertions about the limits of language and meaning, but about the severely limited possibility (or near-impossibility) of communication and thus of community. From this it follows that questions about the truth or falsity of the thesis of essential contestability are of more than abstract or academic interest but are, in fact, of profound political import. For if the essential contestability thesis holds true about political concepts, then the prospects for meaningful communication, and hence community, would appear to be exceedingly bleak.

Happily, however, our predicament appears, on closer examination, not to be so grim, after all. As I have argued elsewhere,[37] the essential contestability thesis is itself contestable and problematic; and, if not false, then circular and logically vacuous. One cannot derive a claim about essentiality from a (set of) empirical or contingent statements (or, in an older idiom, an analytic statement from a synthetic one). It is quite clear that claims about conceptual contestability are well-supported by empirical evidence from a variety of sources. Even granting that, the thesis of *essential* contestability is circular and commits the fallacy of *post hoc, ergo propter hoc*. That is, the evidence cited in support of the claim that (say) 'power' is an 'essentially' contested concept is that some people have *in fact* disagreed about its meaning and application. But all that can be inferred from an enumeration of individual instances of disagreement, no matter how long the list, is that there *have been* disagreements, and not that there *must always* or *necessarily* continue to be. At most, all that can be concluded is that 'power', 'freedom', and the like, are what I call *contingently contested* concepts.[38]

If we look, not at Lukes's and Connolly's pronouncements but at their actual practice, we quickly discover that their practice does not square with their preaching. Taking their text from Gallie, they preach a sermon about essential contestability; but they soon stray from their own *profession de foi*. For they – like Oppenheim – offer criticisms (often very telling ones) of competing conceptions of power and other concepts, and arguments (some of which are quite persuasive) in defence of their own alternative accounts. Lukes, for example, contends that his conception of power is 'superior' to rival accounts, and he advances arguments to support his claim that they are of 'less value' than his own.[39] Coming from one who holds that political concepts are *essentially* contested, this seems surprising, to say the least. It is not that Lukes has no grounds for judging one view or conception to be *better* than another. He has perfectly good reasons, grounded in an essentially Kantian theory of autonomy and a structural conception of power. The fact that arguments *are* advanced and judgements actually arrived at suggests that the thesis of essentially contestability, as Lukes and Connolly conceive of it, is both untrue and untenable.

Having said that, however, I want to conclude by suggesting that the essential contestability thesis is not without some value. For it might best be viewed, not as a valid philosophical thesis about the essential nature of political language and meaning, but as a rhetorical stratagem for reminding us of a persistent and recurring feature of political discourse – namely the perpetual *possibility* of disagreement. This possibility is intermittently actualized, and nowhere more frequently and vehemently than in disputes over 'freedom' and 'power' and the other concepts to which Felix Oppenheim has paid close and careful attention. But it is important to remember that these disagreements cannot be resolved by fiat or by force of arms or ideological conversion but only by that uniquely human 'power' – the power of reason, of close and careful argument, and rational persuasion. And it is this peculiarly human and humane power that Felix Oppenheim possesses in such ample measure.

Notes

* For their very helpful and incisive comments on an earlier version of this essay I am much indebted to Ian Carter, Richard Dagger, David Miller and Serena Olsaretti.
  1. Felix E. Oppenheim, '"Power" Revisited', *Journal of Politics*, 40 (1978), pp. 589–608; Terence Ball, '"Power" Revised: a Comment on Oppenheim', ibid., pp. 609–18; Oppenheim, '"Power"; One More Visit: a Response to Terence Ball', ibid., pp. 619–21.
  2. Bertrand de Jouvenel, *Sovereignty: an Inquiry into the Public Good*, trans. J. F. Huntington (Chicago: University of Chicago Press, 1957), p. 304.
  3. Oppenheim, *Political Concepts: a Reconstruction* (Chicago: University of Chicago Press, 1981), p. 202.
  4. Locke, *Essay Concerning Human Understanding* (1690), Epistle to the Reader.
  5. Oppenheim, *Political Concepts*, pp. 189–94.
  6. G. A. Cohen, *Karl Marx's Theory of History* (Oxford: Oxford University Press, 1978), p. x.
  7. Karl R. Popper, *The Open Society and its Enemies* (London: Routledge, 1969), pp. 95–6. For a further explication, see James Farr, 'Popper's Hermeneutics', *Philosophy of the Social Sciences*, 13 (1983), pp. 157–76, and his 'Resituating Explanation', in Terence Ball (ed.), *Idioms of Inquiry* (Albany: State University of New York Press, 1987), ch. 2.
  8. Oppenheim, *Moral Principles in Political Philosophy* (New York: Random House, 1968), pp. 145–51.
  9. Strictly speaking, Hobbes was the first to translate Thucydides directly out of the original Greek rather than from earlier and badly corrupted Latin or French translations which, Hobbes complained, 'traduced' instead of 'translated' Thucydides.

10. Thucydides, *History of the Peloponnesian War*, trans. Richard Crawley (New York: Modern Library, 1951), Bk. III, ch. 10, pp. 189–91; for Hobbes's translation see William Molesworth (ed.), *English Works of Thomas Hobbes* (London, 1838), VIII, pp. 348–9. Cf. further James Boyd White, *When Words Lose Their Meaning* (Chicago: University of Chicago Press, 1984), ch. 3, and my review-essay, 'When Words Lose Their Meaning', *Ethics*, 96 (1986), p. 620–31.

11. Ernst Cassirer, *The Myth of State* (New Haven: Yale University Press, 1945), pp. 282–4. For a frightening but illuminating glossary, see Henry Pachter et al. (eds), *Nazi-Deutsch* (New York: Frederick Ungar, 1944).

12. Hobbes's most explicit accusations along these lines are to be found in his later *Behemoth*, ed. Ferdinand Tönnies, 2nd edn (London: Frank Cass, 1969), esp. Dialogue I.

13. See Christopher Hill, *The World Turned Upside Down: Radical Ideas During the English Revolution* (Harmondsworth: Penguin Books, 1972).

14. John Aubrey, *Brief Lives*, ed. O. L. Dick (Harmondsworth: Penguin Books, 1972), p. 230.

15. Thomas Hobbes, *De Cive*, Epistle Dedicatory, *English Works*, II, pp. 3–4.

16. Quentin Skinner, *Reason and Rhetoric in the Philosophy of Hobbes* (Cambridge: Cambridge University Press, 1996). I owe a very great debt to Skinner's seminal studies of Hobbes and the history of 'liberty' (see nn. 20 and 22, below).

17. Hobbes, *Leviathan*, ed. C. B. Macpherson (Harmondsworth: Penguin Books, 1968), Part II, ch. 19, p. 240.

18. *Leviathan*, Part II, ch. 21, pp. 261–4.

19. It might be objected that whilst Hobbes offers descriptive redefinitions of some terms – 'power' and 'liberty', for example – he supplies an emotivist account of others, e.g. 'good'. I attempt to answer this objection in my *Reappraising Political Theory* (Oxford: Oxford University Press, 1995), ch. 4, esp. pp. 104–6.

20. Skinner, *Liberty Before Liberalism* (Cambridge: Cambridge University Press, 1998), pp. 7–11, 59–60.

21. Oppenheim, *Political Concepts*, pp. 162–4.

22. See Skinner, 'The Paradoxes of Political Liberty', in David Miller (ed.), *Liberty* (Oxford: Oxford University Press, 1991), esp. pp. 186–91. It bears mentioning that *we* can now locate Hobbes in the liberal tradition, even though *he* was in no position to place himself in that tradition.

23. Charles L. Stevenson, *Ethics and Language* (New Haven: Yale University Press, 1944), ch. 9. A persuasive definition is one which elides 'emotive and descriptive meaning [to bring about] a redirection of people's attitudes' (p. 210). Contrary to a widespread misreading, Stevenson did not reject such definitions out of hand: 'The practical question is not *whether* to reject persuasion, but which persuasion to reject. Not all persuasion is that of the mob orator; and the evaluation of persuasion, like the evaluation of any-thing else, is not a matter that lends itself to hasty generalizations' (p. 215).

24. Charles Taylor, 'Neutrality in Political Science', *Philosophical Papers*, 2 vols (Cambridge: Cambridge University Press, 1983), vol. II.

25. Or, as Hobbes translates κτῆμα ἐς ἀεί, 'a possession for everlasting'.

26. For a modern restatement and reconstruction – one might almost say reha-bilitation – of the civic republican view, see Philip Pettit, *Republicanism*

(Oxford: Oxford University Press, 1997); for a modern communitarian version of this view, see Henry Tam, *Communitarianism: a New Agenda for Politics and Citizenship* (New York: NYU Press, 1998).

27. Oppenheim, *Political Concepts*, p. 162; for Hobbes's version of this argument, see *Leviathan*, Part II, chapter 21, pp. 266–8, and *Behemoth*, pp. 3–4, 23, 26–8, 33, 36–8.
28. See Oppenheim, *Political Concepts*, p. 164. On this point Oppenheim agrees with the late Isaiah Berlin's endorsement of 'negative' liberty and his abiding hostility to its 'positive' counterpart. For Berlin's now-classic statement of this view, see his 'Two Concepts of Liberty' in *Four Essays on Liberty* (Oxford: Oxford University Press, 1969). It also bears mentioning that there are interesting and suggestive parallels between Berlin's life-experiences and Oppenheim's. For the former, see Michael Ignatieff, *Isaiah Berlin: a Life* (London: Chatto and Windus, 1998).
29. See Otto Brunner, Werner Conze and Reinhart Koselleck (eds), *Geschlichtliche Grundbegriffe: Historisches Lexikon juridisch-sozialen Sprache in Deutschland* (Stuttgart: Klett-Cotta, 1978-), 7 vols. See, further, Koselleck, *Futures Past: On the Semantics of Historical Time*, trans. Keith Tribe (Cambridge, MA: MIT Press, 1985). For a useful introduction and overview, see Melvin Richter, *The History of Social and Political Concepts* (Oxford: Oxford University Press, 1995). Amongst Anglo-American contributions to 'conceptual history', see my *Transforming Political Discourse* (Oxford: Blackwell, 1988); Terence Ball, James Farr, and Russell L. Hanson (eds), *Political Innovation and Conceptual Change* (Cambridge: Cambridge University Press, 1989); and Terence Ball and J. G. A. Pocock (eds), *Conceptual Change and the Constitution* (Lawrence: University Press of Kansas, 1988). For a recent comparison and contrast of Anglo-American and German *genres*, see Iain Hampsher-Monk et al. (eds), *History of Concepts: Comparative Perspectives* (Amsterdam: Amsterdam University Press, 1998).
30. Koselleck, *Futures Past*, pp. 74, 77.
31. Alasdair MacIntyre, *A Short History of Ethics* (London: Macmillan, 1966), pp. 2–3.
32. W. B. Gallie, 'Essentially Contested Concepts', *Proceedings of the Aristotelian Society*, 56 (1955–6), pp. 167–98.
33. Steven Lukes, *Power: a Radical View* (London: Macmillan, 1974); William E. Connolly, *The Terms of Political Discourse*, 2nd edn (Princeton: Princeton University Press, 1983), ch. 3.
34. Connolly, *The Terms of Political Discourse*, p. 128.
35. John Dewey, *Democracy and Education* (New York: Free Press, 1916), p. 4.
36. See my *Reappraising Political Theory*, ch. 4.
37. In my *Transforming Political Discourse*, pp. 13–14.
38. Ibid., p. 14; cf. further Andrew Mason, *Explaining Political Disagreement* (Cambridge: Cambridge University Press, 1993), who, taking issue with me, quite plausibly argues that political concepts are essentially contest*able*, albeit contingently contest*ed* (pp. 58–9).
39. Lukes, *Power*, pp. 9, 30.

3
Essential Contestability and the Claims of Analysis

Mario Ricciardi

1. Analysis contested

Does analytic philosophy rest on a mistake? Since its beginnings this intellectual movement has been an object of much disagreement regarding its merits (and demerits) among friends and foes alike. Those who regard themselves as belonging to the second group normally do so because they hold that the whole business of clarifying philosophical issues through the analysis of the use of words rests on a misunderstanding of the machinery of language and of the nature of philosophy itself. Analytic philosophy is said to be unware of the historical dimensions of language (given that the meanings of words change over time). Analytic philosophers stand accused of thinking that there is such a thing as the set of necessary conditions for the use of a given word. This is regarded as a theoretical delusion, which produces idle distinctions bearing no relation to the 'real life' of a natural language.

If the nature of language is historical, the method of philosophy should be historical too. There is no point in analysis. What philosophers should do is reconstruct the genetic processes leading to a particular idea or theory. Analysis might be appropriate for the natural sciences, but when dealing with human affairs, what philosophers need is history – a kind of collective biography. In political philosophy, this thesis has taken a distinctive form known as the 'essential contestability' of political concepts, after the title of an oft-quoted article by W. B. Gallie.[1]

Since its publication in the 'golden era' of analytic philosophy, Gallie's article has been widely read and discussed. More than thirty years on, in a new climate of opinion quite hostile to analysis, it is still regarded as a seminal contribution by those arguing against analytic philosophy. It is now almost a commonplace, among philosophers on both sides of the Atlantic, that 'there is a crisis of analytic philosophy', or that 'analysis is not enough' or even that we should 'give up the principle of non-contradiction as a practice of rationality'. These statements are often coupled with allusions to 'essential contestability'.

My aim in this paper is to take seriously some of the most articulated expressions of this attitude in order to provide a critical assessment of their theoretical import. Two different philosophical sects are travelling our *fin-de-siècle* intellectual landscape under the banner of 'essential contestability'. As a review of the literature shows, authors belonging to both sects mention 'essential contestability' (though with different meanings, and in the course of pursuing distinct lines of argument), and are hostile to analytic philosophy. In my view both sects are wrong, though for different reasons. I shall call their two theses: (i) the *Primacy of Historical Understanding Thesis*; and (ii) the *Essential Contestability Thesis*. I will ascribe the first thesis to W. B. Gallie and other like-minded philosophers, and the second to W. E. Connolly.

According to Gallie, the main contemporary advocate of the first thesis, the fact that there are *some* essentially contestable concepts (defined in a rather complicated way) is evidence of the limits of analysis as a candidate for being *the* method of philosophy. What is essential contestability? Gallie's point might be summarized by saying that a concept is essentially contestable when it 'stands for' an open-ended activity, like a game with no end-state, where all or some of the participants disagree on who, among the actual participants, is best doing what he or she (or it) is supposed to be doing according to the rules of the game. Moreover, some of them disagree about which are the features that are necessary to qualify a particular action in the game as the best performance of that kind of action (i.e. the one that is closest to the ideal). There are no criteria available on which to settle this second disagreement. But the participants do neverthless agree on the fact that this is a genuine disagreement and not a breakdown of communication. This is not a delusion, as some might say; the participants in the game do share a common background of assumptions that is the condition of possibility of a disagreement.[2] For example, they might agree on their positive evaluation of certain patterns of action in the game, but disagree on the particular behaviour that counts as an instance of that pattern of action. Gallie's point is that there are disagreements that cannot be settled by reference to the rules of the game because the pattern of action on which the participants disagree is not itself defined by the rules. This seems true of knowledgeable football fans, who often disagree less about who has won a match (something which is usually settled by looking at the rules of the game), than about questions like which is the best team in the recent history of the game. This second disagreement is not settled by reference to who, according to the rules, has won the most matches. According to Gallie, in these situations, historical understanding is not just useful, or even necessary, but is 'proper' understanding. Gallie holds that following a story is the primary mode of understanding in human affairs. Looking back at the history of football, one should compare a team's achievements today with those in its past, compare each team's achievements with those of the others, and choose the best, giving particular weight to the reknowned exemplars of outstanding performances.

Those advocating the primacy of historical understanding thesis, like Vico, Hegel, Croce and Collingwood, are not committed to a complete denial of the utility of analysis (e.g. in the natural sciences or in formal thought), but they think that analysis *is not enough* (expecially when dealing with human affairs), and so philosophy needs historical understanding at a fundamental level. They hold that historical understanding is *real understanding* (some kind of 'deeper' understanding as opposed to 'mere' analysis). They think that you cannot say you have understood 'democracy' if you are not able to follow different stories reporting practices that are qualified by competent speakers as being 'democratic', and if you are not able to figure out what people in these different settings do, or will do, or might have done. This ability to follow a story is logically preliminary to any understanding of a particular democratic practice. Understanding is always the understanding of a particular story. To say that an action is democratic, one needs to have compared it with outstanding instances of democratic behaviour in the past. The closer it is to the original item, the more democratic it will be. This is what I call the *Primacy of Historical Understanding Thesis*. Those holding this thesis do not argue for the essential contestability of whole areas of language. On the contrary, they hold that what are essentially contestable are certain concepts used in ordinary language like, for example, those of 'art', 'justice' and 'democracy'.

According to the advocates of the second thesis it is *the language of a whole area*, that of politics, *that is essentially contestable*. They seem to hold this thesis as part of *a wider thesis on the nature of philosophy*, aiming at substituting analysis with other methods (e.g. 'genealogy' or 'deconstruction'). This is the *Essential Contestability Thesis* proper. Their definition of 'essential contestability' is – despite their reference to Gallie – importantly different from Gallie's. According to Connolly, the main advocate of this second approach, a concept is essentially contestable when it is a concept involved in a disagreement. In his book on *The Terms of Political Discourse*, he explains his definition by stating that a concept is essentially contested when it 'is *appraisive* in that the state of affairs it describes is a valued achievement, when the practice described is *internally complex* in that its characterization involves reference to several dimensions, and when agreed and contested rules of application are relatively *open* enabling parties to interpret even those shared rules differently as new and unforeseen situations arise'.[3] Connolly states (like Gallie) that only some political concepts are essentially contestable, but his definition of essential contestability is so broad that one can safely conclude that it applies to all political concepts alike.

As those familiar with his writings know, Felix E. Oppenheim is an analytic political philosopher and a staunch opponent of 'essential contestability'. Oppenheim has given what he regards as a refutation of the essential contestability of political concepts in his book *Political Concepts: a Reconstruction*. I agree with much of what Oppenheim says in this book. But I do not wish to follow his path in arguing against essential contestability as a thesis about political language alone. It is my intention in this essay to deal with both (i) essential contestability as a general thesis about the semantics of particular words (a thesis which forms part of a broader philosophical outlook), and (ii) essential contestability as a thesis about the language of politics. I hope that in this way the wider theoretical implications of such anti-analytic theorizing in political philosophy as well as in other fields might become clearer. In order to do so, we shall need to return to the ideas of W. B. Gallie on the relevance of essentially contested concepts to philosophical method. According to Gallie, the aim of philosophy is historical understanding, that is, the understanding of human reality and of the social world, an unfolding of the narrative structure of our knowledge of these facts.[4]

The fact that there are concepts that are essentially contestable is seen by Gallie as evidence of the insufficiency of analysis as the method of philosophy. I think that some of Gallie's claims are wrong, and his accusations misplaced. It is my intention to show in the second part of this chapter that, when wrong, his claims are based on the same errors as those that are characteristic of historicism.

As I have said, in contemporary political philosophy, the expression 'essential contestability' is usually associated with W. E. Connolly's claims about the essential contestability of the language of politics.

Connolly's idea of essential contestability is different from Gallie's but he arrives at similar conclusions. He is even more hostile than Gallie to the claims of analysis in political philosophy (and, it seems, in philosophy in general) because he implies that, not just many, but all the concepts of ordinary language are essentially contestable. Political philosophers should drop analysis altogether and engage in more rewarding activities like 'deconstruction' or 'genealogy'.[5] To support his argument, Connolly quotes several 'authorities' (from Quine, Kuhn and Putnam to Wittgenstein and Stuart Hampshire), mounting an attack on several philosophical dichotomies (facts vs. values, norms vs. descriptions, analytic vs. synthetic). I think that Connolly, too, is wrong. But, given that his argument is different from Gallie's, his errors are partly different too. The third part of this chapter is devoted to a criticism of Connolly's claims. I hope that, seen together, my criticisms of Gallie and Connolly will be regarded by those who agree with my arguments as a 'negative defence' of analysis. In the conclusion of this essay, I shall put forward a reformulation of the notion of 'essential contestability' which I think might be of some help for political and social philosophers. I shall argue that essential contestability is a property of words, not of concepts; and it might be helpful to identify a particular class of words of our ordinary language (i.e. language commonly used in human affairs) that 'stand for' open-ended activities. The meaning of these words is essentially contestable because their use depends in part on singling out the correct solution to the question of which is the best among the various possible actions made available by the rules underlying the activities that these words 'stand for'. The lack of uncontroversial criteria on which to settle the disagreement over how to single out those actions that are correct with respect to the rules, results in essential disagreement on the proper use of these words. Examples I would give of essentially contestable words are 'philosophy', 'politics', 'law', 'art', 'democracy', 'Christianity', 'war', 'socialism' and 'liberalism'. It is my intention to show that the fact that there are words whose meaning is essentially contestable is evidence of the limits of analysis; but that this does not establish the priority of historical understanding. It is just an argument for the importance of history in the explanation of the different uses of a word.

2.   The primacy of historical understanding thesis

Gallie introduces the notion of an essentially contested concept by means of an example: the concept of 'championship' in a fictitious game. In this championship (i) 'each team specialises in a distinctive method, strategy and style of play of its own, to which all its members subscribe to the best of their ability'; (ii) the championship 'is not adjudged and awarded in terms of the highest number' of scores, but 'in virtue of level of style or calibre'; (iii) the championship 'is not a distinction gained and acknowledged at a fixed time and for a fixed period. Games proceed continuously, and whatever side is acknowledged champion today knows it may perfectly well be caught up or surpassed tomorrow'; (iv) 'there are no official judges or strict rules of adjudication'. Instead, each side has 'its loyal kernel of supporters, and in addition, at any given time, a number of *floating* supporters who are won over to support it because of the quality of its play – and, we might add, the loudness of its kernel supporters' applause and the persuasiveness of their comments'. So, at any given time, one side will have the largest and loudest group of supporters who will effectively hail them as the champions; (v) the supporters of each contesting team regard and refer to their favoured team as 'the champions'. This last point means that there is no such thing as the universal recognition of the outstanding excellence of one team's style and calibre of play. The supporters of each team regard their team as being the champions while competing with the other teams' supporters for the recognition of their criteria for 'championship' as the proper ones.[6] As I have suggested, Gallie's example can be easily understood by thinking of the attitude of football fans and of the importance that these people attach to the idea of their team being, not simply the actual winner, but the quintessential representative of the ideal of an outstanding football team.

Which are the 'formal' or 'logical' (in Gallie's obscure 'loose sense') conditions for a concept to be an essentially contested one? After his description of the imaginary game with champions but no winner, Gallie enumerates four conditions: (i) the concept in question must be appraisive, i.e. it should mean 'some kind of valued achievement'; (ii) the 'achievement must be of an internally complex character' and its worth should be 'attributed to it as a whole'; (iii) any explanation of the achievement's worth 'must therefore include reference to the respective contributions of its various parts and features; yet prior to experimentation there is nothing absurd or contradictory in any of a number of possible rival descriptions of its total worth, one such description setting its component parts or features in one order of importance, a second setting them in a second order and so on'; (iv) the achievement must be of a kind that 'admits of considerable modification in the light of changing circustances; and such modification cannot be prescribed or predicted in advance'. The last two conditions receive a further qualification from Gallie as (iii) the condition of being initially 'variously describable'; and (iv) that of being 'open'. According to Gallie, these conditions are sufficient to explain how it is possible that different groups of people might cheer their teams for their respective style in doing the same thing, i.e. playing the same game. But they are insufficient to define what it is to be an essentially contested concept. For this purpose a further condition is necessary: (v) each person should recognize that his own use of the concept 'is contested by those of other parties', and 'each party must have at least some appreciation of the different criteria in the light of which the other parties claim to be applying the concept in question'.[7] To sum up, the first group of five conditions is sufficient to define an essentially contested concept and to explain the nature of the disagreement. But this is not the end of Gallie's argument. There are two further conditions that, according to Gallie, are necessary to distinguish an essentially contested concept from a concept that is 'radically confused'. These are: (vi) 'the derivation of any such concept from an original exemplar whose authority is acknowledged by all the contestant users of the concept'; and (vii) 'the probability or plausibility, in appropriate senses of these terms, of the claim that the continuous competition for acknowledgement as between the contestant users of the concept enables the original exemplar's achievement to be sustained or developed in optimum fashion'.[8]

As I have said, Gallie's use of the logical jargon of necessary conditions is a bit shaky. In particular, it is not clear how conditions (i) to (v) might be sufficient to define an essentially contestable concept if conditions (vi) and (vii) are necessary to distinguish it from one that is just 'radically confused'. Definitions *are* means of distinction.[9] Unless, of course, one thinks that the concept of definition is in itself essentially contestable. But I don't think that Gallie's text could be understood in this way. On a charitable reading, perhaps the best interpretation of Gallie's text is given by regarding all the necessary conditions, taken together, as jointly sufficient for a concept to be essentially contestable. Even in this way, however, Gallie's argument is far from being cogent.

This can be shown by looking at one of Gallie's examples, that of the concept of art. It is hard to deny that the word 'art' satisfies all the conditions for being essentially contestable in Gallie's sense. Indeed, we all praise art as an achievement, and many of us disagree on the appropriate features of a work of art while thinking that this disagreement is genuine. The history of aesthetics is a catalogue of such disagreements.

To take just one contemporary instance of these disagreements, think of the everyday hunting tools of a primitive tribe as seen by Arthur C. Danto in the New York Center for African Art: 'The first object that strikes the eye upon entering the ground-floor gallery is a hunting net, folded and tied, hauled back as an artifact of the Zande people by Herbert Lang in 1910. There is little doubt that were you to see an identical object displayed and illuminated just as the net is, but placed in one of the alcoves of the Guggenheim Museum or in a chaste corner of the Museum of Modern Art, it would be instantly accepted as a work of art – dense, mysterious, even beautiful, perhaps by Jackie Windsor or Eva Hesse. That something just like it could be a work of art does not – or does it? – make this object, of conspicuous utility to its makers, a work of art. The catalogue entry says the Zande net "bears a completely spurious resemblance to a work of modern art". Well, nothing the eye can tell you will tell you whether it is art or artifact, and in order to get some purchase on the difference – and on the difference it makes – you may need recourse to a long catalogue essay by Arthur C. Danto.'[10] So is Gallie right when he says that in order to understand art one needs the history of art? Yes, if one wants to know how a new group of arti-facts (in the example, everyday hunting tools) becomes a commodity in the art market. To make sense of this, one needs to know what Picasso did and what Roger Fry wrote.

But the story is nevertheless the story of a material object, a body. To tell the story (or to follow the narrative) one needs a description of that item. One needs to know what it is made of, its shape, its colour and its position in space. These are requirements for knowing that the object in the New York Center for African Art is the same as that used by the Zande hunters to catch their prey at the beginning of the century. Gallie's narrative is the story of the making of an object and of the different uses of it. It is the story of different ways of seeing it, of interacting with it, of considering its importance and scope as seen by different people in various times and places. This story might be inter-esting, and might enable one to answer all sorts of important ques-tions. But Gallie's point is not just that it is interesting or important. He holds it to be fundamental, which is to say, primary with respect to conceptual analysis. It should be clear by now that it is not so. At the more fundamental level, before the story, there is the description of an item, and this activity involves a lot of analysis: analysis of perception, visual and auditory reports, proposals of classification. This in turn implies identification, an act of judgement of the form: this is an x, because of its features a, b, c; therefore it is not a y or a z. Conceptual analysis is the precondition of such a judgement, and hence the precondition of the story itself. To tell (or follow) a story of something, one needs to know what sort of thing that something is. Every narrative is *about* items in a world (real or fictitious), and there is no way of talking (or thinking) about these items unless one uses words and concepts. Isaiah Berlin summarizes this point nicely: 'it needs no deep reflection to realise that all our thought is shot through with general propositions. All thinking involves classification; all classification involves general terms. My very notion of Napoleon or hats or battles involves some general beliefs about the entities which these words denote. Moreover, my reasons for trusting an eye-witness account or a document entail judgements about the reliability of different kinds of testimony, or the range within which the behaviour of individuals is or is not variable and the like – judgements which are certainly general'.[11] Even if following a story is always the understanding of a particular event, this does not imply that one can grasp anything purely singular without using concepts. As Ludwig von Mises pointedly says: 'history is a sequence of phenomena that are characterized by their singularity. Those features which an event has in common with other events are not historical. What murder cases have in common refers to penal law, to psychology, to the technique of killing.'[12]

Even granted that there are essentially contestable concepts as defined by Gallie, this is not a sufficient reason to accept the Primacy of Historical Understanding Thesis. Gallie summarizes his project by saying that he hopes that 'intellectual history could be developed in such a fashion that it could take the place of, and (among other things) fulfil the only valid functions of traditional metaphysical statements and systems'.[13] I suppose Vico, Hegel, Croce and Collingwood would agree with this bold statement. However, I think that the argument about the primacy of identification with respect to narrative proves them to be wrong. Historical knowledge, *qua* knowledge of the development of an item in the world, is logically dependent on conceptual kowledge, *qua* knowledge of kinds of items; and not the other way round as Gallie holds.

3. The essential contestability thesis

As I have said, Connolly's definition of essential contestability is broader than Gallie's. While Gallie pays considerable attention to the question of what kinds of things we talk about when using essentially contestable words, Connolly (despite his mention of this question) seems to be more interested in the kinds of disagreements that result from essential contestability. According to Connolly, these are disagreements over the evaluation of something – value-disagreements. But, on a closer reading, it is not clear if these value-disagreements regard the way our shared criteria of value-judgements are applied in making judgements, or the values themselves. The first interpretation would be closer to Gallie's view. Indeed, Connolly seems to hint at this interpretation when he says that the concept of politics is essentially contestable because it is 'an internally complex concept with a broad and variable set of criteria but each criterion itself is relatively complex and open'.[14]

However, Connolly does not pursue this line of argument very far. He seems more interested in the connection between essential contestability and the supposed rebuttal of three philosophical dichotomies: (i) analytic vs. synthetic; (ii) facts vs. values; and (iii) description vs. evaluation. Here his argument becomes a curious mixture of highly technical points taken from writers such as Quine, Kuhn, Putnam and Hampshire (to mention just a few) and a Derrida-style campaign against dichotomies. While it is easy to see the connection between essential contestability and the rejection of the semantic analytic vs. synthetic distinction, it is much more difficult to make sense of the connection between essential contestability and the rejection of two dichotomies belonging respectively to ontology (facts vs. values) and the theory of intentionality (description vs. evaluation). There is of course a connection between the second and third dichotomies, namely that if the second does not hold then the third is not likely to either. But Connolly's argument seems more far-reaching than this. He seems to hold that the recognition of the collapse of the three dichotomies should be taken as evidence that there are essentially contestable concepts, and that this, in turn, will show that political philosophy (but, again, the argument seems wider) needs a new methodology based on genealogy and deconstruction. If my reconstruction is correct, it is easy to test the argument by checking the premises. I shall start with the first of these, namely the collapse of the analytic vs. synthetic distinction supposedly demonstrated by Quine. According to Hilary Putnam (one of the authorities quoted by Connolly), Quine's argument conflates two notions of analyticity. According to the first, 'a sentence is analytic if it can be obtained from a truth of logic by putting synonyms for synonyms'. According to the second, an analytic truth is one 'that is *confirmed no matter what*' (the traditional idea of a priority). While Quine's argument against the first version of the dichotomy relies on his contention that he does not know how to define 'synonymy' (and this claim, argues Putnam, is far from beyond reasonable doubt), his second and more promising argument establishes the revisability of any statement in our conceptual endowment, including statements about logical laws. Putnam holds that this is not an argument against analyticity at all, but instead an argument for the revisability of the laws of logic (traditionally regarded as being a priori).[15] If Putnam is right (as Connolly seems to assume) it is not easy to see why the rejection of a priority should have any consequence for the question of the essential contestability of political concepts. No one in their right mind would claim that political concepts are known a priori. Hence, under scrutiny, the first premise of Connolly's argument collapses.

Let us turn to the second and third premises. I think it is safe to check both together because Connolly himself seems to imply that the third depends on the second. He uses what looks like a semantic argument to challenge an ontological dichotomy: 'a description does not refer to data or elements that are bound together merely on the basis of similarities adhering in them, *but to describe is to characterize a situation from the vantage point of certain interests, purposes, or standards'*.[16] This statement is elucidated by means of an example: 'a table might be round or any of several other shapes; it might have four legs or none, be made of wood, metal, or other materials, be solid or soft. But various combinations of these elements unite to form a table if in combination they make a convenient place for us to eat from or to work on and are characteristically used in these ways. Similarly, a stick of wood, a metal rod, or other elongated object becomes a lever when it is put to the use of prying, and a large and indefinite set of plants, chemicals, and pills become medicine when they are taken with the reasonable expectation that an unhealthy condition will thereby be remedied'.[17] It seems that there is no fact of the matter in the way we use our language; our choice of words is parasitic on our motives, interests, hidden preferences. Connolly's choice of examples is the main source of the apparent solidity of his argument. A table is whatever one happens to use as a table. And the same holds for a lever. But does the argument hold for a tree? or a telephone? or one's sister? or the Queen of England? Does a painkiller, mistakenly prescribed during a heart attack, lose its capacity as a medicine even if, in that particular case, it fails to relieve the patient's condition? Should a promise always be in someone's interests? I doubt it, but I am even more doubtful when Connolly seems to claim that a broken promise is not always wrong. Connolly's interest-driven semantics cannot carry the weight of his argument, and are also the source of several mistakes (for instance, Connolly's definition of 'murder' as 'intentionally taking the life of another for personal advantage' has the puzzling consequence of ruling out murder in a third party's interest, or random 'disinterested' murder).

I think that the reason for this failure is that Connolly's point is not to establish the philosophical legitimacy of essential contestability at all. His argument is wider, and amounts to a radical rejection of the traditional understanding of philosophy as conceptual analysis. According to Connolly, this is a kind of ideology (in the Marxist sense) and should be rejected in favour of a more politically aware attitude.[18] I confess a lack of sympathy with this idea, but this is not the proper place to engage with it. As far as essential contestability is concerned, Connolly's argument fails to establish its connection with his general thesis on the need to reject analysis as the method of philosophy.

A textual remark might support my reconstruction of Connolly's argument. According to J. P. Day, in the expression 'essentially contestable' the word 'contestable' means 'can be contested', not 'ought to be contested' ('contestable', here, is used like 'visible' and unlike 'desirable'). Hence, the modifier 'essentially' means 'necessarily'.[19] I concur that this is the best reading of Gallie's text and that Gallie's use of the word 'contested' instead of 'contestable' is a mere slip of the pen. Connolly's view of the matter is different. He claims that the predicate 'essential' is ambiguous (like almost anything else, one might say), and so he gives the reader his own interpretation of the word: 'not only does the predicate signal that these disputes are central rather than trivial or peripheral, some have interpreted it to mean that they are *demonstrably* interminable rather than reasonably expected to be so and that there are no rational grounds whatsoever to guide and inform these debates. I wish to affirm the disputes to be centrally important, to deny that it is demonstrable that they are in principle irresolvable, and to deny that there are no criteria at all to illuminate these contests.'[20] The differences with Gallie's argument are striking. Gallie shows, with great ingenuity, that disputes about the meaning of essentially contestable words depend on the nature of such words. According to Gallie, the essential contestability of 'art' is here to stay. Connolly, by contrast, says that a word is contingently contested. One might wonder why a disagreement that is not demonstrably interminable should be reasonably expected to be so. More radically, one might wonder why one should bother with the *notion* of essential contestability at all, if it amounts to nothing more than saying that people sometimes happen to disagree. I suppose Connolly's answer to be: 'because those people disagree about things they regard as important'. Again, the idea of one's motives, interests and hidden preferences, seems to be central in Connolly's argument. On a closer reading, this amounts to the substitution of a traditional understanding of philosophy as conceptual analysis (by means of the analysis of language or otherwise) with a quasi-political, confrontational, rhetorical idea of this intellectual activity.

Even though Gallie fails in his attempt to use essential contestability as evidence of the Primacy of Historical Understanding Thesis, his ground-breaking treatment of these problems should be regarded as a major contribution to conceptual analysis. In particular, Gallie's idea that there is a kind of disagreement that depends on conceptual incommensurability can be very helpful to the social philosopher. Think, for example, of Ronald Dworkin's idea of law as an interpretative concept and of the similarities with Gallie's approach. According to Dworkin, the old question about wicked legal systems (are they really law?) can be given a satisfactory answer by focusing on the interpretative character (the essential contestability, I would say) of the word 'law'. Dworkin says: 'we need not worry so much about the right answer to the question whether immoral legal systems really count as law. Or rather we should worry about this in a different, more substantive way. For our language and idiom are rich enough to allow a great deal of discrimination and choice in the words we pick to say what we want to say, and our choice will therefore depend on the question we are trying to answer, our audience, and the context in which we speak. We need not deny that the Nazi system was an example of law, no matter which interpretation we favor of our own law, because there is an available sense in which it plainly was law. But we have no difficulty in understanding someone who does say that Nazi law was not really law, or was law in a degenerate sense, or was less than fully law.'[21] We can make sense of our intuition that the institutionalized aspect of legal activity does not help one to answer any of the possible questions about the application of the law unless it is supplemented by a substantive theory of the law itself. This option is not open on Connolly's reading of essential contestability. In Dworkin's example, according to Connolly, the advocates of the different answers to the question of the legal character of wicked legal systems will be arguing at cross-purposes.

4. Essential contestability restated

The Primacy of Historical Understanding Thesis is wrong in its claim of primacy. Historical understanding is different from analysis: *they answer different questions* (analysis: what is it? historical understanding: where does it come from?). The Essential Contestability Thesis is wrong in its claim that genealogy or deconstruction can supersede analysis. No amount of genealogy or deconstruction can tell one the difference between 'contract' and 'promise', only analysis can. Both are wrong because they are *not aware of the difference between words and concepts.*[22] Many words might appear to be essentially contestable, but it is their meaning that is *vague* or their use that is *ambiguous*. Vagueness and ambiguity are two features of ordinary language that cannot be completely eliminated. It is one of the great achievements of Felix E. Oppenheim to have shown the importance of definitions in reducing vagueness and ambiguity in ordinary language as used in the realm of politics.[23]

Nevertheless there are, as Oppenheim himself acknowledges, genuine cases of essential contestability. These depend on semantic properties, and hence are akin to vagueness (a semantic notion), not to ambiguity (a notion belonging to pragmatics). My suggestion is that there are words whose meaning is essentially contestable, but that a concept cannot be essentially contestable as a matter of logic. Sadly, the importance of the difference between words and concepts is often underestimated, and many confusions arise out of this misjudgement.

No concept can be essentially contestable, because concepts are used in judgements. A judgement is a mental act (expressed in a language or not) that can be true or false. This thesis was clearly stated by Frege in *Grundgesetze der Arithmetik*: 'a definition of a concept (of a possible predicate) must be complete; it must unambiguously determine, as regard any object, whether or not it falls under the concept (whether or not the predicate is truly assertible of it). Thus there must not be any object as regards which the definition leaves in doubt whether it falls under the concept; though for us men, with our defective knowledge, the question may not always be decidable. We may express this metaphorically as follows: the concept must have a sharp boundary. If we represent concepts in extension by areas on a plane, this is admittedly a picture that may be used only with caution, but here it can do us a good service. To a concept without sharp boundary there would correspond an area that had not a sharp boundary-line all round, but in places just vaguely faded away into the background. This would not really be an area at all; and likewise a concept that is not sharply defined is wrongly termed a concept. Such quasi-conceptual constructions cannot be recognised as concepts by logic; it is impossible to lay down precise laws for them. The law of excluded middle is really just another form of the requirement that the concept should have a sharp boundary. Any object Δ that you choose to take either falls under the concept φ or does not fall under it: *tertium non datur.*[24] The allowing of exceptions to this law of the excluded middle (as in three-valued logic) does not go as far as to deny it completely. In ordinary language, where vagueness often occurs, Frege's metaphor might be used in a slightly modified form that I borrow from Wittgenstein *via* Peter Geach: to represent a vague predicate P one should draw two concentric boundary lines, A and B; P will be definitely true inside the inner boundary, and the negation of P will be definitely true of what lies outside the outer boundary. Even if the boundary is arbitrary, because there is an area where one does not know if P is true or not, the concept will have sharp boundaries where it is still possible to draw a clear line (i.e. where there are criteria available). This means that a word whose meaning is vague can have sharp boundaries and hence have precise logical properties without any second-order vagueness. Even if the meaning of 'oak' and 'elephant' is vague, it is certain that no oak-tree is an elephant. So, the statement: 'this is an oak-tree, therefore it is not an elephant' is true despite vagueness, if asserted about something that is tree-like and oak-like enough to satisfy the relevant tests. Without these arbitrary, but reasonable, boundaries there will be no room for judgements. Without boundaries one cannot tell trees from elephants.[25] The area of vagueness is an area of suspended judgement for lack of criteria, not a mysterious third realm. For our purposes, it is safe to say that one cannot make a judgement with an essentially-contestable-thing-in-the-mind. By means of analysis and reconstruction, one can reduce the vagueness or the ambiguity of a word insofar as it is possible to use it as a concept to make judgements. But language is not just for judgements. We do many things with words, like telling stories or alluding to sequences of events in ways that are not judging in the technical sense. There is no point in asking if a story is true in the strict sense. A story might be interesting, moralizing, persuasive or incredible without being strictly true or false. This is where the area of irreducible vagueness comes in. Most of the words we use in ordinary language keep their vagueness in everyday discourses without damage for the various purposes of such discourses. No one would say that Gibbon or A. J. P. Taylor should not be read because they mostly use words that are irreducibly vague. The same point applies to essential contestability, this being simply a particular case of vagueness.

Essential contestability is a property of certain words. When a word is essentially contestable it is a kind of cluster-word used in ordinary language to allude to different activities (in space and time) that go under the same name because they have some relation of similitude, analogy, genetic derivation or rhetorical connection. Allusion, or even mention, are different from predication. These words are thought of as 'standing for' activities whose identity depends on rules the interpretation of which leaves partly open the question of which actions are correct with respect to the rules themselves. Think again of the example of football. The rules leave open the question of what counts as 'outstanding' or 'elegant' in the game. This is where disagreement comes in. It is genuine disagreement because the participants do share a common background of assumptions (their knowledge of the rules and of the history of the game, their reference to exemplars in the past); but they lack criteria that are beyond question to settle this disagreement. This is the reason why the meaning of the word is contested. Such a feature explains why political scientists, sociologists, historians and anthropologists (and like-minded philosophers) are so fascinated by the notion of essential contestability. The notion of essential contestability seems indeed to capture nicely the semantic properties of some of the words they use in talking about social groups and human affairs in general. In these cases, one cannot use material continuity as the principle of identification over time of objects belonging to the same kind. Think, for example, of words like 'socialist' or 'conservative' as used in talking about parties or political movements. According to Alasdair MacIntyre, to speak about the identity or the continuity of a political party 'involves no reference, explicit or implicit, to law-governedness. The historic continuity of a political party is compatible with large-scale changes in regularities of behaviour; what is crucial is a certain kind of continuity in belief and in practice informed by belief. The continuity and identity of a planet or an atom is quite different from the continuity and identity of physics or of the Royal Society, of politics or of the Conservative party. Part of the continuity and identity both of such a form of social practice and of such a form of social organization is the continuity of institutionalized argument, debate, and conflict.'[26] In this sense, it is true that in order to grasp the differences in the way in which, say, 'democracy' is understood in Italy – as opposed to the United Kingdom – one needs a certain amount of historical reconstruction. But this is not necessary in order to make a judgement about the democratic nature of the Italian government; rather, it is necessary in order to grasp which are the ideas, the narratives and the images that are associated with the use of the word 'democracy' for an Italian native speaker. It might be the case that they are noticeably different from those of the average British or German citizen.

To sum up my argument: one can judge if a government is democratic or not, but in order to do so one needs a theory of democracy articulated around a concept of democracy. This is a product of analysis and reconstruction (including the elimination, by redefinition, of some of the contradictory features of the ordinary use of the word 'democracy'). Both the advocates of the Primacy of Historical Understanding Thesis and those of the Essential Contestability Thesis fail to notice that (in order to make judgements) one needs to ask, when confronted with an open-ended process: Is this the same thing as the thing that it reminds me of? In order to say if something is 'the same thing' one needs the concept of that thing. Only a definition (i.e. the set of necessary and jointly sufficient conditions of application of a concept) can specify a concept. A definition is necessary not for the use of a word, but for that of a concept. Thus, in order to know which concepts one is using, and whether they are used properly, one needs analysis.

Notes

1. A revised version of this article was published as ch. VIII of Gallie's book *Philosophy and Historical Understanding* (London: Chatto & Windus, 1964). All references in the text are to this version of the essay.
2. See Stuart Hampshire, *Thought and Action* (London: Chatto & Windus 1959), p. 229.
3. W. E. Connolly, *The Terms of Political Discourse* (Oxford: Blackwell, 3rd edn 1993), p. 10.
4. Gallie, *Philosophy and Historical Understanding*, pp. 140–56.
5. Connolly, *The Terms of Political Discourse*, pp. viii–ix.
6. Gallie, *Philosophy and Historical Understanding*, p. 159.
7. Gallie, *Philosophy and Historical Understanding*, p. 161.
8. Gallie, *Philosophy and Historical Understanding*, p. 168.
9. See Richard Robinson, *Definition* (Oxford: Clarendon Press, 1950), pp. 27–34.
10. Arthur C. Danto, 'African Art and Artifacts', in Danto, *Encounters and Reflections. Art in the Historical Present* (Berkeley: University of California Press, 1986), p. 168.
11. Isaiah Berlin, 'The Concept of Scientific History', in Berlin, *Concepts and Categories*, ed. Henry Hardy (London: Chatto & Windus, 1999), p. 113.
12. Ludwig von Mises, *Theory and History* (London: Jonathan Cape, 1958), p. 212.
13. Gallie, *Philosophy and Historical Understanding*, p. 224.

14. Connolly, *The Terms of Political Discourse*, p. 14.
15. Hilary Putnam, '"Two Dogmas" Revisited', in Putnam, *Realism and Reason. Philosophical Papers*, vol. III (Cambridge: Cambridge University Press, 1983), pp. 87–97.
16. Connolly, *The Terms of Political Discourse*, p. 23, italics in original.
17. Connolly, *The Terms of Political Discourse*, p. 23.
18. Connolly, *The Terms of Political Discourse*, p. 225.
19. J. P. Day, 'Is the Concept of Freedom Essentially Contestable?', in Day, *Liberty and Justice* (London: Croom Helm, 1987), p. 182.
20. Connolly, *The Terms of Political Discourse*, p. 230.
21. Ronald Dworkin, *Law's Empire* (London: Fontana Press, 1986), pp. 103–4.
22. This distinction is made in Peter Morriss, *Power: a Philosophical Analysis* (Manchester: Manchester University Press, 1987), pp. 202–4. However, Morriss seems to use 'concept' simply to mean that which words express or to which they refer. On my account, we use concepts only when we make judgements. Thus, I would not say that all words stand for concepts.
23. Felix E. Oppenheim, *Political Concepts: a Reconstruction* (Chicago: Chicago University Press, 1981), pp. 182–5.
24. Gottlob Frege, 'On Definitions', in Frege, *Philosophical Writings*, ed. P. Geach and M. Black (Oxford: Basil Blackwell, 1952), p. 159.
25. Peter T. Geach, *Logic Matters* (Oxford: Blackwell, 1972), pp. 86–7.
26. Alasdair MacIntyre, 'The Essential Contestability of Some Social Concepts', *Ethics*, 84 (1973), pp. 4–5.

4
Freedom and Bivalence*

Hillel Steiner

As has been true of so many others, my own first encounter with Felix Oppenheim's path-breaking work, *Dimensions of Freedom*, proved to be a watershed in the development of my thinking on this subject.[1] Even now, over thirty years later, it continues to illuminate and inspire reflection on the profound complexity of that concept.

What Oppenheim aims to do in that book is to supply social scientists and others with an analysis of the meaning of freedom that possesses two key attributes: (i) that it is devoid of any valuational connotations and can thus enable that term to figure in statements which are testable solely by reference to empirical evidence; and (ii) that the relation it refers to is solely an interpersonal one. To do this, he painstakingly explores the many diverse senses in which 'freedom' is commonly used and distills out one usage, which he labels *social freedom*, the presence of which depends upon whether persons' actions are prevented or punished by others. This analysis is then amplified and refined so as to distinguish this concept clearly from other apparently similar ones.[2] The main burden of this essay is to argue the need for a further refinement.

Having isolated the concept of *social freedom* as uniquely referring to an empirical relation between actors, Oppenheim is concerned to avert what he considers to be a possible misapprehension of its logic.

> Our first reaction might be to interpret social freedom as the opposite of unfreedom ... If I am not being made unfree to do something, am I not left free to do it?[3]

Failure to appreciate that the answer to this question is 'No' has, he suggests, licensed much ideologically-driven distortion.

57

Historically, freedom has all too often been equated with absence of unfreedom. The expression 'freedom to propagate the truth' has been used as if it meant the same as not being unfree to spread the 'truth'; but what is really meant is: unfreedom to advocate 'error'. 'Freedom to worship God' is often another way of expressing the view that agnostics should not be permitted to voice their convictions. 'Freedom to work' in a dictatorship often means compulsory labor. Because of the favorable connotation of the word 'freedom' it is politically expedient for the advocates of unfreedom to parade their ideology under the banner of liberty.[4]

So, wishing to deprive these ideologues of their licence to mount such parades, Oppenheim argues that

it becomes, thus, necessary to distinguish between being unfree to do something and not being free to do it.[5]

Accordingly, he draws that distinction in the following way:

With respect to Y, X is not free to do x, to the extent that X is, with respect to Y, either unfree to do x or unfree to abstain from doing x. It follows that, whenever X is unfree to do x, he is not free to do so. But the contrary implication does not hold. If it is mandatory for X to do x, X is not free to do x; yet he is not unfree to do so.[6]

If this is the case, then it follows that

[s]ocial freedom is the contradictory, not of unfreedom, but of not being free to do something. If it is not the case that X is not free to do x, then he is free to do so. With respect to Y, X is free to do x to the extent that X is, with respect to Y, neither unfree to do x nor unfree to abstain from doing x.[7]

And X is thus describable as free as long as Y does not do any of the following:

(a) prevent X from doing x; (b) make it necessary for X to do x; (c) make it punishable for X to do x; (d) make it punishable for X to refrain from doing x.[8]

Now, one way of framing the question we need to address here might be thought to be this: Can it really be true, as Oppenheim's account claims, that X is *both* not free to do *x and* not unfree to do so? Can there be actions which we're *neither free nor unfree* to do? Isn't it the case – as we were all taught by our primary school grammar teachers (who were not logicians) – that two 'negatives' make a 'positive'?

We now know, of course, that the answer to the last of these questions is 'Not necessarily'. But that fact does not, in itself, give us an unequivocally clear answer to the preceding questions. And, indeed, no such answer is available. For what is evident – and what Oppenheim's book precisely displays – is the enormous variety of opposed conceptions of freedom sustained by ordinary language: opposed, in the sense that these conceptions frequently yield mutually contradictory judgements about whether a particular person is free to do a particular action in a particular circumstance. And among this plurality of freedom conceptions, the ones which most familiarly eschew the *bivalency* of our early grammar lessons are those which are value-laden.

For, on such conceptions, an action's *positive eligibility* (on some scale of evaluation) is a necessary condition of its figuring in freedom/unfreedom judgements at all. Hence persons, whether unprevented or prevented by others from doing actions which lack such eligibility, are describable as neither free nor unfree to do them, under those conceptions. Such conceptions fail to conform to the 'Principle of Bivalency'. They deviate from it, not for the standard reason – namely, that there can be vagueness about whether some actions are in fact subject to prevention (or punishability) – but rather because those actions simply don't count one way or the other. They are not *freedom-relevant* – in just the same way as raspberry jam, being neither tall nor short, is not height-relevant. Accordingly, we might call such conceptions of freedom 'trivalent' ones.

To draw attention to these differences, however, is not to counsel despair. For as long as we take care to distinguish these various conceptions and to avoid sliding back and forth between them in our reasoning, we have no grounds to fear the sort of confusion that otherwise can and often does result.

The point of the foregoing remarks is simply to serve as a prologue to two suggestions: one weak, the other strong. The weak suggestion is that, among the many conceptions of freedom embedded in ordinary language, there may be *two* – rather than only one – that exhibit the pair of attributes which Oppenheim claims are distinctive of *social freedom*: namely, that (i) it refers to a relation between actors, and one that (ii) can be empirically identified without recourse to evaluative judgements. So, next to Oppenheim's *social freedom* conception, we can juxtapose another conception which I'll call *bivalent freedom*. *Bivalent freedom* is the conception implicit in the lessons of our grammar teachers. My strong suggestion, for which I'll argue more hesitantly, is that Oppenheim's *social freedom* lacks the independence from valuational connotations that he attributes to it.

Consider an example of doing *x*. Suppose that my doing *x* is my entering the precincts of a nuclear power station. And suppose, not unreasonably, that I, as a thoroughly unauthorized person, would be prevented by Y from doing so. Hence, I am (on both *social freedom* and *bivalent freedom*) describable as *un*free to do so and also as *not* free to do so. The question we need now to ask is whether my *abstaining* from doing so is something which I am free to do.

Not according to *social freedom*. On Oppenheim's analysis, as we've seen, Y's prevention of my entry makes me not only unfree to enter but also not free to abstain from entering. That I have a strong desire and every intention not to enter this or any other nuclear power station, and that I avail myself of every opportunity to abstain from entering them, in no way impairs the description of me as not free to abstain from doing so. So the implication of this account is that I am not free *both* to enter *and* to abstain from entering. My being free to enter is actually a *necessary condition* of my being free to abstain from entering. And since I lack the former freedom, I lack the latter one as well.

The same holds when *x* is itself an abstention. Oppenheim notes that, in Belgium, persons are unfree to abstain from voting in elections. If this is so, they are also (on both *social freedom* and *bivalent freedom*) not free to abstain from voting. But a further implication of *social freedom* alone is that they are also appropriately described as not free *to* vote. And they are so, despite the fact that their voting is neither prevented nor punishable. To be free to vote, Belgians would have to be free to abstain from voting – which they're not.

The affinities and differences between these two conceptions of freedom can be seen more precisely if we examine the following six propositions and some of their logical relations to one another.

(1)   Belgians are free to abstain from voting.
(2)   Belgians are not free to abstain from voting.
(3)   Belgians are unfree to abstain from voting.
(4)   Belgians are free to vote.
(5)   Belgians are not free to vote.

(6)   Belgians are unfree to vote.

What is uncontroversial between the two conceptions is that

(3) implies (2)   (2) contradicts (1)
(6) implies (5)   (5) contradicts (4).

However, they differ inasmuch as they respectively entail the following:

Social Freedom	*Bivalent Freedom*
(3) implies (5)	(3) implies (4)
(6) implies (2)	(6) implies (1).

And consequently, the two conceptions are mutually contradictory. For if (3) is true, then

Social Freedom	*Bivalent Freedom*
(4) is false	(4) is true
(5) is true	(5) is false.

So what can be said about the comparative merits of these two conceptions?

Oppenheim correctly observes that, with respect to voting, Americans are more free than Belgians because Americans are free both to vote and to abstain from voting. And it's true, of course, that in implying that Belgians *are* free to vote, *bivalent freedom* counterintuitively implies that Belgians are no more free than, say, Burmese with respect to voting. This is because Burmese, being unfree to vote, are possessed of a freedom which Belgians lack: namely the freedom to abstain from voting.[9]

But I would suggest that whatever counterintuitiveness there is in this equivalence, it rests entirely on an evaluative premiss which most of us happen to share: that is, the belief that the freedom to vote is usually far more valuable than the freedom to abstain from voting.[10] In this regard, two things need to be said. The first is that it may not be open to proponents of an *empirical* conception of freedom to invoke evaluatively-based counterintuitions in support of such conceptions. And second, the nomination of this as a counterintuition itself presupposes that, contrary to *social freedom*, Belgians are indeed appropriately described as free to vote.

Now descriptive inappropriateness, we must immediately concede, is simply too blunt an instrument to be decisive in arguments about concepts which display as much non-univocality as freedom does. Yet we do need some explanation of why there is some strain involved in embracing the implication, say, that Belgians are not describable as free to vote. So what sorts of reason can be given for why we should embrace it? As far as I can see, Oppenheim's argument for doing so consists entirely in the previously cited suggestion that this embrace is necessary if we are to deny the banner of liberty to parading ideologues. We just don't want the Ys of this world to be linguistically enabled to parade their sponsorship of the 'freedom to abstain from entering nuclear power stations'.

Yet we may well wonder whether this proposed linguistic disablement is not thereby purchased at too high a price. Oppenheim was previously quoted as remarking that

> [t]he expression 'freedom to propagate the truth' has been used as if it meant the same as not being unfree to spread the 'truth'; but what is really meant is: unfreedom to advocate 'error'.

This is no doubt, and regrettably, quite correct. But imagine a group – perhaps within a prison or on the internet – whose members are prevented from communicating with one another at all, and irrespective of the veracity of whatever communication they would undertake if they were not so prevented. Now suppose that their bonds are loosened, but only to the extent that they are thence unprevented from communicating the truth; communicating error is still prevented. Should we not want to say, in the interests of descriptive accuracy, that they have indeed acquired a freedom which they previously lacked – namely, the freedom to propagate the truth? Should we reject a conception of freedom, *bivalent freedom*, that licenses us to offer this description of that emancipatory development? In general, should we regard the freedom to abstain from an action as a necessary condition of the freedom to do it?

I should, perhaps, note here that not all *trivalent* conceptions of freedom operate in this way. Not all conceptions that sustain the view, that actions can be ones which we're either (i) free or (ii) unfree or (iii) neither-free-nor-unfree to do, are conceptions that make our freedom to abstain from an action a necessary condition of the freedom to do it. Most trivalent conceptions, as was previously observed, are evaluative ones. For them, actions which get into the 'neither-free-nor-unfree' category do so because they are of a type which lacks positive eligibility on some scale of evaluation.[11] Actions which are inauthentic or which fail to reflect the General Will or which violate moral rights or which run counter to our higher-order preferences are only a few among the many types that have been nominated, by various political theories, as being ones which we can be neither free nor unfree to do, regardless of whether others prevent us from doing them or not.

The trivalency of Oppenheim's *social freedom* is not at all like this. No type of action is ruled out as an eligible subject of freedom/ unfreedom judgements. Actions get into Oppenheim's 'neither-free-nor-unfree' category, not by virtue of their theory-selected (relational) properties, but rather because their abstentions are in the 'unfree' category.[12] In this sense, we might describe the eligibility criteria of those other trivalent conceptions as *exogenous*, whereas Oppenheim's is *endogenous*.

Or is it? What other motivation might there be – other than wanting to stop ideologues parading under the banner of liberty – for insisting that the freedom to abstain from doing x is a necessary condition of the freedom to do x? Well, perhaps we think that, unless Belgians were like Americans and were free not to vote, what they do on election day can't *really* be described as voting. This seems highly implausible, so let's try an example that looks more promising and presses harder. If you, as a night-club bouncer, push me out of the club, it's clear that I'm describable as unfree to abstain from leaving the club. Yet we're further tempted to say – and *social freedom* does say – that I'm also not free to leave the club. Why say this? Maybe because my leaving the club in these circumstances isn't really something I *do*; rather, it looks more like something that's done to me. Our first instinct would definitely not be one to describe the bouncer as respecting my freedom to leave the club.

But first instincts are not infallible. What, after all, is the difference between the bouncer and Belgian cases? What has the bouncer prevented? Has he prevented the behavioural event of my leaving the club from occurring? Evidently not. Has he prevented me from forming the intention to bring about that event? Again, no. Can we say, then, that what he's prevented is that intention's being the cause of that event? Once again, no, because nothing in this story rules out the possibility of that intention including his pushing me as the means of bringing that event about[13] – just as my intention to be checkmated in a game of chess or to make a killing on the stock-market similarly includes the actions of others. Belgians, unfree to abstain from voting, perform the

behavioural event of voting and, presumably, do so with the accompa-
nying intention. Why should we treat the bouncing case differently?
What the bouncer *has* done, we can all agree, is to prevent me from
leaving 'under my own steam': I was indeed unfree to leave the club
under my own steam. But that freedom, which the bouncer denied me,
is just not the same as the freedom to leave *per se* – just as the freedom
to fly business class to New York is not the same as the freedom to fly
to New York *per se*. I can be unfree to do the former without being
unfree to do the latter.

Why, then, insist on the freedom to abstain from doing x as a necessary condition of the freedom to do x, and *vice versa*? On the basis of
what we've just seen, we might conjecture that the motivation to do so
is supplied by a belief in the relevance, for freedom, of our doing
actions *under our own steam* or, in less metaphoric terms, *voluntarily* or
willingly. Yet that abstaining freedom is neither a necessary nor a
sufficient condition of doing an action voluntarily, as the existence of
many enthusiastic Belgian voters amply indicates.

An alternative motivational conjecture might be that we're reluctant
to describe ourselves as free to do actions which we don't want, or
have no reason, to do. This indeed was the thesis advanced by Isaiah
Berlin in his seminal lecture *Two Concepts of Liberty* – a thesis which he
later came to reject in the revised version of that lecture. In the original
version, Berlin proposed:

> If I am prevented by others from doing what I want I am to that
> degree unfree.[14]

As many commentators have since remarked, and as Berlin himself
came to acknowledge, this formulation both flies in the face of a fairly
entrenched feature of common usage and generates a serious paradox.
It opposes common usage inasmuch as we think that the prisoner,
locked in his jail-cell, is unfree to go to the theatre *regardless* of whether
he wants to do so, is indifferent to doing so, or wants not to do so.
More worryingly, perhaps, Berlin's original formulation paradoxically
licenses the inference that my unfreedom can be reduced by my suppression of those desires which others prevent me from satisfying. And
conversely, it implies that my unfreedom can increase merely by virtue
of an increase in my desires and without any alteration whatsoever in
the restrictive treatment meted out to me by those others. In short, this
formulation suggests that ultimately one's oppressor is oneself. And in
so doing, it presents a conception of freedom lacking the attribute

which Oppenheim seeks, inasmuch as it refers not to a purely *inter*personal relation but rather to an (at least partially) *intra*personal one. To avoid these consequences, what we need is something like the following amended version of Berlin's original formulation:

> If I am prevented by others from doing what I *might* want I am to that degree unfree.[15]

And since voting is something any Belgian might want to do, since I might want to leave the club by means of the bouncer's push, and since these are not prevented, this revised formulation supplies no grounds for denying that the Belgians and I are free to do them.

So my own best guess, as to the motivation for insisting on the freedom to abstain from doing *x* as a necessary condition of the freedom to do *x*, and *vice versa*, remains the one mentioned earlier: that we just don't want the Ys of this world parading under the banner of liberty. If they want to carry on with those parades then, on Oppenheim's analysis, they had better stop preventing us from, say, entering nuclear power stations. Had the drafters of the current Belgian constitution been serious about vesting Belgians with the freedom to vote, they should have given them the freedom not to vote.

It seems to me, however, that this kind of reason for withdrawing that parade license has much more to do with *values* – perhaps ones often associated with liberalism, such as autonomy or pluralism[16] – rather than having much to do with considerations of what counts as interference with actions. This is, to be sure, merely a suggestion and not at all a knock-down argument. *Social freedom*'s eligibility criterion, for whether we can be described as free to do an unprevented (or non-punishable) action, is the impeccably empirical one of whether we're prevented from (or punishable for) abstaining from it. And this is still very different from the eligibility criteria of other trivalent conceptions – criteria which exogenously select some favoured property of that type of action itself. Yet it remains unclear to me why the freedom to abstain from an action should be an eligibility criterion at all and, for that matter, why an empirical conception of freedom should entertain *any* eligibility criterion. To that extent, there may be some doubt as to whether *social freedom* is entirely devoid of valuational connotations.

Suppose, then, that our language does indeed sustain an empirical conception of freedom that is bivalent: a conception such that 'unfree to do *x*' *implies* 'free to abstain from doing *x*', and that 'unfree to abstain from doing *x*' *implies* 'free to do *x*'. This fact has important consequences for the range of conditions under which persons can be regarded as unfree. For recall that, under *social freedom*, it is not only *x*'s prevention by others, but also *x*'s punishability, that count as sufficient conditions of X being unfree to do *x*. Can this be true under *bivalent freedom*?

Let's return to the nuclear power station which Y prevents me from entering. And let's further suppose that there is a notorious terrorist, Z, who has kidnapped my family and who will kill them unless I carry a bomb which he has given me into that power station. On both *social freedom* and *bivalent freedom*, I'm unfree to comply with Z's threat because I'm unfree to enter the power station. On *bivalent freedom*, I am free to abstain from complying with that threat because – being bivalent and implying that 'unfree to do *x*' *implies* 'free to abstain from doing *x*' – it thereby implies that I'm free to abstain from entering the power station. However, on *social freedom*, according to which punishability is a sufficient condition of unfreedom, I am unfree to abstain from entering the power station. On Oppenheim's analysis, then, I am unfree both to enter and to abstain from entering.[17]

Now we know, *ex hypothesi*, that this affair is going to end very badly indeed and that what is going to happen is my abstention from entering the power station. One significant feature of *bivalent freedom* is that, unlike *social freedom* and most other conceptions of freedom, it does not logically commit us to denying that people are free to do things which they actually do. On the contrary, it commits us to affirming that. Because abstention from any prevented or punishable action can itself be punishable, a bivalent conception of freedom must reject punishability as a sufficient condition of unfreedom.[18] Of course, the punishability of doing *x* does entail that, once I've done *x*, I shall be made unfree to do – prevented from doing – a great many other actions (including many which are not punishable or otherwise prevented). But, at least on *bivalent freedom*, that fact does not imply that I am unfree to do *x*. Indeed I must do it, and hence be free to do it, if I am to incur that subsequent unfreedom.

Nor, on reflection, is this quite as counterintuitive as some have wanted to suggest. For it's plain that, when we claim that we're free to do a certain type of action, we don't mean that we're free to do *all* actions of that type. My being free to give lectures does not mean that I'm free to stand up and deliver a lecture in the middle of a religious ceremony or a war zone. It means, rather, that there is *at least one action* which fits the description of 'giving a lecture' and which I'm free to do. Hence even if the punishability of giving lectures applied to all actions fitting that description, this would not imply my unfreedom to lecture. As the legal maxim has it, 'No punishment without a crime'.

So I'll conclude by simply observing that, although our early grammar teachers were certainly incorrect to insist on the necessity of bivalence, it's very doubtful that the bivalent conception of freedom can be eliminated without loss from the promiscuous usage of our ordinary language.

Notes

* I am grateful to Ian Carter, Jerry Cohen and Matthew Kramer for their helpful comments on several arguments used in this essay.
1. Felix E. Oppenheim, *Dimensions of Freedom: an Analysis* (New York: St. Martin's Press, 1961).
2. An abbreviated version of this analysis is presented in Oppenheim's subsequent work, *Political Concepts* (Chicago: University of Chicago Press, 1981).
3. Oppenheim, *Dimensions of Freedom*, p. 110.
4. Oppenheim, *Dimensions of Freedom*, pp. 110–11.
5. Oppenheim, *Dimensions of Freedom*, p. 111.
6. Oppenheim, *Dimensions of Freedom*, p. 111.
7. Oppenheim, *Dimensions of Freedom*, p. 111.
8. Oppenheim, *Dimensions of Freedom*, p. 111.
9. Note that *social freedom* generates the same counterintuition, though for different reasons. For under that conception, while Belgians are describable as 'neither free nor unfree to vote', Burmese are describable as 'neither free nor unfree to abstain from voting'.
10. '*Usually* far more valuable', because this may not be true in one-party electoral systems, especially ones in which persons are unfree to abstain from voting.
11. One *non*-evaluative trivalent conception imposes its *technological possibility* as a condition of an action's eligibility to figure in freedom/unfreedom judgements: actions which are technologically *im*possible are thereby ones which we're neither free nor unfree to do. This conception is, however, not unproblematic, for the following reasons. Often, one action's, A_1's, occurrence is a necessary causal condition of another's, A_5's: my sharpening my pencil is a necessary condition of my using it to play noughts and crosses. Accordingly, if I'm prevented from doing – unfree to do – A_1, I am thereby also unfree to do A_5. Conversely, if I am free to sharpen my pencil, then (barring other interferences) I'm also free to use it to play noughts and crosses, regardless of whether or not I sharpen the pencil. Hence to claim that a technologically impossible action, A_5, is one which we're neither free nor unfree to do, is to presuppose that A_5's impossibility is *not* due to the unfreedom to do an action, A_1, in a relevant technology-devising chain of actions (A_1, A_2, A_3, A_4). For if it *were* due to such unfreedom, A_5 would indeed be an action eligible to figure in freedom/unfreedom judgements:

that is, we would be unfree to do it. And so it's simply unclear why, if persons are in fact free to do all the actions ($A_1 - A_4$) in that technology-devising chain of actions, we should not describe them as also free (barring other interferences) to do any action (A_5) made possible by that chain, regardless of whether or not they do all those technology-devising actions.

12. And conversely, abstentions from actions get into his 'neither-free-nor-unfree' category because those actions are in the 'unfree' category.

13. Bored with being in the club, I might wish to leave it in a manner that would not make my companions (who are enjoying themselves) feel that I was simply abandoning them.

14. Isaiah Berlin, *Two Concepts of Liberty* (Oxford: Oxford University Press, 1958), p. 7.

15. Cf. Isaiah Berlin, *Four Essays on Liberty* (Oxford: Oxford University Press, 1969), pp. xxxviii–xl; Hillel Steiner, *An Essay on Rights* (Oxford: Blackwell, 1994), ch. 2(A).

16. Thus in electoral systems where voting is mandatory, contestants have *ceteris paribus* less incentive pluralistically to cater to diverse minority preferences, because they know that the 'exit' option – abstention – is blocked. Theirs is a constrained rivalry and voters' choices may, perhaps, be correspondingly described as possessing constrained autonomy.

17. Note that this analysis yields the same conclusion even if Y does *not* prevent my entry, but only makes it punishable.

18. Elsewhere, I've offered reasons independent of the present ones for why an action's punishability does not make one (empirically) unfree to do it; cf. *An Essay on Rights*, ch. 2(B).

5
Dimensions of Nomic Freedom

Amedeo G. Conte

> We do not know the boundaries because none have been drawn.
>
> Ludwig Wittgenstein[1]

The title of this paper, 'Dimensions of Nomic Freedom', is a variation on the title of Felix E. Oppenheim's fundamental contribution to eleutheriology,[2] *Dimensions of Freedom*.[3] I shall deal, more specifically, with *nomic* freedom,[4] that is, freedom in relation to *nómoi*, to *rules*, as opposed to the kind of freedom dealt with by Oppenheim (which we might call *non-nomic* or, simply, *ontic* freedom).

1.   Nomic (or rule-relative) possibility

1.1.   Wittgenstein's 'freedom of the pieces'

1.1.1. In the posthumous *Wittgenstein's Lectures, Cambridge 1932–1935*, Ludwig Wittgenstein (1889–1951) writes: 'The rules of chess [...] constitute the freedom of the pieces'.[5] The rules Wittgenstein is referring to are *eidetic-constitutive* rules. In the case of eidetic-constitutive rules, action is *made possible* by its rules; in other words, the rules are a *necessary condition of possibility* of action.

1.1.2. *Eidetic-constitutive* rules do not prescribe a piece of behaviour, as deontic[6] (i.e. regulative) rules do,[7] but constitute the *eidos* (the idea, the type) of their object.[8]

For instance, the rules of a praxis like the game of chess constitute both the *praxis* itself and (in the praxis) its *praxemes*. (The term 'praxeme' is modelled on 'phoneme', and stands for 'unit of praxis'. The praxemes of chess are the *pieces* (for instance, the rook); the *pragmemes* (for instance, castling); the *game-situations* (for instance, check).)

In my research on eidetic-constitutive rules, I have developed *two* definitions of this concept: an *ontological* one (in terms of *condition*) and a *semiotic* one (in terms of *connotation* or *intension*). The two definitions are as follows:

1.1.2.1. The *first* definition (the *ontological* one) is in terms of *condition*: eidetic-constitutive rules are a *necessary condition* of a praxis and of its praxemes.

In eidetic-constitutive rules there is a paradoxical inversion of the relationship between the *rule* and the *ruled*. For instance, the rules of chess are the necessary condition both of the *praxis* called chess and of its *praxemes* (in particular, of the *pieces*; of the *pragmemes*; and of the *game-situations*) in the sense that neither this praxis nor its praxemes exist independently of (prior to) the rules.

In the case of *eidetic-constitutive* rules, the relation between *rule* and *action* is the reverse of that found in the case of *deontic* rules:

(i)   *deontic rules* (such as the rule prohibiting one to drive past a red traffic-light) limit the nomic possibility of action. In this sense, they *limit* freedom;

(ii) *eidetic-constitutive rules* (such as the rule according to which one ought to move the rook in a straight line), on the other hand, do not limit the nomic possibility of action. They do not limit freedom; rather, they *constitute* it.

1.1.2.2. The *second* definition of eidetic-constitutive rules (the *semiotic* one) is in terms of *connotation* or *intension*: eidetic-constitutive rules are those that determine the *connotation* (or the *intension*) of those terms that (in the formulation of the rules) designate the praxemes (the units of praxis) which are governed by the rules.

For example, the rules of chess are eidetic-constitutive because (and in the sense that) they determine the connotation (the intension) of the terms ('rook, 'castling', 'check', ...) which designate the praxemes (pieces, pragmemes, game-situations) of the game.

1.1.3. An enlightening instance of the thesis that eidetic-constitutive rules constitute what Wittgenstein calls 'the freedom of the pieces' is to be found in the work of the Polish philosopher Czesław Znamierowski (1888–1967).[9]

1.1.3.1. Znamierowski explicitly asserts that there are rules which render action *possible*, rules which create new *possibilities* of action ('nowe możliwości działania'), rules which are a necessary condition for the *possibility* of action. Znamierowski calls these rules 'constructive rules'. (The Polish for 'constructive rule' is a transparent phrase of Latin origin: 'norma konstrukcyjna'.)

1.1.3.2. Znamierowski clarifies his concept of a constructive rule by citing as an example the rules of chess: constructive rules create 'new *possibilities* of action', which would not exist without them. More specifically, without the rules of chess, the moves of the chess-men would be *impossible*. 'Without the rules of chess, there would be no moves of the rook, of the pawn, or of the king.'[10]

1.1.3.3. The reason for using the adjective 'constructive' ('konstrukcyjny') in the phrase 'constructive rule' ('norma konstrukcyjna') is indicated by Znamierowski where he says that constructive rules 'construct' ('konstruują') new acts.[11]

Constructive rules, Znamierowski points out, produce not only the *necessity* ('konieczność') of an action (as *deontic* rules do), but also its *possibility* ('możliwość').[12]

1.2. Kant's dove

1.2.1. Following Kant, we might say that eidetic-constitutive rules are to action as air is to the flight of a dove. Feeling the resistance of the air as it flies, the dove might perhaps think that it would be easier to fly in air-free space ('im luftleeren Raum'), failing to recognize that it is exactly the air that makes its flight possible.[13] (By the same token, a train-driver might think that his train would move more freely were it not for the rails, despite the fact that it is exactly the rails which (although they undoubtely limit and constrain the movement of the train) make it possible for the train to advance.[14])

1.2.2. Both *deontic rules* and *eidetic-constitutive* rules are determinants of action and impose *constraints* on it. However, they are related to freedom of action in two opposite ways.

Some light may be thrown on this difference between *deontic* rules and *eidetic-constitutive* rules by means of an analogy. Think of the free flow of the water in a river. There are two kinds of entity that can limit this free flow of the water:

(i)   dams
(ii) river-banks.

Both dams and river-banks limit the free flow of the water, but they do so in opposite ways. *Dams* prevent (render *impossible*) the flow of the water; *river-banks*, on the other hand, make it *possible*. (Were there no banks, the water would spread out in all directions and the river would cease to be such, would no longer exist as a river. The banks are, in other words, *constitutive* of the river.)

Now, the relation between *deontic* rules and *eidetic-constitutive* rules is analogous to that between *dams* and *river-banks*:

(i)   *eidetic-constitutive* rules are like *river-banks*, which limit the flow of the water while at the same time making it possible (they are *constructive rules*);[15]

(ii) *deontic* rules, on the other hand, are like *dams*, which prevent the flow of the water (they might be called *constrictive* rules).[16]

2.   Nomic (or rule-relative) impossibility

2.1.   Deontic rules, anankastic-constitutive rules, eidetic-constitutive rules

But what, more technically, *is* rule-relative (i.e. nomic) possibility? In what, exactly, does nomic possibility consist?

2.1.1. In order to answer this question, it is best to start by asking another one: what is the meaning of nomic *im*possibility, of rule-relative *im*possibility? What is the difference between *nomic* impossibility and *non-nomic* or *ontic* impossibility (for example, the ontic impossibility of squaring the circle, or the ontic impossibility of working out the square root of 785 910 273 in one's head in less than 18 seconds)?

2.1.2. There are at least three kinds of nomic impossibility (of rule-relative impossibility). I shall call these three kinds of nomic impossibility '*deontic* impossibility', '*anankastic* impossibility' and '*eidetic* impossibility'.

The names of these three kinds of nomic impossibility make reference to the three kinds of rule in relation to which nomic impossibility holds. These three kinds of rule are:

(i) The *deontic* rule – a central concept in the study of deontics. An example is the rule of the highway code: 'It is forbidden to drive past a red traffic-light'.[17]

The ought, the *Sollen* of *deontic* rules is a *deontic ought* (a *deontisches Sollen*).

(ii) The *anankastic-constitutive* rule. Anankastic-constitutive rules (from the Greek *anánke*, meaning 'necessity') are rules that impose a *necessary condition* for their object. An example is the rule: 'One cannot enter a doctoral programme without having previously achieved a Bachelor's degree'. Another classic example of an anankastic-constitutive rule is: 'Wills ought to be signed by the testator'.

The difference between anankastic-constitutive rules and eidetic-constitutive rules is that while the latter determine the *intension* of the term referring to their object, the former determine its *extension*. Anankastic-constitutive rules do not constitute a *type*; rather, they determine (place constraints on) the *tokens* of pre-existing types.[18]

The ought, the *Sollen* of *anankastic-constitutive* rules is an *adeontic* ought (an *adeontisches Sollen*). To provide a name for the adeontic ought of anankastic-constitutive rules, Giampaolo M. Azzoni and I have introduced the term 'anankastic ought', *anankastisches Sollen*.[19]

(iii) The *eidetic-constitutive* rule. As explained in §1, eidetic-constitutive rules constitute the *eidos* (the idea, the type) of their object. An example is the rule of chess: 'One cannot castle when the king is under check'. Other examples are the rule: 'The bishop ought to move diagonally', or the rule: 'The king ought to be moved from check'.

The ought, the *Sollen* of *eidetic-constitutive* rules is an *eidetic ought* (an *eidetisches Sollen*). This ought, like that of anankastic-constitutive rules, instantiates the (in some sense paradoxical) notion of an *adeontic* ought (an *adeontisches Sollen*).

2.2. Deontic impossibility, anankastic impossibility, eidetic impossibility

2.2.1. It is worth commenting briefly on the three kinds of nomic impossibility (deontic, anankastic and eidetic impossibility).

(i) *Deontic impossibility* is nomic impossibility relative to a *deontic* rule and consists in *deontic illegitimacy*, i.e. the straightforward *prohibition* of an action by a *deontic* rule.

An example of deontic impossibility is the following. According to a deontic rule of the British highway code, it is *deontically* impossible (i.e. it is prohibited, forbidden) to drive past a red traffic-light.[20]

(ii) *Anankastic impossibility* is nomic impossibility relative to an *anankastic-constitutive* rule and consists in the *unsatisfiability* of (at least) one of the necessary conditions imposed by an *anankastic-constitutive* rule.

An example of anankastic impossibility is the following. According to the *anankastic-constitutive* rules of most doctoral programmes, it is *anankastically* impossible to enter the doctoral programme without having first achieved a Bachelor's degree.

(iii) *Eidetic impossibility* is nomic impossibility relative to an *eidetic-constitutive* rule and consists in the *non-instantiation* by an action of an *eidos* constituted by eidetic-constitutive rules.

An example of eidetic impossibility is the following. According to the *eidetic-constitutive* rules of chess, it is *eidetically* impossible to castle if the king is under check. (Castling when under check does not instantiate the rule-constituted act-type called 'castling'.)

Eidetic-constitutive rules rule out any action that does not conform to them. Thus, while the act of passing a red light falls under the deontic rule that forbids one to pass a red light, any movement of the king and the rook which does not conform to the eidetic-constitutive rules of castling does not instantiate the rule-constituted type of castling. Such a material movement is not a *move* in chess. This point was already noted by Ludwig Wittgenstein, in *Zettel*:

> Do not say 'One cannot', but say instead: 'It doesn't exist in this game'.
> Not: 'One can't castle in draughts' but – 'There is no castling in draughts'.[21]

2.2.2. I have distinguished *deontic* nomic impossibility (impossibility relative to a deontic rule) from two kinds of *adeontic* nomic impossibility (impossibility relative to an *anankastic*-constitutive rule, and impossibility relative to an *eidetic*-constitutive rule). These three kinds of nomic impossibility can be represented graphically by means of two dichotomies:

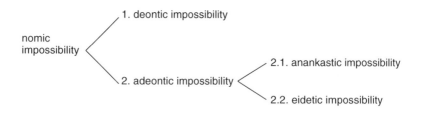

nomic impossibility
- 1. deontic impossibility
- 2. adeontic impossibility
  - 2.1. anankastic impossibility
  - 2.2. eidetic impossibility

3.   Nomic vs. ontic impossibility, agent-relative vs. act-relative impossibility

The notion of *nomic* (or rule-relative) impossibility examined in the previous section can be usefully contrasted with its opposite, that of *non-nomic* (or *ontic*) impossibility (i.e. impossibility that is not relative

	Source of impossibility	
Kind of impossibility	Ontic	Nomic
Impossibility *a parte subiecti* (*agent-relative impossibility, subjective impossibility*)	1. *ontic* impossibility *a parte subiecti* (agent-relative *ontic* impossibility; subjective *ontic* impossibility) Examples: the *physical* impossibility for a prisoner of leaving his cell once locked in by the guard (one of Oppenheim's examples of 'social unfreedom'[22]); the *neurological* impossibility for a mathematics student of working out the square root of 785 910 273 in his head in less than 18 seconds.	2. *nomic* impossibility *a parte subiecti* (agent-relative *nomic* impossibility; subjective *nomic* impossibility) Examples: the *deontic* impossibility for a motorist of passing a red traffic-light; the *anankastic* impossibility for an undergraduate student of entering a doctoral programme.
Impossibility *a parte obiecti* (*act-relative impossibility, objective impossibility*)	3. *ontic* impossibility *a parte obiecti* (act-relative *ontic* impossibility; objective *ontic* impossibility) Examples: the *physical* impossibility of building a Penrose-triangle in a three-dimensional space; the *geometric* impossibility of squaring the circle.	4. *nomic* impossibility *a parte obiecti* (act-relative *nomic* impossibility; objective *nomic* impossibility) Examples: the *eidetic* impossibility of castling if the king is under check; the *eidetic* impossibility of moving the rook diagonally.

to rules). Furthermore, both nomic and non-nomic (i.e. ontic) impossibility can be either *a parte subiecti* (i.e. *agent-relative*), or *a parte obiecti* (i.e. *act-relative*). By combining the two opposites (nomic vs. ontic; *a parte subiecti* or agent-relative vs. *a parte obiecti* or act-relative), we get four combinations, which are represented in the table.

Notes

1. 'Wir kennen die Grenzen nicht, weil keine gezogen sind'. Ludwig Wittgenstein, *Philosophische Untersuchungen. Philosophical Investigations*, ed. G. E. M. Anscombe and Rush Rhees, trans. G. E. M. Anscombe (Oxford: Blackwell, 1953, 1958), I.69, p. 33.
2. The term 'eleutheriology', which derives from the Greek adjective *eleútheros* (meaning 'free') and noun *eleuthería* (meaning 'freedom'), was introduced into philosophical language by Johann August Heinrich Ulrich in his book *Eleutheriologie, oder über Freyheit und Nothwendigkeit* (Jena: Cröker, 1788). Immanuel Kant introduced the term *Eleutheronomie* (*Freiheitsprinzip der inneren Gesetzgebung*) in *Die Metaphysik der Sitten* (Königsberg: Friedrich Nicolovius, 1797). A third, etymologically cognate term, 'eleutheriometry', might be used to refer to the measurement of freedom, which is the subject matter of Ian Carter's book *A Measure of Freedom* (Oxford: Oxford University Press, 1999). *Eleútheros* ('free') and *eleuthería* ('freedom', 'liberty') are etymologically related not only to the Latin adjective *liber* ('free') and to the Latin noun *libertas* ('freedom', 'liberty'), but also to the German *Leute*, the Croatian *ljudi*, the Czech *lidé*, the Russian *ljud* and the old-English *lēod* and *lēode* (all meaning 'people'). The etymological link of *Leute*, *ljudi* etc. with *eleútheros* and *liber* may reflect the philosophical insight that freedom is a *constitutive feature* of persons.
3. Felix E. Oppenheim, *Dimensions of Freedom: an Analysis* (New York: St. Martin's Press, 1961).
4. 'Nomic' derives from the Greek *nómos* (meaning 'rule' or 'norm').
5. Ludwig Wittgenstein, *Wittgenstein's Lectures, Cambridge 1932–1935*, ed. Alice Ambrose (Oxford: Blackwell, 1979), p. 86.
6. 'Deontic' derives from the Greek *déon* (meaning 'duty' or 'obligation'). (The same root occurs in Jeremy Bentham's noun 'deontology', in John Grote's noun 'deontics' and in Ernst Mally's noun *Deontik*.)
7. Cf. John Rawls, 'Two Concepts of Rules', *Philosophical Review*, 64 (1955), pp. 3–32, reprinted in Rawls, *Collected Papers*, ed. Samuel Richard Freeman (Cambridge, Mass.: Harvard University Press, 1999), pp. 20–46; John R. Searle, *The Construction of Social Reality* (London: Penguin, 1995), pp. 27–9.
8. Cf. Amedeo G. Conte, 'Variationen über Wittgensteins Regelbegriff', in Rudolf Haller (ed.), *Sprache und Erkenntnis* (Vienna: Hölder-Pichler-Tempsky, 1981), pp. 67–78; 'Semiotics of Constitutive Rules', in Michael Herzfeld and Lucio Melazzo (eds), *Semiotic Theory and Practice*, Vol. 1 (Berlin: Mouton, 1988), pp. 143–50.

9. Cf. Czesław Znamierowski, *Podstawowe pojęcia teorji prawa. I.* (Poznań: Fiszer i Majewski, 1924, 2nd edn 1934).

10. 'Norma konstrukcyjna stwarza nowe możliwości działania, bez niej nie istniejące; bez norm szachowych nie byłoby ruchów wieży, pionka, królowej'. Znamierowski, *Podstawowe pojęcia teorji prawa. I.*, p. 103 (2nd edn, without alteration, p. 149).

11. Znamierowski, *Podstawowe pojęcia teorji prawa. I.*, p. 72 (2nd edn, without alteration, p. 107). (The Polish verb corresponding to the English verb 'to construct' is *konstruować*.)

12. 'Norma konstrukcyjna musi tworzyć nietylko tetyczna *konieczność* działania, lecz i tetyczna *możliwość*. Znamierowski, *Podstawowe pojęcia teorji prawa. I.*, p. 103 (2nd edn, without alteration, p. 149). Znamierowski's verb *tworzyć* ('to create' or 'to produce') resembles, by chance, another verb that has an opposite sense: *twierdzić* ('to assert' or 'to affirm'). Correlatively: the neuter noun *tworzenie* means 'creation', or 'formation'; the neuter noun *twierdzenie* means 'assertion', or 'affirmation' (and also 'thesis' and 'theorem': for instance, the Polish for 'Pythagoras's theorem' is *twierdzenie Pitagorasa*).

13. 'Die leichte Taube, indem sie im freien Fluge die Luft teilt, deren Widerstand sie fühlt, könnte die Vorstellung fassen, daß es ihr im luftleeren Raum noch viel besser gelingen werde'. Immanuel Kant, *Kritik der reinen Vernuft* (Riga: Hartknoch, 1781, 1787), Einleitung, III, trans., Norman Kemp Smith, *Critique of Pure Reason* (London: Macmillan, 1929), Introduction, III. Kant's *dove* is one of the three birds I have met in the course of my philosophical life. The other two are Hegel's *owl* (which 'spreads its wings only with the falling of the dusk') and Borges's *goofus bird* (which always flies backwards since it wants to return to where it has come from). Cf. Georg Wilhelm Friedrich Hegel, *Grundlinien der Philosophie des Rechts* (Berlin: Nicolai, 1821), Vorrede, trans. T. M. Knox, *Hegel's Philosophy of Right* (Oxford: Clarendon Press, 1952), Preface, p. 13; Jorge Luis Borges, *Manual de zoología fantástica* (Mexico: Fundo de Cultura Económica, 1957).

14. It is interesting to note that the term 'rail' comes from the Latin *regula* (as does the term 'rule'!).

15. Albert Einstein wrote that it is the rules of a game that *make possible* (*möglich machen*) the game itself; it is the *Bestimmtheit*, the determinacy of the rules, that *makes* the game *possible* (that *das Spiel erst möglich macht*). 'Physik und Realität', *Franklin Institute Journal*, 201 (1934), pp. 315–16.

16. The play on words 'constructive' vs. 'constrictive' can be rendered in Italian (*costruttivo* vs. *costrittivo*), but not in Znamierowski's language, for the Polish counterparts of 'constrictive' (*zmuszający* and *przymuszający*) are in no way similar to Znamierowski's adjective *konstrukcyjny*. (The nouns *przymus*, *zmuszanie*, *zmuszenie* and *przymuszanie* correspond to the French noun *contrainte*; the verbs *zmuszać* and *zmusić*, *przymuszać* and *przymusić* correspond to the French verb *contraindre*.)

17. 'Forbidden' is one of the so-called *deontic modalities*. The logic of deontic modalities is *deontic logic*. The founder of deontic logic, the Finnish philosopher and logician Georg Henrik von Wright, has given two slightly different definitions of 'deontic modalities' ('deontic moods') in his first two essays on deontic logic.

First definition: '*Deontic moods* or modes of obligation are concepts such as the *obligatory* (that which we ought to do), the *permitted* (that which we are allowed to do), and the *forbidden* (that which we must not do).' G. H. von Wright, 'Deontic Logic', *Mind*, 60 (1951), pp. 1–15, at p. 1.

Second definition: 'The *deontic modalities* are about the mode (or way) in which we are permitted or not to perform an act. They are used in phrases such as "it is *obligatory* to ...", "it is *permitted* to ...", or "it is *forbidden* to ...".' G. H. von Wright, *An Essay in Modal Logic* (Amsterdam: North-Holland, 1951), p. 36.

18. I refer to Charles Sanders Peirce's opposition: *type* vs. *token*.
19. Cf. Amedeo G. Conte, 'Fenomeni di fenomeni', in Giuseppe Galli (ed.), *Interpretazione ed epistemologia* (Turin: Marietti, 1986), pp. 167–98, reprinted in Amedeo G. Conte, *Filosofia del linguaggio normativo. II. Studi 1982–1994* (Turin: Giappichelli, 1995), pp. 313–46; Giampaolo M. Azzoni, *Il concetto di condizione nella tipologia delle regole* (Padova: CEDAM, 1988). Perhaps the most extensive investigation of anankastic ought is that of Giuseppe Lorini. Cf., for instance, his paper 'Deontica tra logica e filosofia', *Rivista internazionale di filosofia del diritto*, 70 (1993), pp. 599–633.
20. *Deontic impossibility* presupposes *ontic possibility*. (It is a pragmatic presupposition of a prohibition that the forbidden action is ontically possible.) It would be pragmatically odd to forbid an ontically impossible action (for instance, to forbid someone to touch heaven with his finger). My thesis ('*Deontic impossibility* presupposes *ontic possibility*') means: 'The deontic impossibility of an act presupposes the ontic possibility of its *commission*'. It differs from a *second* thesis, viz. the thesis: 'The deontic impossibility (i.e. the forbiddenness) of an act presupposes the ontic possibility of its *omission*'. This second thesis is a straightforward application to the *omission* of acts of a third thesis, viz. the thesis: 'Ought implies can' (*Sollen impliziert Können*). (This third thesis is ascribed to Immanuel Kant (1724–1804).) The third thesis is discussed by Ian Carter in this volume.
21. 'Statt: "Man kann nicht", sage: "Es gibt in diesem Spiel nicht". Statt: "Man kann im Damespiel nicht rochieren", sage: "Es gibt im Damespiel kein Rochieren".' Ludwig Wittgenstein, *Zettel* (Oxford: Blackwell, 1967), §134, p. 315.
22. Felix E. Oppenheim, *Political Concepts: a Reconstruction* (Oxford: Blackwell, 1981), p. 54.

6
'Ought' Implies 'Practical Possibility'*

Ian Carter

It is common among moral, political and legal philosophers to claim or assume that 'ought' implies 'can'. By this, they mean that if an agent cannot perform a given action, then it cannot be the case that such an action is required of the agent. In short, one cannot have the duty to do the impossible.

1.   Two interpretations of '"ought" implies "can"'

I am interested in whether the claim that 'ought' implies 'can' (hereinafter, OC) should be interpreted as an ethical norm or as a non-ethical, purely semantic norm. This question will in turn depend on how we interpret the words 'ought' and 'can'. I shall concentrate here in particular on the meaning of 'can'. But first, a few words about the meaning of 'ought'.

It is rarely said that 'ought' implies 'can' for *all* meanings of 'ought'. For example, we often use the word 'ought' to attribute blame to people who are responsible for their own inabilities. Where I owe you money, but cannot repay the debt because I have gambled everything away at a casino, we are still inclined to say that I 'ought' to repay my debt, despite the fact that I cannot do so.[1] Here, 'ought' does not imply 'can', because 'ought' is used in a purely evaluative sense, rather than prescriptively. This illustrates the way in which our interpretation of the word 'ought' will affect the truth value of OC. But I do not propose to discuss this issue here; rather, I shall simply assume that in the context in which OC is uttered, 'ought' has a prescriptive, action-guiding meaning, and that in this case OC is true.[2] Even where 'ought' is interpreted in this way, it remains an open question whether OC is an ethical or a semantic norm.

Another issue in the interpretation of OC has to do with the meaning of 'implies': OC might be taken to mean either that 'ought' *entails* 'can' or that 'ought' *presupposes* 'can'. As Walter Sinnott-Armstrong has pointed out, if 'ought' entails 'can', then it is *false* that an agent who cannot do x ought to do x, whereas if 'ought' presupposes 'can' then it is *neither true nor false* that such an agent ought to do x.[3] Although I shall not discuss this issue directly here, it nevertheless has some bearing on the nature of OC as an ethical or non-ethical norm: if the implication in question is one of presupposition, then OC must be interpreted as a non-ethical, semantic norm; and while it is logically coherent to see OC as a semantic norm expressing an entailment, this is not normally the case in the literature on OC.[4]

Let us now look at the two interpretations of OC. The interpretation of OC as a semantic implication is best exemplified in the work of R. M. Hare and G. H. von Wright.[5] To quote Hare, the idea here is that 'the impossibility, or the inevitability, of doing something stops the question of whether to do it arising'.[6] Thus, 'ought' *presupposes* 'can' in exactly the same way as the question 'Is the King of France wise?' *presupposes* that there is a King of France. If there is no King, then 'the question does not arise whether the King is wise'.[7] Similarly, if I cannot do x, then the question whether or not I ought to do x does not arise. On this first interpretation OC is not itself an ethical norm, even though it refers to ethical norms.[8] Its function is to describe one of the semantic properties of prescriptive ethical norms, thus filtering out some of the norms which cannot fall into this category.

The second interpretation under examination is that OC should be seen as itself an ethical norm. More precisely, it is that OC should be seen as a *second-order* ethical norm – an ethical norm about ethical norms. On this interpretation, we do not see OC as simply holding for any prescriptive use of 'ought'. Rather, we see it as holding because we believe that its denial is wrong – because we think it ethically mistaken to prescribe impossible actions. This interpretation is endorsed by Rem Blanchard Edwards, Manfred Moritz and K. E. Tranøy.[9] According to Blanchard Edwards, we can certainly imagine action-guiding senses of 'ought' according to which OC does not hold: for example, in the perfectionist strand of Christian ethics, where 'we are morally required *to act* to make ourselves perfect even though we know we shall not succeed'.[10] OC is therefore 'itself a substantive, normative moral principle'. In its negative form, it might be reformulated as follows: 'It is morally wrong to hold a person under obligation to do something which he does not have the ability and opportunity to do ... and it is morally wrong to blame or punish a person for not doing something if he was not obligated to do it'.[11] A similar view is taken by Manfred Moritz and K. E. Tranøy, although they limit themselves to calling OC a second-order *norm*. This is a weaker claim than that OC is a second-order moral principle, as the reasons in this case for supporting OC might be non-moral. Thus, OC might simply be taken as a prudential second-order norm for rulers: 'do not command your subjects to do what they cannot do'. Moral reasons can of course also lie behind this advice. For example, Moritz appears to hold that endorsing OC would be morally wrong as well as pointless or imprudent, because it would be morally wrong to censure or punish someone for not having done what he could not do.[12]

On this second interpretation, OC cannot be a semantic implication, for it does not hold of all moral prescriptions. Rather, it is itself a claim that takes an ethical stand: it is an ethical claim about ethical claims. It is of a higher order than first-order ethical claims, like 'It would be wrong for you to kill me', but of a lower order than metaethical claims like 'Moral principles are neither true nor false'. It is a claim on which the supporters of various incompatible (first-order) ethical norms can agree, but it remains an ethical norm, and therefore (in turn) a norm on which people can disagree while agreeing over certain other metaethical claims (for example, that moral principles can be shown to be true or false).

That the above two interpretations of OC are mutually inconsistent should be clear from the fact that on the first interpretation, where 'ought' semantically presupposes 'can', OC serves to *circumscribe* our ethical prescriptions. It stands outside our prescriptive ethical discourse, so to speak, and partly determines whether or not ethical prescriptions are applicable in given situations. On the second interpretation, on the other hand, OC is itself *one* of our ethical prescriptions – if a second-order prescription – and is, so to speak, part of our prescriptive ethical discourse. On the second interpretation, but not the first, the extension of the set of pieces of behaviour on which we can pass ethical judgement, as determined by OC, is itself an ethical question.

In what follows, I want to bring to bear a particular consideration that weighs in favour of the second interpretation, according to which OC is (insofar as it refers to prescriptive 'oughts') itself an ethical norm rather than a presupposition that serves to circumscribe the applicability of ethical norms. This consideration has to do with the interpretation of 'can' in OC. It is my view that on a particular meaning of 'can', the second interpretation must be the correct one.

In the context of OC, it is plausible to see 'I can do x' as having one of at least three different meanings. One such meaning is 'it is logically possible for me to do x'. Thus, it is logically possible for me to travel from Milan to Pavia, but not for me to be in both Milan and Pavia at the same time. Another such meaning is 'it is physically possible (in an absolute sense) for me to do x'. It is, for example, physically possible (in an absolute sense) for me to travel from Milan to Pavia in 45 minutes, but it is absolutely physically impossible (though logically possible) for me to do so in 10 seconds. These are the two meanings of 'can' which seem to be assumed in most discussions of OC. Logical and absolute physical possibility may be called forms of 'strict' possibility.

But there is also a third, weaker meaning of 'I can do x', according to which 'I can do x' implies that the performance of x is not too costly or too painful or too difficult for me. Imagine, for example, a captive spy who is under pressure from his enemies to reveal a certain piece of information. If the method used for extracting the information is torture, we might well say that he cannot remain silent. Under torture, or the threat of it, we say, he 'cannot but' reveal the information. If this is a valid meaning of 'cannot', then there are situations in which it makes sense to say that I 'cannot' do x, even though it is both logically and physically possible (i.e. it is 'strictly' possible) for me to do x. Following Felix Oppenheim, we may say that in such situations, although my doing x is both logically and physically possible, it is nevertheless *practically* impossible.

My contention is that at least where the 'can' in OC has this third meaning, OC must be interpreted as itself an ethical norm.

I suppose this conclusion to have some general relevance for normative analysis. But I am particularly interested, in the context of this essay, in the notion of practical impossibility in the political thought of Felix Oppenheim – its role in his theory of freedom, and the way it affects our moral judgements of political actors.

Oppenheim appears to endorse the first of the above-mentioned interpretations of OC.[13] For Oppenheim, that is, OC is a non-ethical norm that circumscribes action-guiding normative discourse, showing where we can and cannot meaningfully make prescriptive judgements about the conduct of individuals or groups. He applies this view, in particular, to the behaviour of governments, so as to guage the relevance of moral judgements about foreign policy. However, the meaning of 'can' Oppenheim has in mind includes not only the first and second of the meanings mentioned above but also the third, according to which a sufficient condition for it being 'impossible' for me to do x is that x be too costly or painful or difficult for me. In other words, for Oppenheim, 'ought' implies 'practical possibility'. It is this combination of views that I wish to contest. My aim, then, is to argue that '"ought" implies "practical possibility"' is an ethical norm. In order to do so, it seems reasonable to begin with a closer examination of the concepts of practical possibility and impossibility.

2. Oppenheim on practical impossibility

Oppenheim uses the concept of practical impossibility as one of the building blocks in his analysis of unfreedom.[14] The idea of an option being 'too difficult, or too costly, or too painful' originally comes from Alvin Goldman, although Oppenheim is the first to use the term 'practical impossibilty' to express this idea.[15] A useful sister-concept is that of practical necessity, which can be defined in terms of practical impossibility: if an action is practically necessary, then its avoidance is practically impossible.

It is worth making the concept of practical impossibility a bit more precise at this point. Defining this concept in terms of difficulty, cost and pain seems to me over-complicated. Pain can certainly itself be thought of as a kind of cost. Difficulty can also be understood in terms of costs, although only partially. To describe an action as very difficult to perform *might* mean that it is very costly to perform: for example, if I say that it is very difficult for me to push a car up a hill, I might mean that it would take me a great deal of time to do so, or that doing so requires a great deal of energy. The action is therefore costly in terms of time and energy. However, some uses of the term 'difficult' can instead be taken as references to low degrees of probability of success: this seems to be what I mean when I say that it is difficult for me to hit the bull in a game of darts. On reflection, then, it seems best to define practical impossibility in terms of the costliness and low probability of success of actions.

It is important to distinguish the description of an action as 'practically necessary' in the above sense from two other kinds of imperative. First, the term 'practically necessary' has often been used by moral philosophers – especially by Kantians – to describe that which is *morally required* – i.e. that which is necessary according to moral prescriptions.[16] But this is to use the term in quite a different way from that in which Oppenheim uses it. Indeed, to interpret 'can' in OC in terms of Kantian practical possibility would be to interpret OC in a rather eccentric way – i.e. as meaning that the obligation to do something implies the permission to do it. For Oppenheim, far from representing the sphere of the morally required, the notion of practical necessity serves to delimit it. Far from being morally required, that which is practically necessary *cannot* be morally required, given that the performance of a practically necessary action is not something about which the agent has a choice. Secondly, that which is practically necessary in Oppenheim's sense is to be distinguished from that which is rational.[17] Oppenheim adopts an instrumental conception of rationality, whereby rational action is action that constitutes the best available means to given ends. One is not constrained – one is not unfree – simply because one acts rationally in this sense; on the other hand, one is constrained – one is unfree – to the extent that one acts out of practical necessity.[18] The various available tokens of a practically necessary act-type can be more or less rational, in that some provide better means than others to realizing the agent's ends. But the agent remains free to perform any of these act-tokens, including the least rational of them.

On Oppenheim's definition of social freedom, P (an agent) renders R (another agent) unfree to do x (an action) if P renders x either physically or practically impossible for R. One way in which P can render x practically impossible for R is by rendering x punishable for R . To say that x is punishable for R is to say that there is a high probability that R will be punished by P (with a sufficient degree of severity), should R choose to do x. Thus, on Oppenheim's definition of social freedom, we can be unfree to do certain things that we then nevertheless go on to do. Absolute physical impossibility is not a necessary condition for unfreedom: x might be merely practically impossible for R (for example, too costly, given a threat on the part of P that has a reasonable probability of being carried out), and this will be a sufficient condition for R being 'unfree' to do x. Despite the fact that it may seem strange to say that a person was socially unfree to do a thing that she then went on to do, the intuition behind the practical impossibility clause in Oppenheim's definition of social freedom should be clear: we do not normally want to say that a person remains as free as before when she is subjected to a severe threat that is aimed at deterring her from doing something. To return to the example of the spy threatened with torture in case he does not provide a certain piece of information, ordinary language tells us in such a case that the spy is not really free, despite it being physically possible for him either to talk or to remain silent. We would ordinarily say that he is forced to talk, despite the fact that his captors do not (indeed, probably cannot) make it absolutely physically impossible for him to refrain from doing so.

Let us return, now, to '"ought" implies "can"'. Oppenheim interprets OC as meaning that 'ought' *presupposes* 'can', and adopts the explanation given by Hare, that where an action is impossible, the question of whether one ought to do it does not arise. Therefore, 'if A cannot do X, my propounding that A nevertheless ought to X is not logically false, but it is pointless as advice'.[19] A difference with Hare, however, is that Oppenheim explicitly states that 'these considerations are applicable, not only to strict [i.e. logical or physical] but also to practical necessity and practical impossibility'.[20] Thus, the semantic interpretation of OC – the first of the two interpretations I mentioned at the outset – gets extended to include 'can' in the sense of practical possibility. OC remains a semantic implication, because OC remains a claim about the *province* of moral prescriptions, whatever their nature: 'to fall *within the purview* of ethics, actions must be practically possible (neither practically necessary nor practically impossible). Only when the agent has a practical choice is it relevant to advise him what he ought to do on moral grounds.'[21]

The interpretation of 'I cannot do x' as meaning 'x is practically impossible for me', together with the interpretation of OC as a semantic (and thus non-ethical) implication, does a great deal of work in determining Oppenheim's view of the proper place of morality in our judgements of political actors. (Although he restricts himself here to the relevance of *moral* prescriptions, if his conclusions go through in the sphere of morality they will also concern the relevance of prescriptions in general, given the more general scope of OC.) Oppenheim has attempted to make use of OC in exploring the moral implications of what international relations theorists (but not moral philosophers) call 'realism',[22] and has illustrated this use in an argument about the scope of moral judgements in matters of foreign policy. When making foreign policy decisions, he says, a government cannot but pursue the national interest (defined as the territorial integrity, military security and economic well-being of a nation). Pursuit of the national interest is practically necessary for governments as actors. Therefore, the question of whether they ought or ought not to pursue the national interest does not arise. Only foreign policies that accord with the national interest can be an object of moral judgement, and this only where there is more than one such policy – that is, where the government has a real choice. The fact of governments pursuing or not pursuing their national interest cannot itself be an object of moral judgement. All that can be said is that a government which pursues its national interest acts rationally, and that a government which does not pursue its national interest acts irrationally. We cannot, for example, say that a government ought to avoid a bellicose foreign policy if this foreign policy is not in any case in accordance with the national interest (we can only say that it is not rational to adopt such a foreign policy); and we cannot say that a government ought to pursue some humanitarian goal if that goal conflicts with the national interest. Neither can we say that a government ought *not* to do such things in such conditions or even that it is morally permissible for it to do so. The relevance of moral judgements in the sphere of foreign policy is indeed, in Oppenheim's view, much more limited than it is commonly thought to be, and the reason for this lies in the practical necessity of the government's pursuing the national interest, together with the fact that 'ought' semantically implies 'can'.

In what follows, I shall examine the relationship between practical impossibility and unfreedom (section 3), and the question of how we should interpret the claim that 'ought' implies 'practical possibility' (section 4). The aim of my argument is, as I have said, to show that '"ought" implies "practical possibility"' is itself an ethical claim – if a second-order ethical claim. In the conclusion, I shall return briefly to the implications of my argument for Oppenheim's view about the proper scope of moral prescriptions.

3.   Practical impossibility and unfreedom

Something Oppenheim and I certainly agree on is the importance of defining social freedom in a purely empirical way. Oppenheim's work has been importantly influential in this respect, and we need not share the belief in the possibility or desirability of a completely 'value-neutral' political science, expressed in his early work on freedom, in order to take heed of this basic point. Defining 'freedom' empirically is in any case desirable if we wish to fix the meaning of certain political terms as a means of clarifying the ways in which different political prescriptions diverge, for without certain common meanings it will never be possible to recognize agreements and disagreements as such; we shall simply be talking past each other.

An empirical definition of freedom is also required if freedom is to have an independent role in determining the meaning of our political prescriptions (for example, in determining the meaning of our principles of justice). And it is true of liberal political philosophers, at least, that they do wish freedom to have such an independent role, because, as I have argued elsewhere, they generally see freedom as a fundamental good. They see freedom as being *independently* valuable, which is to say, as having value independently of the other values it might bring about or of which it might be partly constitutive.[23] To the extent that we define and measure freedom in terms of other values, we deny freedom's independent value.[24] Only an empirical definition of freedom is compatible with freedom being a distinct and fundamental good, rather than a normatively redundant term that can be defined using other, more fundamental normative terms (such as rights or justice). Liberals therefore have strong value-based reasons – not just social-scientific reasons or reasons of conceptual clarification – for wanting to define freedom empirically.

This said, it is not so clear that practical impossibility should be seen as a form of unfreedom, for it is not so clear that practical impossibility can be defined in purely empirical terms. The problem is to distinguish between that which is practically possible and that which is simply undesirable, for we should not like to say that a person is forced to do everything that she most desires to do and is unfree to do that to which she is most averse. This would be once again to confuse unfreedom with irrationality. It therefore seems inescapable that the judgement of a form of behaviour as being 'necessary' (in less than the strict sense) must involve some kind of value judgement assigning a particularly strong weight to the costs associated with its avoidance. Would this not involve a departure from a purely empirical definition of freedom?

Oppenheim has attempted to avoid this problem by referring to the values of an empirically determinate normal or 'average' agent.[25] But this surely only pushes the question a step back. The question of which costs render an action practically impossible will only be an empirical one after we have first fixed the confines of the group of individuals from which we are to construct the normal or average agent. Are such confines those of our nation or our continent or our planet? Are they those of the 1990s or those of the last five centuries? The answers to these last questions are again inescapably normative. As Tranøy writes, 'our ideas about what is possible, impossible, and necessary [for human beings] have changed, and [given OC] these ideas very much determine our *moral* attitudes to them'.[26]

Another way of suggesting that practical necessity can be defined empirically might be by saying that the practically necessary is that which is rationally necessary as a means to any end whatsoever.[27] However, it is difficult to think of a good or action that is a necessary means to *any* end.[28] Even if we concentrate on the most obvious examples, such as physical survival, we can always think of another end that contradicts the set of ends to which it is a necessary means: in the case of physical survival, the relevant counter-example is the end of suicide. The concept of practical necessity cannot therefore be *purely* instrumental; in order to make sense of that concept, some reference must be made, however implicitly, to a set of background norms by which to evaluate the 'necessity' of ends.

It seems to me that the relationship between unfreedom and the different kinds of impossibility discussed here can be usefully clarified by distinguishing between 'the freedom to act' and 'acting freely' (or 'free action'). Oppenheim has himself emphasized the importance of this distinction,[29] despite also claiming that we are unfree to act in practically impossible ways. The difference is essentially that in the case of the freedom to act, freedom is attributable to agents, whereas in the case of acting freely (or free action), freedom is attributable to actions. One *is* free *to do* that which is practically impossible; we must say this, in my view, in order to make sense of the fact that people do sometimes do what is practically impossible. But this is not to deny the possibility that when a person is doing something which it is practically necessary for her to do, she is doing so *unfreely*. She might indeed be doing so unfreely – for example, if she does so merely out of a fear of punishment.[30] The concept of freedom to act can be defined in a purely empirical way, because it can be defined purely in terms of the absence of (absolute) physical impossibility. The concept of acting freely, on the other hand, cannot be defined in a purely empirical way, because it must be defined at least in part by reference to the relative values of the alternatives open to the agent. On an empirical account of freedom to act, we should say that the captive spy who is threatened with torture is free to talk and free to remain silent. We can make sense of the constraint to which he is subject by saying that he does not reveal the information freely.[31]

Distinguishing in the above way between the freedom to act and acting freely brings out more clearly the *point* of making judgements about practical impossibility, and with it the normative nature of the latter. The concept of acting freely, in which the concept of practical impossibility plays a clarificatory role, concerns actually or hypothetically *performed* actions, unlike the concept of the freedom to act, which concerns only hypothetical actions – actions that it is *open* to the agent to perform. The *point* of the concept of acting freely is to determine which actually (or hypothetically) performed actions are performed by fully *responsible* agents, and which are instead performed less than fully responsibly, or with no degree of responsibility. And the point of making judgements about degrees of responsibility for action is to be able to know when agents can be properly praised or blamed for their actions. Diminished responsibility excuses a person for having performed an otherwise blame-worthy action, and this, as we shall see, is one of the assumptions behind the claim that '"ought" implies "practical possibility"'.

4. 'Ought' implies 'practical possibility'

Another point on which I *agree* with Oppenheim regards the interpretation of 'can' in OC. I think it highly plausible to say that a person can become exempt from what might otherwise have been considered a duty because of the practical impossibility of performing the action in question. Despite a person having been free *to do* something which he refrained from doing, we tend to think it inappropriate to blame him for not doing it (or appropriate to blame him less) if his refraining from doing it was practically necessary. Most of us would think it normatively over-demanding to say that the captive spy threatened with torture nevertheless 'ought' to remain silent. Most of us would say that his 'inability' to remain silent under torture exempts him from such a duty.

  Some confirmation of this view can be gleaned from the literature on 'ought' and 'can'. Goldman discusses a number of examples where 'inability' (in terms of excessive difficulty or costliness) is seen as 'excusing', and he points out that this idea might be formulated as implied by OC (despite the fact that not all cases of inability excuse).[32] James Griffin has extended the morally relevant sense of inability to cover that which is emotionally difficult. He argues, for example, that complete moral impartiality is too demanding, given the 'limits of the will', to count as a moral requirement. It is simply not 'possible' for beings like us to show complete impartiality between, say, our own children and other children: 'we should not know how to produce someone emotionally detached to that extreme degree, yet sane. We are incapable of such fine-tuning'.[33] Given that 'ought' implies 'can', complete impartiality is not something that we 'ought' to aim for. This, despite the obvious fact that complete impartiality is strictly (both logically and physically) possible. To take one other example, Tranøy explicitly introduces the concept of basic human needs in his discussion of OC. According to Tranøy, needs are things one 'cannot' avoid pursuing: 'I think there are human actions which can be said to be necessary ... It is necessary for any person ... to seek and/or obtain satisfaction of his vital and legitimate needs'.[34] No doubt it is important to distinguish between '"ought" implies "strict possiblity"' and '"ought" implies "practical possibility"'. But this is not to deny the plausibility of the latter claim.

It is my additional contention, however, that when a person does what is practically (but not strictly) necessary, we nevertheless often judge this fact in moral terms. This happens when our judgement consists in *condoning* the action in question (in as much as it is practically necessary). In such a case, it is felt that the agent has a *prima facie* duty to perform an action but, because of the practical impossibility of that action, it is also felt that the agent is *exonerated* from this duty. The practically impossible action is not one that the agent can be *reasonably expected* to perform. To say in such circumstances that 'ought' implies 'can' is to suggest that because the agent could not perform the action in question, it is *morally acceptable, or permissible*, for the agent not to perform it.

This contention needs defending, for it is not immediately obvious that from the lack of duty to do x, we must derive the conclusion that not-x is morally acceptable. The position defended by Oppenheim is that where x is practically impossible, *no* moral evaluations of not-x can be made, and that not-x is therefore neither morally acceptable nor morally unacceptable. What is meant by there being no duty to do x (where x is practically impossible), he will say, is simply that x cannot be judged morally, and the same must therefore be said of not-x. It is only in this sense, if any, that we can see not-x as 'permissible'.

In order to clarify our difference on this point, it will be useful to draw on a distinction made by von Wright between 'weak' and 'strong' permission. A weak permission to do not-x is simply the absence of the duty to do x, and does not itself imply a practical norm, whereas a strong permission to do not-x is itself a practical norm. A strong permission has independent normative validity, and is not simply defined as the absence of an obligation. An action is permitted in the strong sense 'if the authority has considered its normative status and decided to permit it'. Weak permission, on the other hand, 'is not an independent norm-character'.[35] My contention is that to categorize an action as practically necessary is often to permit that action in the *strong* sense.

To arrive at this conclusion we must begin by noting that we sometimes morally evaluate practically *impossible* actions. Evidence of this can be found in the fact that people sometimes exercise their freedom to do the practically impossible, and are morally judged for it. This is

what happens when a person is said to have performed a 'supererogatory' act – that is, an act that is praiseworthy but not required, usually
because of the degree of self-sacrifice involved.[36] Here, rather than
refraining from passing moral judgement, we elevate the person to
the status of a saint, and say that she has acted 'above and beyond
the call of duty'. The judgement of an action as supererogatory
should certainly be seen as a moral judgement, inasmuch as
supererogatory actions are 'encouraged by morality' despite not being
required by it.[37]

The existence of supererogatory actions shows that we do not consider it pointless to evaluate practically impossible actions positively in
moral terms. Rather, the effect of '"ought" implies "practical possibility"' is to counterbalance this evaluation, excusing or exonerating a
person for not conforming to it. What we imply in saying that a *prima
facie* good action is nevertheless practically impossible is that despite
being morally encouraged, such an action is beyond what can reasonably be expected of a normal agent – because it is too difficult or costly
or, as Griffin puts it, because it is too demanding on the will.

Despite supererogatory acts having a high positive value, they are not
things that we 'ought' to do, and the reason for this is that there is an
important sense in which we 'cannot' do them. Does this mean that
the omission of such acts lies outside the scope of morality – that we
cannot pass moral judgement on such omissions in the same way as
we pass moral judgement on the acts themselves? Such a conclusion is
surely unwarranted: the fact that we pass moral judgement on practically impossible actions shows that we can also pass moral judgement
on practically necessary actions. Part of the positive moral value of
supererogatory acts is independent of their practical impossibility – not
all practically impossible acts qualify as supererogatory, for some such
acts are no doubt morally bad – and the permission not to perform a
supererogatory action derives from the way in which its practical
impossibility counterbalances this independent positive value. Thus,
while the mere practical impossibility of doing x leaves us with merely
a weak permission to do not-x, the practical impossibility of doing x in
combination with the independent judgement of x's *prima facie* moral
superiority implies more than a weak permission to do not-x. In the
latter case, the permission is implied by the very description of x as
supererogatory, which is itself the expression of a moral judgement.
Given that the permission is implied by a moral judgement rather
than by the mere absence of a moral judgement, it must be interpreted
as a strong permission. The 'not-ought' implied by calling an act

supererogatory is a *moral* 'not-ought'. It is a not-ought that condones, where to condone is to 'approve or sanction ... reluctantly'.[38]

It follows that '"ought" implies "practical possibility"' is itself an ethical norm, as stated in the second of the interpretations of OC examined at the outset. If the first interpretation were correct – if '"ought" implies "practical possibility"' were a semantic presupposition that circumscribes prescriptive discourse rather than being a part of it – then the question of what we 'can' do would be logically prior to the question of what we 'ought' to do. In Hare's words, where we cannot do something, or cannot avoid doing it, the question of whether it ought to be done would 'not arise'. This excludes the possibility of moral evaluations of impossible or necessary behaviour, allowing at most for the weak permission of what is necessary. While such an interpretation of OC may remain plausible where the kinds of impossibility and necessity assumed are limited to strict (i.e. logical and physical) impossibility and necessity, it ceases to be plausible where the kinds of impossibility and necessity assumed include practical impossibility and necessity, for we have seen that practically impossible actions are sometimes performed and morally evaluated. Only the second interpretation of OC is logically consistent with this last fact. Given that people sometimes do perform practically impossible actions, the question of whether or not they ought to do so does arise. Given OC, part of the answer to that question is that they are morally justified in not doing so.

5.   Conclusion

'"Ought" implies "practical possibility"' is a claim about what can be reasonably required of the normal agent, and is therefore itself an ethical claim – if a second-order ethical claim. The reasons for this lie in the value-laden nature of judgements about practical necessity and the fact that we can and do pass ethical judgement on practically impossible actions. This conclusion has implications both for Oppenheim's conception of freedom and for his view of the proper scope of moral judgements. First, I have said that an advantage of Oppenheim's account of the freedom to act is that it is motivated by a desire to provide a purely empirical definition of the concept. This also means, however, that we would do well to exclude the concept of practical impossibility from our explication of the freedom to act. Secondly, I have said that an advantage of Oppenheim's interpretation of '"ought" implies "can"' is that he interprets 'cannot' so as to include practical as well as strict impossibility. This also means, however, that we should see '"ought" implies "can"' – where this is taken to mean '"ought" implies "practical possibility"' – as itself an ethical norm, rather than as simply stating a logical presupposition of ethical norms.

As far as our moral judgements of governmental actions are concerned, the upshot of the foregoing argument is that all those governmental actions seen by Oppenheim as immune to moral judgement (because practically necessary) can in fact be objects of moral judgement after all. In one sense, this conclusion appears to bring Oppenheim's position much closer than he would like to the doctrine of 'reason of state'. Although he need still not say that the state has a moral duty to pursue the national interest, he should, according to my conclusion, say that it is often morally permissible (in the sense of being morally excusable, or condonable) for it to do so.[39] In another sense, however, it takes Oppenheim further away from the doctrine of reason of state, allowing as it does for the possibility of praising a state for compromising its national interest in favour of the 'supererogatory' pursuit of some morally superior goal.

Notes

* I should like to thank Carla Bagnoli, Felix Oppenheim and Mario Ricciardi for their helpful comments on earlier drafts of this paper.
1. Cf. Michael Stocker, '"Ought" and "Can"', *Australasian Journal of Philosophy*, 49 (1971), pp. 314–15, and *Plural and Conflicting Values* (Oxford: Clarendon Press, 1990), p. 96; Walter Sinnott-Armstrong, '"Ought" Conversationally Implies "Can"', *Philosophical Review*, 93 (1984), pp. 352–4.
2. Drawing on the work of H. P. Grice, Sinnott-Armstrong calls this kind of implication 'conversational' (see his '"Ought" Conversationally Implies "Can"'), given that it depends on the context of the utterance of 'ought' and on the purpose of the speaker. Oppenheim calls the same kind of implication 'pragmatic' (see Oppenheim, *The Place of Morality in Foreign Policy* (Lexington, Mass.: Lexington Books, 1991), pp. 38, 57).
3. Sinnott-Armstrong, '"Ought" Conversationally Implies "Can"', pp. 249–50.
4. Sinnott-Armstrong contrasts conversational implication with semantic implication (where the latter means entailment or presupposition). I shall not follow him in using this distinction; rather, I shall assume that OC can be called a semantic implication where we restrict our attention to a particular, precise meaning of 'ought' (the prescriptive, action-guiding meaning), and that *this* semantic implication can be interpreted as one of either presupposition or entailment.
5. R. M. Hare, *Freedom and Reason* (Oxford: Oxford University Press, 1963), ch. 3; G. H. von Wright, *Norm and Action* (London: Routledge and Kegan Paul, 1963), ch. 7.

6. Hare, *Freedom and Reason*, p. 59.
7. Hare, *Freedom and Reason*, p. 58.
8. Felix Oppenheim would call it a 'metaethical' norm. Cf. Oppenheim, *Moral Principles in Political Philosophy* (New York: Random House, 1968), p.16. However, this term may not suffice to distinguish the first interpretation of OC from the second.
9. Rem Blanchard Edwards, *Freedom, Responsibility and Obligation* (The Hague: Nijhoff, 1969), ch. 6; Manfred Moritz, 'On Second-order Norms', *Ratio*, 10 (1968), pp. 101–15; K. E. Tranøy, '"Ought" Implies "Can": a Bridge from Fact to Norm?', parts 1 and 2, *Ratio*, 14 (1972), pp. 116–30 and *Ratio*, 17 (1975), pp. 147–75.
10. Blanchard Edwards, *Freedom, Responsibility and Obligation*, p. 104, my emphasis; cf. James Griffin, *Value Judgement. Improving Our Ethical Beliefs* (Oxford: Clarendon Press, 1996), pp. 91, 92.
11. Blanchard Edwards, *Freedom, Responsibility and Obligation*, pp. 105–6.
12. Moritz, 'On Second-Order Norms', p. 104.
13. Oppenheim, *The Place of Morality in Foreign Policy*, ch. 3.
14. See Oppenheim, 'Social Freedom and its Parameters', *Journal of Theoretical Politics*, 7 (1995), sec. 2. The notion is also implicit in his *Dimensions of Freedom: an Analysis* (New York: St. Martin's Press, 1961), pp. 63–4, where he gives a broad interpretation of 'impossibility', and in his *Political Concepts: a Reconstruction* (Chicago: University of Chicago Press, 1981), ch. 4.
15. Cf. A. I. Goldman, *A Theory of Human Action* (Englewood Cliffs, NJ: Prentice Hall, 1970), ch. 7. Oppenheim also cites David Braybrooke and Charles Lindblom, Kenneth Arrow and Joseph Raz as sources.
16. For an analysis of impossibility and necessity according to rules (though not only moral rules) see Amedeo G. Conte's contribution to the present volume.
17. Cf. Oppenheim, *The Place of Morality in Foreign Policy*, p. 27.
18. One is *socially* unfree to the extent that this practical necessity is imposed by some other agent.
19. Oppenheim, *The Place of Morality in Foreign Policy*, p. 38.
20. Oppenheim, *The Place of Morality in Foreign Policy*, p. 38.
21. Oppenheim, *The Place of Morality in Foreign Policy*, p. 39, emphasis in original.
22. I take political realism to be (or at least to include) the view that power relations are the basic driving force of political life. (Sometimes, as in the case of Oppenheim, the scope of political realism is restricted to international politics.) Moral realism, which Oppenheim does not endorse, is a metaethical view (in Oppenheim's sense) according to which moral judgements have an objective truth-value.
23. Ian Carter, 'The Independent Value of Freedom', *Ethics*, 105 (1995), pp. 819–45; *A Measure of Freedom* (Oxford: Oxford University Press, 1999), chs 2 and 3.
24. Oppenheim is himself sceptical about the measurability of freedom in overall terms. See for example, *Political Concepts*, pp. 70–1, 78–81. I respond

to Oppenheim on this point in *A Measure of Freedom*, sec. 1.5 and chs 7 and 8.

25. Oppenheim, 'Social Freedom and its Parameters', sec. 4.
26. Tranøy, '"Ought" Implies "Can"', part 2, p. 164.
27. I derive this suggestion from Oppenheim's reference to John Rawls in his exposition of the notion of practical impossibility. Apparently, Oppenheim sees the pursuit of Rawlsian primary goods as practically necessary because they are, in Rawls's words, 'things which it is supposed a rational man wants whatever else he wants'. Cf. Rawls, *A Theory of Justice* (Cambridge, Mass.: Harvard University Press, 1971), p. 92; Oppenheim, *The Place of Morality in Foreign Policy*, p. 38.
28. In *A Measure of Freedom* (ch. 2) I claimed that freedom has a 'wholly non-specific' instrumental value. But I did not mean by this that freedom is a means to any end whatsoever; rather, I meant that freedom has wholly non-specific value as a means to certain given ends, such as happiness or progress.
29. Oppenheim, *Political Concepts*, pp. 88–91. Cf. Serena Olsaretti, 'Freedom, Force, and Choice: Against the Rights-based Definition of Voluntariness', *Journal of Political Philosophy*, 6 (1998), pp. 53–78.
30. Oppenheim in fact makes fear of punishment a necessary condition for unfree action (see *Political Concepts*, p. 90), but one can also reasonably conceive of 'free action' non-socially, in which case the circumstances forcing the agent to act 'against her will' need not be humanly imposed.
31. In *A Measure of Freedom* (ch. 8), I argue that unfreedom to act can be defined purely in terms of (absolute) physical impossibilty without the counterintuitive results that this is often thought to bring. The key to doing so is to conceive of *overall* unfreedom as the physical prevention of *sets of compossible actions*.
32. Goldman, *A Theory of Human Action*, pp. 208–9.
33. Griffin, *Value Judgement*, p. 91.
34. Tranøy, '"Ought" Implies "Can"', part 2, p. 148.
35. Von Wright, *Norm and Action*, p. 86. The 'character' of a norm, for von Wright, depends on whether it obliges, forbids or permits.
36. The most demanding ethical theories, like act-utilitarianism, deny the category of supererogatory acts, since they assert that agents are always required to maximize the good. Such theories fall outside the scope of my argument, since they deny that 'ought' implies 'practical possibility'.
37. I quote from Bernard Gert's entry on 'supererogation' in the *Cambridge Dictionary of Philosophy*, ed. R. Audi (Cambridge: Cambridge University Press, 1995), p. 777.
38. I quote from the *Concise Oxford Dictionary*.
39. On the other hand, this is not to say that anyone who accepts my arguments must condone all such state actions; only that they must do so where they agree with Oppenheim that the state, as a perfect analogue of the individual, really 'cannot' do otherwise. This issue is discussed by George Kateb in his contribution to the present volume.

7

Clarifying the Science Wars: the Concept of Scientific Authority

Mark R. Weaver

1. Oppenheim's approach to political philosophy

It is unfortunate that some theorists will judge Felix E. Oppenheim's contributions to political philosophy solely in terms of his meta-theoretical stances on such issues as the separation of facts and values, a non-cognitivist view of moral values, and the construction of a value neutral political science based upon the reconstruction of ordinary language. While Oppenheim certainly did articulate and defend these positions in the face of a fundamental shift in the basic orientation of Anglo-American political theory, these metatheoretical arguments do not constitute the core of what he offered to political theory in his writing and teaching. Instead, what is most essential to understanding Oppenheim's own approach to political philosophy, and what remains most relevant to contemporary social and political theory today, is his conception of the nature and central tasks of political theory as a critical and reflective enterprise.

Oppenheim's approach to political theory, both in the classroom and in his scholarship, emphasized that cogent political argument and successful political inquiry are inevitably dependent upon careful attention to the clarity and precision of the basic concepts used in argument or inquiry. Always sceptical of what normative or empirical conclusions could be reached on the basis of armchair theorizing alone, he saw political theory as an integral part of political science. His interest in the metatheoretical debates about how to do political theory or how to interpret political concepts was always secondary to his primary concern with actually doing political theory, especially the clarification and reconstruction of the key concepts of political inquiry.[1] In Oppenheim's view, it was the usefulness of specific analyses of particular concepts to ongoing political inquiry and political argument rather than metatheoretical debates about interpretation or understanding that would ultimately determine the success or failure of any theoretical perspective.

Of course, the value of Oppenheim's approach to political theory to us today is necessarily dependent upon the context within which we find ourselves. While this question of context raises several difficult issues that are beyond the scope of this chapter, it is useful to think about the continued significance of Oppenheim's vision of political philosophy in terms of two different problems confronting the theorist today. On the one hand, there is the danger of confining oneself to too narrow a conception of the theoretical enterprise and becoming so pre-occupied with questions of definition and clarity that important sub-stantive issues are being neglected. On the other hand, there is the danger of being swept up into issues at such levels of abstraction and with so little attention to questions of definition and specification that communication within the community of theorists as well as with other communities around them becomes increasingly difficult.

Felix Oppenheim's work remains a valuable paradigm to those theor-ists who confront issues of the second kind. As an illustration of this second type of problem in contemporary social and political theory, this chapter will consider an important debate in contemporary US academic discourse, the so-called science wars. Put simply, the science wars is an ongoing battle, which is primarily verbal but increasingly includes struggles over hiring decisions, between a group of feminist, postmodernist and STS (science and technology studies) critics of natural science and an increasingly vocal group of natural scientists and allies in other fields who claim to speak in defence of science.[2] While the science wars is a complex and far-ranging debate, much of it centres in rival claims about the 'epistemic authority' or the 'cognitive authority' of science in modern society.

In short, the science critics challenge, and the science defenders justify, science's claim to a unique type of cognitive authority in contemporary society.[3] However, this debate remains mired in funda-mental confusion because there is virtually no attention directed to explicating the central concept of cognitive authority, and because the implicit concept of scientific authority which underpins the debate is seriously flawed. If this debate is to be resolved, it will require the kind of careful explication and reconstruction of the concept of scientific authority that is demanded in Oppenheim's approach to political philosophy.

2.   The conception of scientific authority in critiques of science

Stanley Aronowitz illustrates the fuzzy conception of scientific authority that is characteristic of the critics of science:

> The sum of these investigations [STS] is to bring science and scientificity down to earth, to show that it is no more, but certainly no less, than any other discourse. It is one story among many stories that has given the world considerable benefits including pleasure, but also considerable pain. Science and its methods underlie medical knowledge, which, true to its analytic procedures, has wreaked as much havoc as health on the human body; and it is also the knowledge base of the war machine. Science has worked its precepts deep into our everyday life. Science as culture is as ubiquitous as is science as power.[4]

In his book *Science as Power*, he develops this conception of the hegemony of scientific authority by arguing that 'claims of authority in our contemporary world rest increasingly on the possession of legitimate knowledge, of which scientific discourses are supreme'.[5] Indeed, Aronowitz holds that scientific discourse now dominates economics, politics and modern culture and that scientific authority operates as a kind of trump card which can be used to dismiss or exclude other discourses describing or evaluating contemporary politics and culture.

Aronowitz's conception of scientific authority as monolithic and hegemonic is, with variations, common among critics of science. Although specific characterizations of scientific authority are seldom offered, a clear illustration of the pervasive implicit conception of scientific authority is provided by Collins and Pinch's *The Golem: What Everyone Should Know About Science*. Collins and Pinch, much like Aronowitz, are primarily concerned with the 'overweening claims to authority of many scientists and technologists' that dominate contemporary society and politics.[6] They contend that this excessive scientific authority is grounded in an idealized popular vision of scientific knowledge as a form of truth which is immune to error and bias. Indeed, the purpose of their eight case studies in the sociology of scientific knowledge is 'to change the public understanding of the political role of science and technology' by deconstructing the almost god-like status of scientific authority in contemporary culture and politics. Thus, by showing how science actually works in their case studies, which range from transfer of memory through transfer of worm brain matter to cold fusion, they attempt to destroy the idealized image of science as truth upon which modern scientific authority rests. We find that science is like a stumbling golem, and that 'scientists are neither Gods nor charlatans; they are merely experts, like every other expert on the political stage'.[7]

Thus, like Aronowitz, Collins and Pinch assume that the authority that the scientific expert exercises in contemporary society and politics flows directly and automatically from the cognitive authority of the scientific community. In other words, you can deconstruct the cultural and political authority of science (Collins and Pinch's goal) by telling the real story of how cognitive authority works within the scientific community (their case studies). Again like Aronowitz, Collins and Pinch assume that scientific authority rests upon a particular view of science which is rooted in a positivist philosophy of science. The authority of science in contemporary politics and society is assumed to be dependent upon this philosophical vision of scientific method as granting privileged access to a single reality, a single truth. Accordingly, they believe that if their sociological account of the production of scientific knowledge reveals that science is a stumbling golem rather than a discovery of the true picture of the real world, then the general public will develop a healthy scepticism of scientific claims in the political realm. For the most part, the critics of science agree with this account of their mission: to deconstruct the cultural and political claims of scientific expertise and authority by exposing the real story of what happens in the scientific laboratory.

3. The conception of scientific authority in defences of science

While the various defenders of scientific authority vehemently reject this critique of science, they generally share the conception of scientific authority that underpins it. Gross and Levitt's *Higher Superstition* provides one of the most developed and explicit formulations of scientific authority among those who respond to the critics of science. Their diagnosis of the present political challenges to the cognitive authority of the natural sciences focuses on what they perceive as current strains of academic anti-scientism which are increasingly dominant in university departments in the humanities and social sciences. In part, they suggest that this anti-scientism represents an opportunity to settle old scores in the continuing struggle for cognitive status and financial resources in the university. By challenging established 'assumptions about the epistemological rankings of various fields', with the hard sciences which produce reliable knowledge at the top and literary criticism ('subjective beyond hope of redemption') at the bottom, these critiques of science represent attempts 'to regain the high ground, to assert that the methods of social theory and literary analysis are equal in epistemic power to those of science'.[8]

Gross and Levitt's central target is 'the academic left', a theoretically diverse movement across the humanities and social sciences that is unified in promoting a common political project: 'to demystify science, to undermine its epistemic authority, and to valorize "ways of knowing" incompatible with it'.[9] They object that these academic left critiques of science do not aim at reforming science and using it to promote progressive causes, but rather seek to destroy the epistemological and institutional foundations of scientific authority. In their view, postmodern scepticism, with its rejection of 'the possibility of enduring universal knowledge in any area' and its consequent reduction of all knowledge projects to forms of power politics, promotes a cognitive relativism that attempts to erase completely the cognitive authority of science.[10]

Thus, at the core of their defence of scientific authority is a defence of a particular philosophy of science, a modified version of positivism which 'is still embraced, at least tentatively, by most working scientists who have reflected at all (as most have) on the issues of knowing and truth'.[11] In addition, they specifically link science, as presented by this philosophy of science, to a standard narrative of the Enlightenment and human progress:

> The Western culture that grows from, extends, and intensifies the Enlightenment proves itself and displays its uniqueness most impressively by its ability to fathom nature and nature's regularities, to a depth unimaginable in prior civilizations. Western culture converts that knowledge into the instruments, conveniences, and perceived necessities of daily life with a swiftness that far outspeeds the traditional pace of historical progress.[12]

This is, of course, exactly the opposite image of science and human progress from that articulated by Aronowitz.

Yet, like the critics of science, Gross and Levitt assume a particular conception of scientific authority in which the authority of science in the realm of politics and culture flows directly and automatically from the cognitive authority of science as a form of knowledge. Thus, to defend the role of the scientist as an expert or authority in modern culture and politics is to defend this epistemic authority of science. In addition, like the critics of science, Gross and Levitt assume that the political and cultural forms of scientific authority rest upon a particular positivist or realist philosophy of science. Thus, to defend scientific authority is to reassert this philosophy of science, largely by attacking as irrational and relativist the philosophical underpinnings of the various critiques of science. In sum, the defenders of science, like the critics of science, ultimately reduce the issues regarding the authority of the natural sciences in contemporary culture and politics to an epistemological debate about scientific method, objectivity, reason and truth. The term 'epistemic authority of science' represents and reinforces this reduction.

4.   Towards an alternative conception of scientific authority

Much of the confusion in the science wars conception of scientific authority results from a failure to examine carefully how the authority exercised by the natural scientist in the political and cultural realm is both similar to and different from more traditional forms of political or social authority. Social scientists commonly define authority as a type of power in which control over behaviour is exercised through giving commands or formulating rules that are obeyed because they are accepted as legitimate. The concept of authority is thus closely connected to both the concepts of legitimacy and obligation which are thought to distinguish authority from coercion on the one hand and rational persuasion on the other.[13] In short, the power of the authority holder is based upon the authority subject's belief in the legitimacy of her authority which generates an obligation to obey her commands or rules. Moreover, since challenges to authority are a common feature of modern political and social life, enduring authority relations are those that are deeply embedded in wider power networks and social structures which make the authority subject dependent upon the authority holder for her life, liberty, employment and so on.

   The kind of authority exercised by scientists is different in that the scientist is *an* authority rather than *in* authority, or an authority based on special knowledge rather than the holder of an office or a special status.[14] This type of authority is labelled cultural authority, cognitive authority, or professional authority because it is based upon claims of knowledge or expertise rather than on giving commands or establishing rules. In contrast to the power to issue commands or to make rules, this cultural authority exercised by the scientist is typically defined as 'the construction of reality through definitions of fact and value' or the power 'to define the true nature of the living and the non-living world around us'.[15]

Defined in this way, the cultural or cognitive authority of science in the modern Western world seems very impressive: 'Science is next to being *the* source of cognitive authority: anyone who would be widely believed and trusted as an interpreter of nature needs a license from the scientific community'.[16] But before we accept this conception of the overweening authority of the scientific expert in contemporary society, and the corollary proposition that such authority flows directly from the epistemic authority of modern science understood in philosophical terms, we must critically analyse this purported power to define reality, and we must examine how scientific authority rests on legitimacy, obligation and dependency relations.

5.   The power to define and interpret reality

The first critical conceptual distinction that must be made is between the authority to define or interpret the physical and biological world and the authority to define or interpret the social and political world. Scientific authority in relation to the interpretation or definition of the biological or physical world through the production of knowledge constitutes the *internal* cognitive authority of the scientific community. Internal cognitive authority refers to the various uses of scientific authority within the scientific community, such as peer review, in the research, discourses and practices involved in the production of scientific knowledge. Scientific authority in relation to the interpretation or definition of the social or political world through social and political practices refers to the *external* cognitive authority or cultural authority of science and of the scientific community. External scientific authority, or the cultural authority of science, refers to the various uses of the scientific authority of the natural sciences to determine the definition and interpretation of the social and political world.

As we have seen, the science wars debate is essentially a debate about the nature of the internal cognitive authority of science. The critics of science tend to collapse this distinction between the internal and external authority of science because it has been used to defend science as a unique form of activity resulting in a unique form of knowledge.[17] They attempt to demonstrate that there are fundamental cultural or social biases at work in the internal cognitive authority in all the natural sciences, especially in biology and medicine, and that these cultural biases undercut science's claims to articulate universal truth. The defenders of science respond to this critique by attempting to demonstrate that scientific methodology remains free of such cultural and social biases and that the unique cognitive authority of science remains intact. By defending the internal cognitive authority of science, they believe that the external authority of science in society and politics is automatically justified.

In short, both sides in the science wars argue about the external cognitive authority of science in terms of the internal cognitive authority of science. The nature and scope of the external authority of science and the scientific community as deployed within the political, social and cultural realms remains largely unexamined and unclear. We need to start with an analysis of the concept of the external authority of science, a concept that entails all the various ways in which the cultural or cognitive authority of the natural sciences is deployed to define and interpret the social, cultural and political world. Although analysis of the complex connections between scientific authority and the construction of the social world is beyond the scope of this chapter, some of the central features and limits of the external cognitive authority of science are well illustrated by the uses of scientific authority in politics and public policy.

The most visible form of such authority is that utilized by scientific advisers who participate in the formation of science policy or other major policy areas such as health policy or defence policy and the larger number of scientists who attempt to communicate to policy makers their applied research as it relates to specific policy issues. This particular type of external scientific authority, 'science-as-counsel', constitutes a form of mediation, undertaken by a small group of scientists, between the scientific community and other professional communities, the public, the media and policy makers.[18]

Science-as-counsel is never simply a disinterested attempt by scientists to present information which is relevant to public policy, but is also an attempt to influence policy in competition with other interests and other forms of cultural authority. One of the primary ways that scientists attempt to establish, exercise and maintain their cultural authority in this competitive policy arena is to utilize a type of boundary strategy:

When an area of intellectual activity is tagged with the label 'science', people who are not scientists are *de facto* barred from having any say about its substance; correspondingly, to label some-thing 'not science' is to denude it of cognitive authority.[19]

Since scientific research is especially important to the issues that now tend to dominate contemporary public policy, especially security, health and environmental policy, it might seem that the cultural authority of science will inevitably become increasingly dominant as scientists utilize this and other boundary strategies to broaden their monopoly of expertise.

However, such a view of the growing dominance of the cultural authority of science is based upon an inadequate conceptualization of the nature of this mediation process. In the first place, this public 'voice' of science-as-counsel is itself a 'boundary object', a product of the complex interactions of the scientific community and the other communities with which it interacts.[20] For example, in the complex interactions between science and politics, scientists are frequently called upon to address problems and issues which go beyond their scientific expertise and which fall between the boundaries of science and politics. In other words, the cultural authority of science is deployed in and constructed by a complex discourse which consists of the language of science applied to public issues as formulated through a complex set of practices, activities, organizations and institutional arrangements. External scientific authority is exercised and produced within these boundary interactions and is not merely a secondary political expression of the epistemic authority of science.

In addition, the ultimate aim of external scientific authority is not to interpret or define the physical world, but to use the cultural authority of science to change or shape the prevailing interpretation of the polit-ical world. In other words, scientific discourse and research are being deployed in an attempt to formulate or revise the basic ideas which define and interpret the political world. As Deborah Stone emphasizes, this use of scientific authority aims at redrawing the boundaries of the basic categories of political reality:

> Ideas are the very stuff of politics. ... Every idea about politics draws boundaries. It tells what or who is included or excluded in a cate-gory. These boundaries are more than intellectual – they define people in and out of a conflict or place them on different sides. In politics, the representation of issues is strategically designed to attract support to one's side, to forge some alliances and break others. Ideas and alliances are intimately connected.[21]

Even if we take the example of the scientist who is attempting to simply report information to the public or to policy makers, she does so in this arena of competing political ideas, boundaries and alliances. The external voice of scientific authority speaks to the public and policy makers not in the context of the more formal rules and practices that typify the internal cognitive authority of science, but rather in the context of a basic political struggle to control the representation of public issues and to control the interpretations through which the 'facts' will be understood. In this arena of conflict over the identification, classification, categorization and definition of political reality, scientific ideas and information are, like the inputs of other cultural authorities, objects of strategic manipulation.[22] Again, even if we focus narrowly on science-as-counsel in the form of a scientist who attempts to inform the public or policy makers on an issue such as global warming, in this process information becomes a strategic resource that may be shared, withheld or selectively released. Scientific authority is exercised in a political arena in which competing political interests strategically manipulate scientific information and ideas to influence how people define their identities, needs and interests; to control the public agenda by ensuring that certain potential issues are never defined or articulated as public problems; and to limit the policy options that are actually considered by policy makers once problems have been defined.

Moreover, this external voice of scientific authority is inevitably mediated by the symbolism, narrative structure, metaphors, paradoxes and ambiguity that characterize the language, reason and practice of politics. Thus, in order to understand the nature and limits of scientific authority, our focus must shift to the narrative structures and metaphors that are used in the strategic representation of the goals, problems and solutions of political decision-making. For example, in political rhetoric and reasoning the search for causes is never simply an attempt to understand a sequence of events or to understand how the world works. Rather, the search for causes in political argument and policy discussion is always linked to the strategic function of assigning responsibility for a particular problem to particular individuals or groups so that they can be punished, required to compensate other individuals or groups, or simply assigned blame for creating certain problems. The cultural authority of science is frequently deployed in this strategic function of assigning blame or responsibility to some and absolving others of such blame and responsibility. In this external discourse of scientific authority, the language of scientific causation is typically used to define or interpret an issue or problem in terms of standard political narratives of oppressors and victims, of control and helplessness, of guilt and innocence, and of winners and losers.[23]

Of course, the cultural authority of science is a particularly powerful strategic resource precisely because it embodies the claimed objectivity and neutrality of scientific research even though it is deployed as part of the narratives and metaphors of political discourse. However, this does not negate the fact that the external authority of science has become, like all other forms of cultural authority, a strategic resource to be deployed to advance or to attack particular political goals or interests. Moreover, far from hegemonic, the claims to scientific objectivity and other special claims of scientific authority can be successfully challenged and overcome by counter-claims supported by competing scientific authorities or by other cultural authorities. The limits of the cultural authority of science become clearer as we focus on the conceptions of legitimacy, obligation and dependency as they are tied to scientific authority.

6.   The different forms of legitimacy

As we have seen, legitimacy is considered one feature of authority that distinguishes it from other forms of power. Certainly, the cultural authority of the scientific community, like the cultural authority of the Catholic Church or the legal profession, is based upon its acceptance as legitimate by the general public and by policy makers. But in this case, citizens or policy makers are making judgements about the individuals and communities that claim specific forms of knowledge or expertise rather than about particular office holders or governments. The critics of scientific authority, such as Collins and Pinch, are correct in assuming that this legitimacy can be, to some extent, challenged by changing the way people think about scientific truth. Similarly, the defenders of science, such as Gross and Levitt, are correct in thinking that defending certain conceptions of truth, objectivity and reason will support, to a limited extent, the legitimacy of science. However, both the critics and the defenders of science rely on a simplistic conception of scientific authority that largely ignores other ways in which scientific legitimacy is constructed and deconstructed.

The science wars model of scientific authority focuses exclusively on struggles over the cognitive dimension of legitimacy. They essentially ask: when natural scientists make claims in the public policy arena, do they really present a kind of knowledge which is on a sounder epistemological foundation than other claims to knowledge? Aronowitz,

Collins and Pinch defend a negative answer, whereas Gross and Levitt insist on a positive response. However, as Paul Starr's examination of the history of US medical authority demonstrates, this type of epistemic authority does not necessarily and automatically confer cultural authority.[24] The legitimacy of scientific authority, like the legitimacy of other forms of cultural or professional authority, rests upon four analytically distinct grounds: 1. the cognitive authority of the type of knowledge or expertise that is being claimed by the professional group; 2. the professional norms of the community that ensure the training and competence of the individual practitioners; 3. the substantive moral and social values served by the individual practitioners as well as the professional community as a whole; and 4. the legitimacy of the social and political institutions that are most closely connected with the rise of particular forms of cultural authority.[25] Although the debate over cognitive legitimation may be central in the science wars debate and in philosophical discourse, the key contemporary political and cultural legitimation battles over scientific authority concern these professional, normative and institutional forms of legitimacy.

The legitimacy of professional norms

First, scientists like other professionals claim authority as members of a community that certifies and validates each member's competence on the basis of shared standards regarding training, discipline and performance.[26] One of the most significant current challenges to the legitimacy of scientific authority in politics today is based upon questioning the professional standards of the physical and life sciences. This challenge to scientific authority as exercised in and by the scientific community is clearest in how policy makers and the media seem preoccupied with questions regarding professional standards and ethics in the sciences. One example of such challenges to the legitimacy of the current standards and practices of the scientific community is the wide coverage of and continuing debate over unethical experiments conducted on human subjects who were not informed or were lied to by physicians or scientists. A second example is the significant media and policy-maker interest in cases of purported falsification of data and other scientific misconduct in some of the world's leading research facilities. A third example is the concern about individual scientists patenting the products of government-sponsored research as well as the potential conflict of interest of research scientists who have large economic stakes in the regulatory approval of products or processes emerging from their laboratories.

This type of challenge to scientific authority is not based on questioning the legitimacy of the cognitive grounding of science, but rather on questioning the legitimacy of the present professional and ethical standards of the scientific community. Many policy makers and members of the general public are genuinely concerned about whether or not the scientific community is able or willing to exercise its internal authority to correct these perceived problems and to ensure the future integrity and reliability of the scientific enterprise. Moreover, these challenges to the professional and ethical standards of the scientific community have clearly served to delegitimate scientific authority. This is so precisely because the legitimacy of scientific authority does not simply flow from the cognitive authority of science, but is also dependent upon public acceptance of the professional ethics of individual scientists and the scientific community.

The legitimacy of social and moral values

Second, scientific authority, like other forms of cultural authority, achieves legitimation through the claim that it serves important values of the larger community or public rather than simply promoting its own interests or the profits of the profession.[27] In other words, the external authority of science also ultimately rests upon claims that it promotes the public good. It is this dimension of scientific authority that has come into question in post-Cold War discussions of US science policy. In the Cold War era, there was a general public consensus that spending on science was justified in terms of three major goals: to provide the knowledge and technology that would be necessary to protect US national security; to provide the driving force for economic growth and the maintenance of a high standard of living; and to provide the biomedical research that would promote the health of the American people.[28]

The end of the Cold War most clearly called for a re-examination of the specific kinds of research and development (R&D) that were considered essential to defeating the Soviet Union. Of course, there are many who would simply find a new security threat to justify continued public support of spending for the existing R&D structure. However, the legitimation of US science policy had become so closely associated with US security as understood within the Cold War paradigm that the sudden collapse of the Soviet Union created a legitimation gap in terms of public support for science as contributing to the public good. As a result, many policy makers began to challenge government support of scientific research as wasteful and inefficient and to look to more market-oriented approaches to R&D. Moreover, although public support for scientific research that can be justified in terms of promoting health remains strong, even science's role in promoting health has been called into question by critics who point to science's failure to win the war on cancer, criticize science's failure to recognize and respond to the AIDS crisis, and raise questions about links between the scientific establishment and the marginalization of alternative approaches to medicine.

These debates represent far more than a contract renegotiation between the scientific community and government because they raise fundamental questions about science's mission or value to society. Since scientific authority is ultimately dependent upon whether or not policy makers and the public accept it as legitimate, and its legitimacy is partially dependent upon its promotion of acceptable social values, a persuasive articulation of the public values that science promotes is an essential part of the social construction of scientific authority. In addition, these debates over support of scientific research as a public value are a product not of postmodern philosophical critiques of science, but rather of a political arena in which the scientific community must compete with other interests for the limited public funds that are available to promote the public good.

Institutional legitimacy

Scientific authority, like other forms of cultural authority, is necessarily embedded within certain social structures and institutions, and its legitimacy is partially dependent upon the legitimacy of these structures and institutions. Scientific authority always entails more than the dyadic relation between an authority holder and an authority subject because the 'power dyad is itself situated in the context of other social relations'.[29] Moreover, the increasing prevalence of scientific authority in modern politics and public policy is not the consequence of the epistemic success of science alone. In general, 'the rise of expertise in contemporary society corresponds to the development of a specific social structure that allows the expert to become a wielder of power'.[30] Scientific authority is exercised within particular social structures and institutions, and challenges to the legitimacy of these structures and institutions frequently involve challenges to the legitimacy of the external authority of the scientist.

One example of institutional legitimacy is the way that scientific authority is frequently entangled in NIMBY (Not In My Back Yard) politics. To many in the scientific community, NIMBY politics represents a kind of neo-Luddite, anti-science movement that is based upon striking ignorance of scientific method and risk assessment. However, case studies of decision-making involved in the siting and management of nuclear power and weapons facilities, the siting and management of various hazardous waste facilities, and the regulation of scientific research with potential community risks reveal a different picture.[31] Both government agencies and corporations have made extensive use of scientific authority as a strategic device to remove decision-making from public forums, to limit public input into decisions, and to attempt to legitimate political decisions by presenting them as scientific or technological issues. The political challenges to the legitimacy of such decisions and the public and private institutions that make them entail powerful challenges to the legitimacy of scientific authority as it has been and is currently deployed.

In more general terms, there is no reason to assume that the types of institutions and forms of decision-making that are good for science (in the sense that they promote rapid scientific progress in the areas deemed most important by the scientific community) are also good for democracy (in that they promote citizen participation in and control over the decisions that most directly affect the public). One of the most important challenges to scientific authority as it is commonly exercised today centres in a complex set of questions concerning whether scientific experts or the public (or its representatives) will make key decisions concerning how public money will be spent on scientific research, or regarding the acceptable level of public risk associated with particular types of research or with siting hazardous waste facilities.

In sum, this set of contemporary policy debates concerning the use of scientific authority to justify processes and outcomes that are perceived to be undemocratic, regarding the justification of government support of scientific research in terms of social values and the public good, and concerning the adequacy of the existing professional or ethical standards of the scientific community are much more critical to the legitimation or delegitimation of scientific authority than is the science wars debate over the epistemological status of scientific knowledge. For example, contemporary debates over research in biotechnology, particularly genetic enhancement in humans, raise fundamental issues of legitimacy in all three areas. The central debate is not about the epistemological status of the science supporting gene technology, but about whether the professional or ethical standards that will guide such research and its applications are adequate, whether scientific progress in this field ultimately serves or undercuts more fundamental human values, and whether the institutions and institutional arrangements that are emerging in this period of remarkable growth in biotechnology can ever be held accountable for the decisions which they are now making.

7. Obligation and the surrender of judgement

There is, in general, considerable disagreement and confusion regarding the relationship between authority and reason. Many political and social theorists, drawing on the distinction between authority and rational persuasion, hold that authority relationships always involve some kind of surrender of judgement on the part of the authority subject. Starr, for example, claims that authority 'signifies the possession of some status, quality, or claim that compels trust or obedience', and that the 'acceptance of authority signifies "a surrender of private judgment"'.[32] He is here following the lead of Hannah Arendt who states:

> Authority ... is incompatible with persuasion, which presupposes equality and works through a process of argumentation. Where arguments are used, authority is left in abeyance. Against the egalitarian order of persuasion stands the authoritarian order, which is always hierarchical.[33]

This point, if pushed to its logical conclusion, converts a useful distinction between two forms of power into a dichotomy between a hierarchical and a democratic social order and suggests that authority relations are possible only in the former. However, it is possible to conceive of authority relationships within a number of different kinds of social orders and political institutions (e.g. aristocratic, bureaucratic and democratic) and to acknowledge the possibility that some authority relations might compel obedience in ways that preclude rational judgement or reflection while others do not.[34]

The conception of scientific authority that prevails in the science wars implicitly accepts this dichotomy between an authoritarian order of hierarchy and an egalitarian order of persuasion. The critics of science seem to assume that the inequality between the scientific expert and the typical citizen compels the citizen to surrender her critical judgement to the superior knowledge of the scientific expert. Moreover, their image of an alternative relation between science and the public requires the destruction of scientific authority and the creation of a new egalitarian relationship between expert and citizen based solely on rational persuasion. Although many of the defenders of science remain rather uncomfortable with the concept of authority, which is often seen as the traditional opponent of the voice of scientific reason, they tend to accept the necessity of a surrender of judgement to the superior knowledge of the scientific expert on the part of a public lacking basic scientific literacy.

However, scientific authority is clearly unlike authoritarian forms of political or social authority that might compel obedience in the form of a surrender of judgement. Moreover, there is simply no obligation to believe the statements of an expert that is parallel to the type of obligation to obey that is thought to be typical of more democratic kinds of political authority. Richard Flathman argues that all forms of cultural authority require some capacity for critical reflection or assessment on the part of the authority subjects in order for them to recognize or accept as legitimate that form of authority.[35] Instead of focusing on a supposed surrender of judgement that is assumed to be typical of all authority relationships, Flathman suggests that we focus on the context and the nature of citizen judgement that is involved in particular uses of scientific authority.

> *An* authority relations are distinguished not by the surrender of judgment on B's part but by the distinctive circumstances under which and the distinctive manner in which B exercises his judgment.[36]

Since there are significant differences in the various types of scientific authority exercised in contemporary politics and culture, there is likely to be a wide range of differences in the extent to which particular circumstances and particular forms of judgement encourage or limit critical reflection.

The science wars' dichotomous treatment of scientific authority and rational persuasion discourages empirical examination of the circumstances and manner in which the public makes judgements about different expressions of scientific authority.

8. Dependency conditions

As we have seen, scientific authority is, like other forms of cultural authority, subject to powerful challenges to its legitimacy that do undermine its authority. In addition, it is a mistake to assume that scientific authority necessarily obligates belief or compels a surrender of judgement. In an age typified by numerous challenges to virtually all forms of authority, the forms of cultural authority that prevail will tend to be those which can mobilize other forms of power, including coercion and persuasion, when their legitimacy is challenged. In particular, effective cultural authority has a second foundation for exercising control that is available if legitimacy fails. Starr labels this second source of cultural authority the 'dependency condition – the dependence [of the citizen or authority subject] upon the professional's [authority holder's] superior competence'.[37]

This dependence of the authority subject is not a function of the perceived legitimacy of particular forms of cultural authority. The level of dependency is determined by the more general networks of power and social structures within which any form of cultural authority is exercised. Instead of assuming the type of monolithic, hegemonic scientific authority pictured by critics of science, we should assume a variety of different attempts to deploy scientific authority whose effectiveness is limited by the corresponding relations of dependency. For example, Starr argues that medicine is a unique form of scientific authority because physicians 'come into direct and immediate contact with people in their daily lives; they are present at the critical transitional moments of existence'.[38] In other words, the cultural authority of the medical profession and its practitioners will differ from that of other scientific specialities, say astronomers, because the physician comes into immediate contact with individuals and the physician's expertise directly concerns the patient's health or life. More generally, different forms of scientific authority will be more powerful to the extent that they are supported by dependency conditions which make authority subjects dependent upon scientific experts for their life, health, liberty or livelihood.

Moreover, the cultural authority of the modern medical profession is hardly monolithic since it varies across societies and historically. In the US, the cultural authority of the medical profession has been very strong because of its ability to translate its cultural authority into a highly effective political organization and extensive economic power.[39] However, shifts in the political economy of health care, including the rise of for-profit corporations and the concentration of ownership of health services, have fundamentally undercut the autonomy of the medical profession and the practising physician. In turn, the basic doctor–patient relationship, including the dependency condition of the patient, has been altered. The cultural authority of the medical profession declines as the relations of dependency shift in favour of the corporate managers of health insurance and health care.

This brief discussion of medical authority and dependency suggests that a comprehensive analysis of scientific authority requires an examination of the dependency relations determined by the networks of power and the social structures within which such authority is exercised. In order to accomplish this, we must move from macro-level arguments about scientific authority that centre on claims about links between scientific epistemology and capitalism, patriarchy or other social structures to micro-level historical and social analyses of the concrete dependency conditions within which scientific authority is deployed.

9. Conclusion: a call for conceptual analysis

Many of the commentators on the science wars, while critical of the inflammatory rhetoric employed by both sides, remain optimistic that something positive will come of this debate because the two sides are at least talking to one another.[40] But, as Oppenheim's political philosophy demonstrates, political argument or political inquiry which is not grounded in systematic attention to the definition of key terms is unlikely to go anywhere. In this case, the science wars debate is trapped by a muddled conception of scientific authority that: conflates the external and internal cognitive authority of science; misunderstands the nature and limits of scientific authority as a strategic resource in politics; neglects the professional, normative and institutional foundations of the legitimacy of scientific authority; treats scientific authority as requiring a surrender of judgement in which citizens are compelled to accept the beliefs presented by scientific experts; and neglects the institutional and structural relations of dependency as sources of scientific authority.

Oppenheim sides with those voices in the Western political tradition, in particular Hobbes, who insist that a failure to define what one is talking about fundamentally undermines one's ability to contribute to political argument or political inquiry. In a time when one of the major current intellectual debates, which focuses on the important issue of the proper role of science in society, flounders around an undefined and confused notion of scientific authority, Oppenheim's rigorous approach to conceptual analysis and political argument remains especially relevant to social and political theory.

Notes

1. See, e.g., Felix Oppenheim, *Political Concepts: a Reconstruction* (Chicago: University of Chicago Press, 1981), pp. 1–3.
2. For relatively neutral summaries of major developments in and positions set out within this science wars debate, see Jay Labinger, 'The Science Wars and the Future of the American Academic Profession', *Daedalus*, 126 (1997), pp. 201–20; and Nick Jardine and Marina Frasca-Spada, 'Splendours and Miseries of the Science Wars', *Studies in the History and Philosophy of Science*, 28 (1997), pp. 219–35.
3. Throughout this paper, I will use the term 'science' as it is used in the science wars debate: to refer to the natural sciences. This debate concerns the cognitive authority of the natural sciences and largely sets aside serious treatment of issues regarding the cognitive authority of the social sciences.
4. Stanley Aronowitz, 'The Politics of the Science Wars', *Social Text*, 46–47 (1996), p. 192. This article appears in the now infamous *Science Wars* volume of *Social Text* in which Alan Sokal's hoax appeared.
5. Stanley Aronowitz, *Science as Power* (Minneapolis: University of Minnesota Press, 1988), p. ix.
6. Harry Collins and Trevor Pinch, *The Golem: What Everyone Should Know About Science* (Cambridge: Cambridge University Press, 1993), p. 142.
7. Collins and Pinch, *The Golem*, p. 145.
8. Paul R. Gross and Norman Levitt, *Higher Superstition* (Baltimore: Johns Hopkins University Press, 1994), p. 12.
9. Gross and Levitt, *Higher Superstition*, p. 11.
10. Gross and Levitt, *Higher Superstition*, p. 72.
11. Gross and Levitt, *Higher Superstition*, p. 86.
12. Gross and Levitt, *Higher Superstition*, p. 217.
13. See, for example, the definitions of authority in Roger Scruton (ed.), *A Dictionary of Political Thought*, 2nd edn (Philadelphia: Trans-Atlantic 1996); Iain McLean (ed.), *The Concise Oxford Dictionary of Politics* (Oxford: Oxford University Press, 1996); and Jack C. Plano and Milton Greenberg (eds), *The American Political Dictionary*, 10th edn (Orlando: Holt, Rinehart and Winston, 1996). For an excellent overview of the more philosophical and analytical debates over the linkages (or lack of linkages) among authority, legitimacy and obligation, see the anthology William A. Edmundson (ed.), *The Duty to Obey the Law* (Lanham: Rowman & Littlefield, 1999).
14. For analytical treatments of this distinction between in authority and an authority, see Richard E. Flathman, *The Practice of Political Authority* (Chicago: University of Chicago Press, 1980), pp. 16–20; April Carter, *Authority and Democracy* (London: Routledge, 1979), pp. 14–18; and E. D. Watt, *Authority* (New York: St. Martin's Press, 1982), pp. 45–54.
15. The first definition is provided in Paul Starr, *The Social Transformation of American Medicine* (New York: Basic Books, 1982), p. 13. The second definition is from Kathryn Pyne Addelson, 'The Man of Professional Wisdom', in Sandra Harding and Merill B. Hintikka (eds), *Discovering Reality* (Boston: Reidel, 1983), p. 167.
16. Barry Barnes and David Edge (eds), *Science in Context: Readings in the Sociology of Science* (Cambridge: MIT Press, 1982), p. 2.

17. See Sandra Harding, *The Science Question in Feminism* (Ithaca: Cornell University Press, 1986), pp. 38–52; Addelson, 'The Man of Professional Wisdom', pp. 165–82; Steven Yearley, *Science, Technology and Social Change* (Boston: Unwin Hyman, 1988), pp. 16–43; and Collins and Pinch, *The Golem*, pp. 142–5.

18. Chandra Mukerji, *A Fragile Power: Scientists and the State* (Princeton: Princeton University Press, 1989), pp. 190–203.

19. Sheila Jasanoff, *The Fifth Branch: Science Advisors as Policymakers* (Cambridge: Harvard University Press, 1990), p. 14. For a critique of scientific authority that focuses on such boundary strategies or 'boundary-work', see Thomas F. Gieryn, 'Boundaries of Science', in Sheila Jasanoff et al. (eds), *Handbook of Science and Technology Studies* (Thousand Oaks: Sage, 1995), pp. 393–443.

20. Mukerji, *A Fragile Power*, p. 194.

21. Deborah Stone, *Policy Paradox and Political Reason* (New York: Harper Collins, 1988), p. 25.

22. Stone, *Policy Paradox and Political Reason*, pp. 21–2.

23. Stone, *Policy Paradox and Political Reason*, pp. 148–65.

24. Starr, *The Social Transformation of American Medicine*, p. 6.

25. Starr labels these first three aspects of the legitimacy of cultural authority the cognitive, collegial and moral. See Starr, *The Social Transformation of American Medicine*, p. 15.

26. See Starr, *The Social Transformation of American Medicine*, p. 12.

27. Starr, *The Social Transformation of American Medicine*, p. 15

28. For an analysis of this social contract between the US government and science which addresses the issues of normative legitimacy, see David H. Guston and Kenneth Keniston (eds), *The Fragile Contract: University Science and the Federal Government* (Cambridge: MIT Press, 1994). Also see Robert N. Proctor, *Value Free Science? Purity and Power in Modern Knowledge* (Cambridge: Harvard University Press, 1991).

29. Thomas E. Wartenberg, *The Forms of Power: From Domination to Transformation* (Philadelphia: Temple University Press, 1990), p. 142.

30. Wartenberg, *The Forms of Power*, p. 154.

31. See, e.g., Charles Piller, *The Fail-Safe Society* (Berkeley: University of California Press, 1991); and Barry G. Rabe, *Beyond NIMBY* (Washington, D.C.: Brookings Institution, 1994).

32. Starr, *The Social Transformation of American Medicine*, pp. 9–10.

33. Hannah Arendt, 'What Is Authority?', in *Between Past and Future* (New York: Penguin Books, 1968), p. 93.

34. See Carter, *Authority and Democracy*, pp. 20–3; and Mark C. Murphy, 'Surrender of Judgment and the Consent Theory of Political Authority', in Edmunson, *The Duty To Obey the Law*, pp. 319–46.

35. Flathman, *The Practice of Political Authority*, pp. 90–108.

36. Flathman, *The Practice of Political Authority*, pp. 100–1.

37. Starr, *The Social Transformation of American Medicine*, p. 15.

38. Starr, *The Social Transformation of American Medicine*, p. 4.

39. Starr traces both the rise and the decline of medical authority in the US. He argues that medical authority is both paradigmatic and exceptional as a form of scientific or professional authority: 'paradigmatic in the sense that other professions emulate its example; exceptional in that none have been

able to achieve its singular degree of economic power and cultural authority'. Starr, *The Social Transformation of American Medicine*, pp. 28–9.

40. See Labinger, 'The Science Wars and the Future of the American Academic Profession', and Jardine and Frasca-Spada, 'Splendours and Miseries of the Science Wars'.

Part II
Political Morality and International Relations

8
On Public Moral Appeals and Identification*

Jean Bethke Elshtain

There are few safe predictions in politics. One is that during the next 'presidential cycle', as the pundits like to call it, we will be treated to the usual homilies and appeals to our patriotism, our fundamental decency, our self-respect, and our capacity to make changes for the better. Such appeals nowadays seem to inspire little but cynicism among the American electorate. That is a pity, but understandable in light of just how low politics seems to have fallen amongst us. Rather than decrying our political cynicism or the sad state of political debate yet another time, I propose to reflect on the question of the nature of appeals made to us in our capacities as citizens and our responses to such appeals.

Let us assume something like a reprise of the energy crisis of the late 1970s. At that time, we were reminded that we were a great, resourceful and resilient people. We were admonished to do our share in order to pull all of us through the crisis. Americans were required by law to drive their automobiles more slowly – laws that have only recently been repealed in a number of states – and to drive them less frequently, asked to lower their thermostats, to conserve electricity, and forced as well to put up with the burden of shortages, rising costs and the possibility of rationing. These sacrifices were presumably made palatable by frequently repeated assurances that we were all somehow 'in this thing together'.

If memory serves, Mr Nixon, followed by Messrs Ford and Carter, attempted to rally citizens and to promote a sense of national unity and purpose in ways reminiscent in their intent, if not their forceful-ness or grandeur, to previous entreaties by leaders in times of national crisis. One recalls Franklin Delano Roosevelt's 'fireside chats' during the darkest days of the Great Depression; Winston Churchill's rousing call to robust defiance which helped to give England her 'finest hour'; and John F. Kennedy's memorable plea in the foreboding moments of that imbroglio known as *Meredith v. Mississippi* ('Who among us would be content to have the color of his changed and stand in his place? Who among us would then be content with the counsels of patience and delay?'), a speech to the nation that remains a high point in the insistence by an American president that American citizens respond as both moral and political persons to the then civil rights crisis.

In each of the latter three instances, it seemed eminently proper for the leaders involved to utter such appeals and to make claims upon citizens. The political legitimacy of Roosevelt, Churchill or Kennedy was never seriously questioned – save by those extremists who would deny legitimacy to any political authority. It is within the purview of legitimate political authority to issue public appeals with a content and purpose which pertains to the welfare of the polity as a whole.[1] A citizen may have major qualms about, or disagreements with, the correctness, efficacy or intent of the appeal made but, in a representative system in which leaders are presumed to be accountable to the electorate that puts them into office, the right of the leader to make such an appeal is pretty much taken for granted. Whether one responds positively or negatively to the exhortation, then, must turn on something else: on one's assessment of the *substantive content* of the appeal.

With Nixon and Ford issues were somewhat clouded because appeals were made by leaders whose legitimacy was in doubt in important, not trivial, ways to many Americans; indeed, public disbelief in President Nixon's legitimacy, as his administration drowned in the brackish backwash of Watergate, paralysed his effectiveness and helped to force his resignation.[2] When Gerald Ford came into office he had to fight public apprehension as he had not been elected by the public to the office he held directly; thus, his 'right' to govern was less secure than that of a popularly elected leader. Nevertheless, the office was his by right of regular constitutional procedures, so no crisis of legitimacy was ever really mounted.

It is the argument of this paper that one's response as a citizen to a public moral appeal should revolve around a set of considerations separable from one's doubts or assurances concerning the leader's legitimacy. (Unless, of course, one confronts an extreme case and these issues are inseparable from one another: the seizure of power by a military leader in a *coup d'état* would present such a case.) A public moral appeal, I shall argue, may possess moral suasion irrespective of the leader who makes it. For example: *X* may be a (sick, incompetent, probably corrupt) leader whose legitimacy is in doubt but who nevertheless was elected to office and continues to hold the reins of power. Suppose

X urges the people in his country to either (*a*) share scarce resources with a neighbouring country in which many are starving, or (*b*) kill babies as there are simply too many of them. What do we make of *X*'s claims on us in case (*a*) or case (*b*)? To answer this question we must distinguish the nature of the claim from the legitimacy of the leader.[3] That requires that citizens give reasons of a certain kind as to why it is they agree to share with their neighbours but refuse to kill babies. These reasons need not refer to the leader at all. What is central is the content of the appeal itself – not whether *X* is sick, incompetent and probably corrupt.[4]

1.   What is a public moral appeal?

If public moral appeals may possess or carry some suasion of their own, one must consider carefully the nature and purposes which distinguish these appeals from other kinds of entreaties or exhortations. There are three criteria which, taken together, comprise a paradigmatic instance of a public moral appeal.

First, such an appeal must be made with reference to those values which 'are not private values, or compounds of private values, or in any way reducible to private values',[5] namely, *social* values. In a society such as our own in which the dominant values are considered 'private', compounded private values may 'seem' or appear to us to be social values. But a social value differs from a private value in this sense: its definition 'makes essential reference to reciprocal states of awareness among two or more persons'.[6] A social value turns on the possibility that there is a general good in which all have a stake. A social framework in question may be a small New England town or the nation-state itself insofar as both are entities which consist of individuals who are linked by reciprocal claims and states of awareness and who are recipients of appeals based on those claims and that awareness.[7] Kurt Baier puts this reciprocity as follows:

> Life in society involves a social framework which multiplies the points of contact between individuals and which can transform the effects of a man's behavior on his fellow men within a given social framework, behavior which may be harmful which is not, from its nature, the infliction of harm on another.[8]

Second, a public moral appeal must be addressed, in the first instance, to persons in their capacities as citizens, not as private persons with self-interests. Persons must be able to respond to the appeal *as* citizens: this involves a recognition of the claims made upon oneself by others as well as an awareness of the claim made upon them by oneself. The category 'citizen' can be distinguished from another political actor, the subject, by the difference between the requirements of active moral agency and the demands of ritualistic rule-following. The citizen is a rule-follower, but an active one. He or she is a participant rather than a simple follower-of-a-rule. The subject, on the other hand, is not required to – and probably could not and need not – give reasons for his or her actions. Outward signs of obedience to rules or commands suffice. For a subject, the decisive and overriding consideration in a political situation is the ruler's legitimacy, *not* the nature of the appeal. The subject may, in this way, consent to many good things but he or she wouldn't know why these were good necessarily and is not required to think about it.[9]

Third, a public moral appeal must distribute any responsibilities or burdens it entails *equitably*.[10] I noted above that public moral appeals must be made to citizens and that considerations as a citizen override issues of one's self-interest, particularly if that self-interest can be seen to conflict with actions required for the common good. The difficulty of this third requirement lies precisely in the fact that public appeals are made to citizens, beings abstracted from the full panoply of particular considerations and constraints of their own place in society. This raises serious problems. In an inegalitarian society, for example, even as the appeal is made to citizens, that appeal must distribute burdens in a way that systematically takes account of those distinctions of wealth, education, occupation, race, class and sex the formal category 'citizen' strips away. An equitable distribution of burdens in an inegalitarian society requires that the costs of responding to the appeal cannot be shared *identically*. I shall return to this point later. For the moment, it is important to remember that if this third criterion is ignored, if the problem of burdens is treated in a formal sense only and the appeal requires that all citizens make an identical sacrifice – mighty and humble alike – the appeal loses one of its powerful claims to be moral and just; indeed, justice will be violated repeatedly if real differences in the objective conditions of the lives of citizens are systematically overlooked.

A public moral appeal, then, is a claim on individuals in their capacities as citizens that invokes social values and that distributes burdens equitably. A public moral appeal cannot be understood or issued in a purely formal manner. In each instance, one must assess the nature and purpose of the appeal and make reference to those considerations which justify actions in accordance with, or in opposition to, that appeal.[11]

2. Citizens and reason-giving

In setting forth his or her reasons for responding in a certain way to an appeal by a political leader, the citizen must divorce his or her considerations, insofar as this is humanly possible, from his or her own self-interest *and* in large part, if not altogether, from the characteristics of the leader himself.[12] It is, for example, logically possible but politically and morally improbable that a leader who had forfeited all claims to legitimacy could issue appeals which met all the criteria for a public moral appeal until he was forced from office. In this unlikely event, the citizen, should he or she affirm the appeal and give substantive reasons for that affirmation, is not following-the-leader but is responding to the nature and intent of the appeal itself.[13]

This distinction between the appeal-giver and the nature of the appeal is critical. If the latter is stressed, it requires that the citizen proffer reasons for his or her actions; moreover, the more likely event than being confronted with appeals from a blatantly incompetent, corrupt or venal leader, is to be faced with appeals issued by more or less attractive, serious and apparently upstanding persons. If their attractiveness, their apparent upstandingness, and their unquestioned legitimacy *alone* serve as grounds for heeding their appeals, nothing precludes the clever demagogue from promoting images of himself as attractive and upstanding in order to gain favourable responses from citizens to measures which may undermine the common good.

The citizen as a responsible moral agent is one who recognizes that unless the appeal makes reference to social values, is addressed to him or her as a citizen, and distributes burdens and benefits equitably, insofar as this is possible, he or she is under no obligation to obey. He or she may, of course, decide to affirm the appeal nonetheless on grounds that involve an overriding moral consideration. What might such an overriding imperative be? A citizen may decide, for example, that although the appeal in question does not meet all of the criteria of a public moral appeal, nevertheless the probable consequences to the social whole should the appeal be ignored, should all citizens act in opposition to it, are so serious that this consideration overrides the flawed nature of the appeal itself.

Baier argues that if an individual believes that others will not refrain from a proscribed action, that individual has a reason not to refrain either 'as my own reason for refraining is my desire to avoid the evil consequences.'[14] For Baier, a citizen needs 'no justification or excuse' for his or her decision not to refrain from doing or performing an act under such circumstances. One's behaviour is wrong 'only if I have no reason to think that others will refuse to make the sacrifice.' Baier continues: 'If I have reason to think they will refuse to make it, then I have reason to think my own sacrifice will be in vain: hence I have reason against making it'.[15] Baier's argument disallows for the possibility that I posed initially, namely, that a citizen who has strong reasons for believing others may not make the sacrifices called for, who has determined that all of the dimensions of a public moral appeal are not present, may go ahead nonetheless on the grounds of an overriding moral principle, say, the survival of a community he or she regards as both a moral and political entity required to protect certain worthy ideals. Baier presumes, as his use of the term 'sacrifice' indicates, that the only alternatives are those values and motivations available to individuals conceived as self-interested persons who have a choice between responding self-interestedly or altruistically, but in either instance they are responding privatistically. The action of the citizen who follows the dictates of an overriding moral principle thus becomes an act of supererogation not considered to be among the normal, ordinary duties and responsibilities of life.

Speaking broadly, the moral rule-following citizen should – it is among the normal duties of a life lived among others – agree to those appeals which meet the defining criteria. If one or two of the criteria are present, the agent must, in giving reasons for his or her action, indicate which of the criteria is missing and thus prevents his or her affirmation of the appeal or, alternatively, articulate those considerations that override the missing criteria or criterion.

An everyday example may serve to illustrate the diverse responses available to the moral rule-following citizen in his or her responses to a public appeal. I return to the energy crisis of the 1970s. Clearly, there was little equity in a situation in which both the average American, Citizen X, and the president of a major oil company, Citizen Y, were both enjoined by the president of the United States to turn down their home heating thermostats as a response to the energy crisis. Because Citizens X and Y bore responsibilities of vastly divergent magnitude for the onset of the crisis and thus could respond in dramatically different ways, a genuine public moral appeal would have to assess which burdens should devolve fairly upon Citizen X and which upon Citizen Y. Citizen X bore an additional burden: given the inflation spurred by the rise in fuel costs, he was placed in the position of suffering an economic sanction as a direct outgrowth of the crisis even as the corporate mogul, Citizen Y, enjoyed a windfall profit from that same crisis. To treat the two identically is inherently unfair.

A full public moral appeal requires both abstracting out from certain particular, specific conditions and demands of everyday life to some purposes, but locating those conditions and constraints in the heart of the appeal for other purposes. Only in this way can those twin imperatives that emerge from one's abstract ties and obligations as a citizen, as well as from the concrete reality of one's social ties and worklife, be met. How, then, could our reason-giving, moral rule-following Citizen X respond to an appeal by the president that made reference to social values and called for responses from individuals in their capacities as citizens but failed, at the same time, to meet the third criterion that burdens be assessed equitably? There are at least two responses that can be defended on ethical grounds.

Citizen X might follow the appeal by arguing that his own assessment of what the 'common good' requires overrides the inequities of burden sharing. In this instance, Citizen X would make a decision in favour of responding because the morally relevant considerations that guided his actions were sufficient to override the rule of equitable distribution. Alternatively, Citizen X might refuse to follow the presidential entreaty on the grounds that the failure of the appeal to distribute burdens fairly absolved him of the responsibilities which would have been his had that criterion, in concert with the others, been met. He would defend his response on the grounds that there are, to him, no considerations which override the failure of equitable burden-sharing.

Citizen X could either refuse or agree to the appeal and act morally in each instance. This reaffirms one of my central points: that public moral appeals and the citizen's duty in response to such appeals cannot be captured in purely formal terms but must be assessed with reference to the substance and content of the appeals themselves, and to the context within which they are made. What becomes 'the moral thing to do' when one is confronted with a public moral appeal turns on a number of considerations that leave open the option of supererogation and thus contain a personal reference which must not be expunged and cannot be captured within a frame of formal universalizability. Formal prescriptions often fail if they are imposed upon the complex moral dilemmas that occur within a social context and make reference to social values. To insist that all moral reasoning can be incorporated within a formalist frame is to distort seriously through oversimplification and a too-radical abstraction from the social realities of human life, the diverse imperatives the citizen must take into account in making a determination on those substantive issues a public moral appeal raises.

3. What is meant by reciprocity among citizens?

I have argued that a public moral appeal involves a genuine social value, one that refers essentially to a reciprocal state of awareness among two or more persons. The concept of reciprocity becomes empty and platitudinous – a kind of hollow incantation – unless one locates that reciprocity in the lives of persons in a compelling and a dynamic way. In order for reciprocity to be tied to reason-giving and rule-following, the links between persons cannot be on the level of surface manifestations of the sort in evidence in *quid pro quo* situations. The dynamic that must underlie Wolff's claim of reciprocity – the more correct term for the links that tie social beings one to the other is *identification* – implicates us in powerful ties that are not reducible to instrumentalism, to interests held in common, but that involve something akin to love.

Identification is one of the powerful, dynamic concepts developed by Sigmund Freud as he moved beyond individual psychology to consider the relationships between persons and their societies. Freud knew that questions of group identity can only be answered within a *social theory*. How, then, do we get from persons to societies?[16] Without explicating the dauntingly complex, developmental intricacies of the concept, it must suffice for now to point out that identification affords that 'community of feeling' without which social life would quickly become brutal and impoverished.[17] Identification binds persons in ways that have the possibility of being long-lasting, resonant and authentically social. The identification of a society's members with one another is built upon or requires a diffused erotic tie, aim-inhibited Eros turned to the task of maintaining civilization in which, ideally, less and less repressive social forms can be realized. Identification, the psychic mechanism that allows for individuals within groups to think and to feel in shared ways and to recognize this sharing as constitutive of the self and society, is the source of the social tie.[18] Without such identification – or reciprocity – individuals within groups would have only thin, contingent and utilitarian connections one with the other. Without an understanding of the ties between persons that the concept of identification affords, assertions of 'reciprocal awareness' remain little but pious hopes and abstractions.

The mode of identification that allows for the intellect or reason to exercise 'a unifying influence on men' might one day, Freud hoped, serve as 'the strongest uniting bond'.[19] But this rule of reason is difficult to achieve. It requires major transformation in the social structure and arrangements that are built upon and require oppression, exploitation and a too high level of cultural hypocrisy, all of which forestall that moment. Freud condemned that hypocrisy in high places which sets up impossibly high standards of morality for citizens from whom is then extracted 'the utmost degree of obedience and sacrifice' only for them to be treated 'as children' in turn. Even as the state forbids wrongdoing to individuals, it monopolizes wrongdoing for itself and engages in 'deliberate lying and deception', particularly in times of crisis and war when 'every such misdeed, every such act of violence, as would disgrace the individual man' are carried out routinely by states.[20]

This erosion of the state's claim to moral credibility can have a devastating effect, or so Freud argued, upon individuals in their twin capacities as private persons and as public citizens. Any society raised upon hypocrisy and grounded in injustice can neither serve to create nor go on to expect that all or even a portion of its members will have internalized the necessary moral restraints that allow them to recognize social values and to accept the responsibilities of moral agency.[21] Instead, persons in repressive, unjust societies will likely remain linked, or bonded together, by a more primitive mode of identification, one tied more closely to repression, that is, dependent upon ties to some leader or higher authority who can praise and reward his 'children' as good or punish them as 'bad' or permit and legitimate their 'bad' behaviour for the good of the state. Those persons who have identified with others through the mediation of a higher authority before whom they are self-effacing and on whom they are dependent will respond to appeals from a leader for one reason: because he is the leader. They will engage in ritualistic rule-following behaviour of subjects, not the reason-giving rule-following of citizens. The 'need for a leader' implied in unreflective obedience to demands from 'higher' authorities is linked to that primitive mode of identification Freud chillingly depicts in his *Group Psychology and the Analysis of the Ego*.[22] Individuals constituted, in part, by such a tie will tend to be passive followers who feel no need to justify their actions with reference either to content or substance. We are all familiar with this mode. It is reflected in such admonitions as 'He's the only president we've got!', or 'I am (am not) doing X because the president says we should (should not) do (not do) X.'[23]

Children who haven't gone beyond a level of primitive identification often respond to commands and claims from higher authorities in this way. Indeed, there are certain stages of development during which a child can respond in no other way. Thus, it should not come as a surprise that during a crisis like the energy crisis of the 1970s, many parents were confronted with serious and avid children who insisted that lights be turned off, heat be turned down, and cars not driven because the president, the principal, or the home-room teacher requested it. For adults to offer such 'reasons' as both necessary and sufficient to explain and to justify their own behaviour would strike us as odd and unfortunate. Persons trapped at the level of developmentally primitive identification with higher authority have given implicitly but nonetheless powerfully (for such ties serve intrapsychic needs of great complexity and thus serve as wishes, motives and beliefs) that blanket 'promise to obey' Rousseau insisted was inconsistent with the concept of the citizen as a moral agent.[24]

A state that would encourage the development of genuinely moral and responsible citizens must promote those social conditions which allow for a variety of diverse, rich identifications among persons and thus enable persons to transcend more primitive command-obedience modes of identification. Then and only then will genuine reciprocity prevail and the rule of reason hold sway. That societies, including our own, seem either unwilling or unable to take such steps postpones, perhaps indefinitely, the day Freud looked to when reason would rule in the hearts of human beings. Until gross inequalities of power and privilege are eliminated, Freud's ideal remains unattainable but not, for that reason, either unworthy or wholly utopian. The claims of the intellect must be constantly reaffirmed in order that unthinking obedience to authority buttressed by primitive identifications not go unchallenged. There is, and can be, a better way.

Notes

*   A word, or two, of explanation. I discovered an early version of this previously unpublished piece when I was going through files from my 'University of Massachusetts years', years spent engaging Professor Oppenheim as well as my other distinguished colleague, William Connolly. I recall this essay as an attempt, in a sense, to respond to the approaches and concerns of each. It seemed fitting, in a tribute to Felix Oppenheim, to resurrect this essay and to polish it up for the purpose of this volume. It

holds many happy memories for me of years of engaging, respectful collegiality. The volume by Professor Oppenheim with which this piece was, and is, in closest dialogue is *Political Concepts: a Reconstruction*.

1. For counterpoint on the issue of self-interest and public interest, see Professor Oppenheim's discussion in *Political Concepts: a Reconstruction* (Chicago: University of Chicago Press, 1981), pp. 123–49.

2. Of course, in a terrible case of historical *redux*, President Clinton's legitimacy in the eyes of a sizeable minority – not yet a majority – of Americans is also being called into question as of this writing. What the upshot will be eventually turns on just how much substantiated evidence emerges of lying under oath, obstruction of justice, etc. Though there are many who would continue to insist on a major difference between Clinton and Nixon by claiming that Clinton's offences were of a private, Nixon's a public, nature, I cannot wade into that dispute here.

3. Certainly a decree urging all citizens to kill babies would serve as powerful evidence of a leader's descent into madness and criminality and all citizens of conscience would begin to take steps to remove him from office. That problem, however, can be kept separate for the purpose of evaluating the specific claims leader X makes upon citizens from the nature of the claims themselves.

4. Again, at first glance, this approach might seem potentially to undermine efforts to dethrone or impeach sick, incompetent or probably corrupt leaders. Not only is this not the case, I shall argue that a focus upon the substance of what one is asked to do or to refrain from doing in one's capacity as a citizen is a firmer foundation for political action, including civil disobedience, than doing or not-doing based upon the single criterion of the leader's legitimacy. Those who do or do not do what a leader requests of them simply because he is the leader will be more likely to respond in a morally indefensible way either by committing clearly immoral acts or by doing the right things but for wrong or insufficient reasons.

5. Robert Paul Wolff, *The Poverty of Liberalism* (Boston: Beacon Press, 1969), p. 170.

6. Wolff, *The Poverty of Liberalism*, p. 184.

7. The affective dimension of these reciprocal states will be a more powerful social bond within smaller social units. Bonds are necessarily more attenuated and abstract within the nation-state than in the local community. But the national tie is powerfully buttressed by the use of charged symbols (the flag, the pledge of allegiance, the presidency, etc.). For more on this see my *Women and War*, written after the original version of this essay but very much on point in the matter of nations and identification (New York: Basic Books, 1987, second edition: Chicago: University of Chicago Press, 1996).

8. Kurt Baier, 'The Moral Point of View', in G. Wallace and A. D. M. Walker, *The Definition of Morality* (London: Methuen and Co., 1970), pp. 188–210, at p. 206.

9. Clearly I am using 'subject' here in a historical sense, as a kind of pre-citizen category of political identity, as in monarchs and their subjects. I am not deploying the term in the contemporary sense of subject-identity and the like.

10. Baier, 'The Moral Point of View', p. 199. Baier argues that observation of moral rules should be for the good of everyone alike. The 'one obvious way in which a rule may be for the good of everyone alike' is if it furthers the 'common good'.
11. Alasdair MacIntyre, 'What Morality is Not', in Wallace and Walker, *The Definition of Morality* (pp. 26–39), *passim*.
12. Save in the most egregious instances when the legitimacy of an entire regime is seriously in doubt.
13. The Donatist schism in the fourth-century Church raised a similar problem – one revolving around the relationship between the sinfulness of a priest and the validity of an ordinance or sacrament. If a sacrament is celebrated by one who may not be a pure priest but a priest in a state of sin, is the validity and sacred character of the sacrament itself thereby destroyed? The Donatists answered 'yes'. They stressed the purity of Administrants and contended that a priest's uncleanness invalidated the sacrament for others. St Augustine, however, the Donatists' chief and most formidable opponent, contended that the rites of the Church had an 'objective and permanent validity' of their own independent of the qualities of those who administered them. Besides, we were all always sinners; no one could claim purity. See the discussion of the Donatist schism in Peter Brown, *Augustine of Hippo* (Berkeley: University of California Press, 1970), p. 222. See also my book, written many years after the original draft of this essay, *Augustine and the Limits of Politics* (Notre Dame: Notre Dame University Press, 1996). It is, of course, interesting to me to see the ways in which I was working the Augustine turf from the beginning of my thinking about all these matters.
14. Baier, 'The Moral Point of View', p. 208.
15. Baier, 'The Moral Point of View', p. 209. In other words, Baier sanctions free-riding, a point much clearer to me now than when I worked on this argument originally. He disallows any acts of moral or civic supererogation. Or at least discourages such.
16. This 'getting to … from' is made more difficult for Freud, of course, given his articulation of the processes of individuation against. Accepting the agonistic nature of individuation, one might begin with a more intrinsically social self, say a Christian anthropology of the Augustinian sort, but that is another argument.
17. Sigmund Freud, 'Why War?' in Philip Rieff (ed.), *Character and Culture* (New York: Collier Books, 1970), pp. 134–47, at p. 144. Freud speaks of 'identification' as an emotional tie that binds human communities and might serve to tie together a 'community of men who had subordinated their instinctual life to the dictatorship of reason' (p. 145), the closest Freud ever came to articulating a utopia.
18. Sigmund Freud, *Civilization and its Discontents* (New York: W. W. Norton, 1962), *passim*. See also the discussion in Richard Wollheim, *Sigmund Freud* (New York: Viking Press, 1971), esp. pp. 259–65. It would be fascinating to compare Freud and Augustine in such matters for Augustine, too, is insistent that interests alone do not a people make but only loving in common. Articulating the diverse anthropologies each brings to bear, one within a horizon framed by a complex uderstanding of the Triune God, the other within a horizon lowered to the point of immanence – something Freud

fretted about – but within which certain 'vertical' points of identification were necessary to forestall the 'psychological poverty of groups' would be fascinating but beyond this essay. This is a promissory note I have made to myself for many years. One day.

19. Sigmund Freud, *New Introductory Lectures on Psychoanalysis* (New York: W. W. Norton, 1965), p. 171. Cf. Sigmund Freud, *The Cuture of an Illusion* (Garden City, New York: Anchor Books, 1962), pp. 87–8. Arguably Freud's most reductionistic work (following Feuerbach on religion), the essay is nonetheless filled with wonderful *bon-mots*, such as: 'The voice of the intellect is a soft one, but it does not rest till it has gained a hearing. ... The primacy of the intellect lies, it is true, in a distant, distant future, but probably not in an *infinitely* distant one.'

20. Sigmund Freud, 'Reflections on War and Death', in Rieff (ed.), *Character and Culture*, pp. 107–33, at p. 112. See also my essay, 'Freud on War/Politics', in James Der Derian and Michael Shapiro, *International and Intertextual Relations* (Lexington: Lexington Books, 1989), pp. 4–68.

21. I am struck, revisiting this argument, with the paucity of 'mediating institutions' in Freud's argument, this despite the fact that the family is his intense focus. Surely, however, families and churches (though Freud reposed no hope there) can sustain persons at least in part against a corrupt regime.

22. Sigmund Freud, *Group Psychology and the Analysis of the Ego* (New York: Bantam Books, 1971), *passim*.

23. Cf. Erik H. Erikson, *Insight and Responsibility* (New York: W. W. Norton, 1964), p. 214. Erikson terms the state that allows for and requires blind obedience to authority a 'pre-rational mechanism' which is linked to that 'vague rage which accompanies a situation of adaptive impotence' (p. 214). In an inegalitarian society, certain classes or categories of persons are perpetually frustrated and damaged in both the private world of family and the public world of work. The structural binds of the society, therefore, shrink the possibility for all or perhaps most persons to move beyond primitive modes of identification to those ties founded on reason and human social purposes. As a note: I'm not at all sure about this argument at this point but this is certainly the implication of Erikson's claims.

24. Jean-Jacques Rousseau, *The Social Contract and the Discourses*, trans. G. D. H. Cole (New York: E. P. Dutton, 1950), p. 29. Cf. Jean-Jacques Rousseau, *The Government of Poland*, trans. Willmoore Kendall (Indianapolis: Bobbs-Merrill, 1972), p. 8. Rousseau notes that the legislators of 'ancient times' all 'sought ties that would bind the citizens to the fatherland and to one another. All three found what they were looking for in distinctive usages, in religious ceremonies that invariably were in essence exclusive and national, in games that brought citizens together frequently, in exercises that caused them to grow in vigour and strength and developed their pride and self-esteem; and in public spectacles that, by keeping them reminded of their forefathers' deeds and hardships and virtues and triumphs, stirred their hearts, set them on fire with the spirit of emulation, and tied them tightly to the fatherland'. Rousseau, of course, favours just such tight identification, one reason his view of the citizen winds up as chilling as it is inspiring.

9
'Anarchical Fallacies': Bentham's Attack on Human Rights*

Hugo Adam Bedau

1. Introduction

For those interested in human rights, the year 1998 deserves to be remembered for at least two convergent reasons. Two hundred and fifty years ago, in 1748, Jeremy Bentham was born in London, and in 1948 the Universal Declaration of Human Rights was adopted by the General Assembly of the United Nations in New York. Thus in 1998 we celebrated two major anniversaries: the birth of an important and influential English thinker – a philosopher, lawyer, reformer and public policy analyst – and the anniversary of the formulation of the most influential manifesto of international human rights.

The conjunction of these two events provides an occasion for reflection on some of Bentham's philosophical arguments regarding what in his day were called 'natural rights' but that we call 'human rights'.[1] This opportunity arises because Bentham wrote an essay titled 'Anarchical Fallacies', in which he attacked the most popular manifesto of such rights in his day, the Declaration of the Rights of Man and Citizen adopted by the French National Assembly in August 1789, six weeks after the storming of the Bastille, the opening salvo of what was to become the French Revolution.

Bentham's essay has a curious history. Apparently written around 1795, it remained unpublished until 1816, when it appeared in print – not in London, but in Geneva, Switzerland, and not in English but in French. It became available in English only in 1834, two years after Bentham's death, when his collected works were published in London.[2]

In light of Bentham's scathing criticisms of the French Declaration, one naturally wonders what he would have had to say today were he in a position to evaluate the United Nations Declaration. Would he say of it what he said of its French predecessor, that it consists of 'execrable trash', that its purpose is 'resistance to all laws' and 'insurrection', that its advocates 'sow the seeds of anarchy broad-cast', and, most memorably, that any doctrine of natural rights is 'simple nonsense: natural and imprescriptible rights, rhetorical nonsense, – nonsense upon stilts'?[3]

2. 'Anarchical fallacies' and the French 'Declaration'

Let us begin at the beginning.[4] Even before the storming of the Bastille in July 1789, the National Assembly had begun debate over the text of a political manifesto that would articulate in a page or two the rights of all persons – or at least of all French men and women. Several different lists of rights were formulated and then bruited about in the National Assembly; these versions were collected and assigned to a committee for review and preparation of a final draft for adoption; this was done late in August of that year. The product of those deliberations was known then and has been known since as the Declaration of the Rights of Man and Citizen.[5]

Bentham's argument in 'Anarchical Fallacies' can be divided into two parts, of very unequal importance and length. By far the greater part of his attention – all but a few scattered sentences, in fact – is devoted to destructive criticism of the French Declaration and by implication to a criticism of almost any possible doctrine of human rights; it is this critical portion of his essay that prompted him to adopt 'Anarchical Fallacies' as the title for the whole. To the philosophically more interesting and important task of offering the reader a constructive alternative theory of rights, built as one would expect upon his fundamental normative principle of utility, he gives much less space. Since I want to concentrate on evaluating this positive contribution, I shall consider his negative criticisms only in a fragmentary manner, in order to put them behind us, so we can turn our attention to his important alternative theory. That theory is of no small philosophical interest, because it is one of the earliest, indeed, perhaps *the* earliest, attempt to give a philosophical analysis (in today's jargon, a deconstruction) of what a natural right is (or would be, if there were any natural rights),[6] something for which one will look in vain in the writings of Bentham's great British predecessors in political philosophy, notably Bacon, Hobbes, Locke and Hume.

3. Fallacies and the French Declaration

So let us turn first to the idea that the French Declaration is riddled with what Bentham calls 'anarchical fallacies'. What, exactly, are 'anarchical fallacies' – what is fallacious and what is anarchistic about them?

In 1824, two decades after Bentham had written the essay under discussion, he arranged to have published (in London and in English) a volume titled *The Book of Fallacies*.[7] In this treatise, the first substantial contribution to the subject since Aristotle, Bentham set out an account of what he regarded as the rhetorical and logical errors to which political discourse was especially vulnerable. One would naturally expect, therefore, to find elucidated in this book the 'anarchical fallacies' he had already discussed many years earlier in his unpublished essay of that name.

But there are at least three problems. The first arises with Bentham's definition of a fallacy. 'By the name of fallacy', he writes, 'it is common to designate any argument employed or topic suggested for the purpose, or with the probability of producing the effect of deception. Or of causing some erroneous opinion to be entertained by any person to whose mind such argument may have been presented'.[8] If fallacies so defined are supposed to lurk in the Declaration, a problem immediately arises: according to Bentham's definition of fallacy, fallacies are the property of a certain class of *arguments*, namely, the invalid ones. But the Declaration is not an 'argument'; it is a manifesto of aspirations, full of imperatives and exhortations addressed to the people of France. So it is not as such an argument, except in the most extended sense of that term, in which *any* propositions asserted on *any* subject constitute an 'argument'.

One might say, to be sure, that the Declaration is the product of an *implicit* argument, in the proper narrow sense of that term, because it rests upon several tacit principles and beliefs from which its manifest content – those imperatives and exhortations – can be derived. But if it is this implicit argument Bentham wishes to attack, it is odd that he doesn't say so and that nowhere in his critique does he attempt to formulate this implicit argument. So I think we may conclude that if the French Declaration is spoiled by 'fallacy', it is not because its *reasoning* is suspect, for a manifesto such as this does not consist of a chain of reasons.

However, even if we charitably agree that there is a loose and familiar sense of the term 'fallacy', in which it is roughly synonymous with 'erroneous belief' or 'mistaken claim' or 'objectionable principle', very little reflection is required to conclude that under Bentham's official definition of 'fallacy', the French Declaration is surely *not* riddled with fallacies of any kind. The loose sense of the term, as Bentham defines it – as a 'topic suggested ... for deception' – does not apply. For it is neither reasonable nor supported by any evidence Bentham cites to believe that the French authors of the Declaration wrote with the 'purpose' of deceiving their intended audience. Bentham's official definition of 'fallacy' simply has to be judged incorrect, because it transforms 'fallacy' into a complex intentional concept; in ordinary usage 'fallacy' is not an intentional concept at all. That is to say, a reasoner can commit a fallacy by means of an invalid argument without the intention to deceive anyone. If, as Bentham insists, the French Declaration suffers from fallacies, we should expect its authors and audience alike to be equally surprised to learn this. To suggest otherwise is to impugn the sincerity of the authors of the Declaration; neither Bentham nor history gives us reason to do that.

As a third and final preliminary point in this context, we should note that one will look in vain in Bentham's *Book of Fallacies* for any account of what he calls the 'anarchical fallacies' in the essay of that name. This appears to be a major oversight and a bewildering omission on his part. Having diagnosed the supposed fallacies in the Declaration years before he wrote his *Book of Fallacies*, why should he fail to mention them in his later and longer work?[9] To be sure, one can find reference in that book to 'anarchy'; Bentham points out that the term 'anarchy' is characteristically used as an abusive epithet in political discourse. This, he says, was especially true of those who oppose any political reforms; their tactic is to condemn as anarchic all new legislation, reforms and ventures. Ironically, Bentham himself is vulnerable to the charge that his denunciation of 'anarchical fallacies' in the Declaration comes rather too close for comfort to being just another example of precisely the rhetorical abuse that he later criticized.

4.   Anarchy and the French Declaration

Against that background, let us turn directly to why Bentham thinks the French Declaration, as he says, 'sows the seeds of anarchy broadcast', why he thinks it is a doctrine of 'the rights of anarchy – the order of chaos'. The Declaration does this, he says, because its tacit message is this: 'People, behold your rights! If a single article of them be violated, insurrection is not your right only, but the most sacred of your duties'.[10]

This is a startling remark; no such radically anarchic language actually appears in the preamble or in any of the seventeen articles of the Declaration. The closest we come is in the second article, where all persons are told they have a 'natural and imprescriptible ... right of resistance to oppression' (*la résistance à l'oppression*),[11] something not found either in the American Bill of Rights of 1791 or in the 1948 United Nations Declaration. This leads Bentham to heap scorn on the very idea of an 'imprescriptible' right – a right that no political or legal authority may or can suspend, modify or nullify – but for present purposes we need not follow Bentham further on the point.[12]

Instead, we need to notice that the Declaration is completely silent on what recourse the French citizens have if in their judgement any of their 'natural and imprescriptible rights' are violated. The measures of resistance it is appropriate for individual citizens (or group of citizens) to take to secure rights disrespected by their government is a question of judgement in the circumstances, not a matter for large-scale constitutional pronouncements. So the silence of the Declaration on this point about legitimate tactics of resistance is neither evasive nor disingenuous; rather, it is evidence of sound political caution. Bentham, putting the worst face on the document, gratuitously assumes that insurrection is the implied (and only) weapon available to persons who judge they are deprived of their natural rights.

Bentham could, of course, point in particular to the Terror, in general to the instability of French society in the aftermath of 1789, and to the evident inability of the French revolutionaries of that day to govern effectively.[13] He could make an argument in defence of his interpretation along the following lines: First, the Declaration does not expressly prohibit violent insurrection as the appropriate response to a government that violates its citizens' rights; second, few if any of the rights proclaimed in the Declaration were operative under law in French society at the time it was promulgated. Therefore, he might conclude, the adoption and publication of the Declaration is a tacit invitation to insurrection, violence and anarchy; it would hardly be surprising if believers in the 'natural and imprescriptible' rights of man and citizen used direct and violent measures in an effort to secure those rights, and were willing to overthrow any government that fails to accord such rights to its citizens.

Thus Bentham might have reasoned. But such an argument cannot be sustained without evidence to back it up, and in the entirety of his critique Bentham never produces any such evidence. He never argues that reformers and critics of the current regime in France, drunk on the intoxicating liquor of 'natural rights', are bound to lose all judgement and – casting prudence aside – will strike at every form of governing authority in their foolish zeal to obtain their rights. He never explains why insistence on 'natural rights', as they are affirmed in the Declaration, is the sole or the dominant cause of political unrest in France.

Not only that, the Declaration's professed right to resist oppression need not be taken (as Bentham no doubt took it to be) as a right of *violent* individual and collective resistance to government officials. We can, after all, think of collective *non-violent* protest, of the sort made famous in the 1960s in the United States during the Civil Rights movement. If that is how citizens intend to act in exercising their alleged 'natural right' to resist oppression, it is not obvious why they should be told they have no such right. Bentham overlooked the possibility of organized non-violent resistance to government oppression. It probably never occurred to him to ponder, as many thoughtful philosophers have argued in this century, whether mass non-violent civil disobedience is a legitimate form of protest in (or in the effort to obtain) a moderately just, liberal constitutional republic.[14] To be sure, Bentham was not an advocate, here or elsewhere, of civil disobedience. He lived in a day in which fear of 'the mob' was a constant preoccupation of the English upper class, a worry made all the more troubling by the excesses of the French Revolution. Nevertheless, is it merely sentimental and anachronistic to suggest that the worst that can be said of the French Declaration on the point under discussion is that its use of the term 'resistance' is subject to several interpretations?

A related but even stronger objection to Bentham's views emerges here. Let us put the French Declaration aside for the moment and think of its American and United Nations counterparts. I challenge anyone to point to any anarchic consequences in political behaviour directly caused by widespread belief among Americans two centuries ago in their Bill of Rights, or among any who believe in the human rights cited in the United Nations Declaration during the half-century since its promulgation. Whatever political actions have been engendered by belief in these rights, there is little or no evidence that their chief effect has been to nourish seeds of insurrection and anarchy where prior to such declarations no such inclinations existed. On the contrary, the violence associated with belief in human rights almost invariably comes from the police and government officials who use their power (as the British did in Amritsar in the 1920s, as the local police across the United States did in anti-union riots of the 1930s, and as the Chinese did in Tiananmen Square in the 1980s) to crush those who non-violently protested violations of their human rights.

Perhaps the aftermath of the storming of the Bastille in the streets of Paris in the summer of 1789 was different; perhaps shrieks and cries of 'natural and imprescriptible rights' did play a prominent causal role in ending Bourbon rule and paving the way for the abuses that culminated in the Terror and then in Napoleon's reign. But if that is what Bentham believed, and what prompted him to denounce the French Declaration within a few years of its promulgation, it is most unfortunate that he so conspicuously failed to say so.[15]

I can only conclude that Bentham has not made out his case for the claim that the French Declaration – or any of the other largely aspirational manifestos of that day and later that were drafted along the same lines – is invalid because of its 'anarchical fallacies'.

5.   The three theses of Bentham's alternative theory

Let us now turn to the positive side of Bentham's essay, his alternative conception of rights.[16] It involves several independent theses, three of which I single out here for special attention. I take them up not in the order in which Bentham stated them but in the order of their increasing interest and importance. The first of these three theses is presented in the following passage: 'In proportion to the want of happiness resulting from the want of rights, a reason exists for wishing that there were such things as rights'.[17] I shall call this Bentham's *eudaemonist* thesis, because of the role it assigns to the pursuit of happiness. We can clarify this thesis if we restate it in the manner Bentham elsewhere calls 'paraphrasis'.[18] Whatever is valid in paraphrasis is to be found in what analytic philosophers a generation ago called 'contextual definition'. Restated in that manner, this is how Bentham's first thesis would look:

> If person A lacks happiness because A lacks a right, R, to do *x*, then the lack of R gives A a good reason for wanting enactment of a law establishing R.

Notice that we can take the term 'happiness' here to refer either to individual or collective happiness. That is, if I suffer from a lack of happiness arising from my lack of a certain right, then according to this thesis that lack gives me personally a reason for wanting the right in question. Similarly, where the members of some group or collective suffer unhappiness from the lack of a certain right, that lack gives the group or collective a reason for wanting the right in question.

Bentham's second thesis is found in the passage in which he claims that there are no such things as rights anterior to the establishment of government:

no such things as natural rights opposed to, in contradistinction to, legal; that the expression is merely figurative; that when used, in the moment you attempt to give it a literal meaning it leads to error ...[19]

In this passage we meet Bentham the legal positivist: he holds that the only rights anyone has or could have are rights conferred by means of positive law enacted, decreed and enforced by some legitimate government. All rights are legal rights, and – he might have added – the rights the law provides today the law can repeal tomorrow. Let us call this his *legalist* thesis. Reformulating it in the paraphrastic fashion he recommends, this is how his second thesis would look:

Person A has a right, R, in society S to do some act *x* if and only if there is a law L in S that permits A to do *x* by conferring on A the right to so act.

We should notice several different things about this thesis. First, Bentham uses the desire to legalize rights as a stick with which to beat advocates of natural rights, since he is convinced that it would be impossible for any government to turn claims of natural rights like those found in the French Declaration into actual legal rights. This criticism, of course, depends essentially on exactly what rights are proclaimed in whatever list of natural rights is in question. Advocates of the American Bill of Rights two centuries ago could claim without running afoul of this criticism that the right of free speech, worship and the rest were natural rights and ought to be protected by law as well, and that none of Bentham's vigorous criticisms of the French Declaration had any application to the American counterpart. Advocates of the United Nations 1948 list of human rights, however, have encountered difficulties in bringing into law all of the rights of that manifesto, especially all the so-called 'welfare' rights. In this regard the French Declaration of 1789 may be more like the United Nations Declaration than it is like the American Bill of Rights.[20]

Second, Bentham might seem to contradict himself when, a few paragraphs later, he says that 'Nature gave every man a right to everything before the existence of laws',[21] a remark reminiscent of Hobbes's claim that in a state of nature each of us has an inalienable natural right (i.e. a privilege) of self-preservation.[22] But Bentham rejects this notion of a right, on two grounds. First, he essentially agrees with Hobbes, that belief in such a right leads to 'the war of all against all'; it is the very paradigm of an 'anarchical' right. This anarchy of the natural right of self-preservation inspires Bentham to utter one of his famous epigrams: '[I]n regard to most rights, it is true that what is every man's right is no man's right'.[23] Second, he objects that this right cannot be a true right because it violates the fundamental principle of true rights, namely, that there is 'No right without a correspondent obligation'.[24] Today, it is commonplace for rights theorists to insist on the correlativity of rights and obligations when discussing so-called 'claim rights'.[25] Bentham believed (as did Hobbes) that the right of self-preservation in a state of nature imports no constraint on anyone's conduct. But if that is so, it cannot be a genuine right at all; at best it is what today we would call a 'liberty' right (as Hobbes did) or (better still) a 'privilege' – that is, person A's privilege-right to do something, *x*, is identical with the lack of any claim by others that A *not* do *x*.[26] As for the silence of the French Declaration on any duties reciprocal to the rights therein asserted, manifestos of natural or human rights have typically been notoriously silent on such responsibilities; witness the American Bill of Rights. In this respect the French Declaration is neither better nor worse than other such manifestos.

Third, it is difficult to be clear about what Bentham means in this passage when he contrasts the 'literal meaning' of talk about natural rights with the 'figurative' meaning of the term. Had he said here (as he does elsewhere)[27] that natural rights are 'fictions', we could more readily understand his objection; his belief that a vast variety of substantive legal and philosophical terms denote 'fictions' is one of his most famous philosophical doctrines. This to one side, it is clear, I think, that when Bentham makes the distinction between the 'literal' and the 'figurative' in this context, his point is that we ought to strive for an understanding of our talk about 'natural rights' in a manner that will not 'lead to mischief – the extremity of mischief', as he thinks a literal interpretation of the doctrine of natural rights does.

This brings us to Bentham's third and most fundamental proposition about the nature of rights:

> What is the language of reason and plain sense upon this same subject? That in proportion as it is *right* or *proper*, i.e., advantageous to the society in question, that this or that right – a right to this or that effect – should be established and maintained, in that same proportion it is *wrong* that it should be abrogated; but ... there is no *right*, which ought not to be maintained so long as it is upon the whole advantageous to the society that it should be maintained, so

there is no right which, when abolition of it is advantageous to society, should not be abolished.[28]

In this passage we meet Bentham the utilitarian, and accordingly I shall henceforth call this his *utilitarian* thesis: our rights are determined by the lawmaker's judgement as to whether it is more or less advantageous to society as a whole that an individual, or class of individuals, or all persons, ought to have a legal right to (or to do) the thing in question. Precise contextual formulation of this thesis requires care. Consider this formulation:

Persons A, B, C, ... Z in society S have a natural right, R, to do x if and only if A, B, C, ... Z
(a) lack any legal right in S to do x, and
(b) wish they had a legal right to do x; and
(c) their government ought to enact a law, L, establishing R, because
(d) doing so would be more advantageous to A, B, C, ... Z than not enacting such a law.

The problem with this four-part formulation is that if its four conditions are satisfied – and there is no reason to think they never could or would be satisfied – then there are natural rights. To put it another way, if we ask 'Under what conditions, if any, are there natural rights?' the answer is 'Under these four conditions'. But this is unacceptable, because – as we have seen – Bentham insists there are no natural rights. And thus his answer to the question, 'Under what conditions, if any, are there natural rights?' must be 'There are no such conditions'. Accordingly, we need to delete any language that appears to refer to natural rights; this can be done only if we cease *using* the term 'natural right' and confine ourselves to the *mention* of that term. This amounts to forswearing what Rudolph Carnap taught us to call the 'material mode' in favour of what he called the 'formal mode'.[29] The way to do this is to reformulate the utilitarian thesis, as follows:

When person A in society S appears to be referring to a 'natural right to (or to do) something, x', what is meant is that
(a) in S not everyone (and perhaps no one) has any legal right to do x, and
(b) A wishes everyone in S did have such a legal right, and
(c) there ought to be a legal right, R_L, in S to do x,

(d)   because it would be more advantageous to the members of S if they had such a legal right than if they did not.

On this interpretation, we do not try to explain what a natural right is, for our ontology includes none. Instead, we explain what people who erroneously say or think there are such rights really mean, whether they are aware of it or not. Or, to put it another way, we have here the four conditions that make it true – not 'literally' but 'figuratively' – to say that there are natural rights.

Superficially, there is some tension (or worse) between part of this thesis if taken in conjunction with Bentham's second, his legalist, thesis. According to that thesis, whatever laws are operative in a society confer legal rights and legal duties on the members of that society. As a matter of fact, however, any actual law may fail the utilitarian test because the law creates a right that is not conducive to the net general welfare. By the utilitarian criterion, it seems such a law and the rights derivative from it cannot be genuine.

We can save Bentham from this apparent contradiction, in which his utilitarianism undermines his legalism, if we avail ourselves of the distinction he makes elsewhere between what he calls 'expository' and 'censorial' jurisprudence.[30] Expository jurisprudence consists of reflections designed to state what the law *is*; censorial jurisprudence consists of reflections designed to state what the law *ought* to be. I suggest we view his legalism as a criterion within expository jurisprudence, telling us what the law is; his utilitarianism, however, is a criterion within censorial jurisprudence, telling us what the law ought to be. If we construe him in this manner, there is no contradiction when he allows, as he surely does throughout his writings, that some laws fail the utilitarian test – provided he goes on to imply that all such laws and the rights they give rise to, ought to be repealed in favour of laws that do satisfy the utilitarian criterion.

6.   Bentham's eudaemonism

The philosophical question now before us is whether these three theses – the eudaemonist, the legalist and the utilitarian – are correct.

Take Bentham's *eudaemonist* thesis first. At face value this thesis seems odd, indeed arbitrary, and even downright wrong. It suggests that *only* a lack of happiness arising from the lack of a certain right gives anyone a reason for wanting that right. And it suggests that the *only* gain for someone from having a legal right is an increase in their net happiness. But why should happiness have this preferred status? Natural rights thinkers such as Immanuel Kant, Bentham's older contemporary, insisted that our rights express and protect our nature as free, autonomous and dignified creatures.[31] Happiness as such plays no role whatever in seeking or enjoying any rights. So why should not the lack of liberty, privacy, autonomy or dignity be a sufficient reason for wanting the relevant rights? Why should a perceived lack of happiness be the *only* good reason for wanting a given right?

Bentham's answer has to be that liberty and the other values I have just mentioned are relevant only to the extent they are the means to, or are hidden constituents in, someone's happiness. Happiness alone is fundamental; as we learn elsewhere in his book *Of Ontology* (written some years after 'Anarchical Fallacies'), happiness for Bentham is the 'real entity' without which there is no meaning in our talk about rights (because they, along with many other moral notions, denote only 'fictitious entities').[32] Happiness and unhappiness are real entities for Bentham because they are experienced directly. (This claim is perhaps more plausible if formulated – as Bentham often does – in terms of pleasure and pain; these are often if not always genuine sensations whereas happiness rarely if ever is a sensation or complex of sensations.) Unless, according to Bentham, we can trace our talk back to some 'real entity' like happiness or unhappiness, we are talking vapid nonsense. Legal rights, Bentham thinks, always can (or ought to) be traceable back to such 'real entities', but so-called natural rights he thinks cannot.

But why should we agree with Bentham that happiness has this paramount status, confining such values as liberty, privacy, autonomy and dignity to a merely intermediate role? Unless one suffers from an excess of enthusiasm for sensationism and reductionism, neither happiness nor pleasure (nor their lack) seems the right sort of thing to cite as the rationale for human rights.

7.   Bentham's legalism

Let us turn now to Bentham's *legalist* thesis. If it is true, then throughout history most people have lacked the rights asserted in the French Declaration of 1789 and the rights asserted in the United Nations Declaration of 1948, because few governments have ever enacted and enforced the laws necessary to turn such alleged rights into legal rights. Bentham is surely correct when he writes: '[as soon as] a list of these pretended natural rights is given, [they] are so expressed as to present to view legal rights'.[33] Of course advocates of natural rights want to see such rights recognized and protected under positive law. But this belief does not imply that no one has the rights in question unless there are laws that provide for them. History assures us, there is no doubt, that most people have lacked the *legal* right to most of the provisions of such manifestos. But Bentham's legalist thesis about rights cannot be sustained by nothing more than the historical fact that clamour for rights (often typically?) occurs where the law fails to identify and protect rights.

First, Bentham's thesis seems highly counter-intuitive and contrary to much that we believe. Surely, I do not need to invoke the law or a legal system to claim a right of self-defence. Surely, it is not the law that gives me the power to promise you $1000 for some landscape gardening around my house, thereby giving you a claim against me for that amount, provided you accept the offer and do the work. And so on. Where is the court or legislature that created such rights? What court or legislature could presume to abolish them? To be sure, these examples of moral rights independent of any legal system do not include any of the rights mentioned in the Declaration. But Bentham's legalist thesis is not confined to those rights; it is a thesis about rights generally and so is vulnerable to counter-examples of the sort I have offered.

Second, Bentham's legalist thesis about rights is as silly or strange, as you wish, as would be a counterpart thesis about other moral concepts. Surely, it is silly or strange to insist that outside the law we have no duties or obligations, outside the law there is no right or wrong, no virtue or vice, outside the law there is no good, better, or best in human conduct. It is simply false – and extravagantly false – to think that there is any good reason for supposing that although we do legitimately refer to *moral* good and evil, moral right and wrong, moral duty and obligation, as soon as we refer to *moral rights* – that is, moral privileges, powers, immunities and claims – either we talk nonsense or we are really referring to our *legal* rights or to what we have good utilitarian reason for wishing were our legal rights. There is not the slightest good reason for supposing that what is true about moral concepts and principles generally is suddenly false where rights are concerned. Moral theory and discourse need, and may use, as they do use, the notion of a moral right, just as much as the law needs and may use the notion of a legal right.

As a final and more constructive point, I think we can say (following James Nickel[34]) that there are human rights norms, and that therefore human rights exist, to the extent that and in the sense that justified moralities contain such norms regardless of what legal norms a given legal system may provide. Better still (following Judith Jarvis Thomson[35]), we can say that there are moral rights apart from the law and any legal system because we are creatures subject to the moral law and because we have inherently individual interests. The claim-rights each of us has against others are created by these two facts about us; the law may or may not also identify and protect such rights. To the extent it fails to do so, to that extent it is morally deficient. Thus, as we know, we can and do use the fact of our moral rights to criticize a legal system for its failure to turn those rights into legal rights.

The only way, in the end, to attack the claim that there are extra- or pre-legal human rights is to argue either that there are no justified moralities, or that such moralities include no human rights norms, or that there is no moral law to which we are subject, or that we have no inherently individual interests. Such an array of denials seems unlikely to prevail except among radical moral sceptics.

8. Bentham's utilitarianism

Let us turn finally to Bentham's *utilitarian* thesis, the most important of the three. First, we should notice that his definition destroys any conception of rights as a fundamental domain or dimension within the whole of morality. Bentham explicitly embraces the adjective 'right' and equally explicitly denounces the substantive 'right'[36] (apart, of course, from legal rights). It is the latter, he says, that 'sets up the banner of insurrection, anarchy, and lawless violence'.[37] He withdraws denunciation of the substantive 'right', as we have seen, provided we confine our talk to legal rights. But trouble begins when he makes it perfectly clear that our legal rights ought to be determined by 'what is *right* or *proper*'. This move repudiates the status and authority of rights, by implying that rights are entirely translatable into assertions about what is right. If Bentham is correct, we do not need a conception of rights, because everything we might want to assert using that vocabulary is replaceable without loss in the vocabulary of what is right – which in turn is replaceable by reference to what is advantageous to society.

Contrary to Bentham, I think we have in our rights a relatively autonomous domain within the larger and more inclusive empire of morality in general. Precisely what connection there is between any given assertion about our rights and some other assertion about what we ought to do needs to be spelled out with care. It cannot be disposed of in the sweeping manner, abstracting from all detail and cases, that Bentham proposes.

Many utilitarians besides Bentham, notably John Stuart Mill[38] and several contemporary philosophers (including Richard Brandt and Wayne Sumner[39]), believe that they can give a moral foundation for rights (and not just for legal rights) by appeal to the principle of utility. But other philosophers (I among them) find it difficult to believe that the rights we have can be grounded on, much less be seen as taking their origin in, utilitarian considerations. This is especially evident where natural or human rights are concerned. Even if it is true, in general, that net social welfare is advanced by recognizing human rights under law, there will be other occasions when the reverse is true – ignoring, denying or otherwise rejecting a claim of someone's human rights will be defended on the ground that net social welfare ought to prevail without exception whenever it clashes with someone's rights. As I suggested earlier, our natural or human rights must be seen as moral conceptions designed to advance our liberty, privacy, autonomy, and in general our dignity – precisely as Kant claimed within a few years of when Bentham wrote his essay under discussion. It seems to me much more plausible to try to derive these rights from a recognition of our common nature as rational, autonomous moral agents for whom liberty, privacy and other goods are paramount, rather than from any collective or aggregative facts about net social welfare or the general happiness.

Note that my objection to Bentham here is not that his theory cannot establish any *absolute* rights. I take it as settled that no theory of human rights can coherently defend a doctrine of absolute rights.[40] I believe we cannot point to a single right, such that once we have identified that right then we *know* what some agent ought to do – as though this right can always be counted on to dominate whatever countervailing moral considerations might arise in a given case. But from the fact (if it is a fact) that none of our rights is absolute, it does not follow that someone's right can always be overridden by appeal to net aggregate social welfare.

Moreover, our conception of ourselves as bearers of moral rights does not owe its origin to applications of the principle of utility. Far from being the product of a calculus of pleasure and pain, as our legal rights are on Bentham's theory, the very nature of human rights is to be the enemy of such calculations. Indeed, it is precisely because of the assault those calculations often require against individuals that we rely on human rights to obviate them.

As for universal political rights such as most of those cited in the French Declaration and the United Nations Declaration, they are designed to protect minorities against neglectful or tyrannical majorities. But if, as under Bentham's theory, rights ought to be created by law if and only if it is to the advantage of some majority to do so, then it appears that rights cannot play the anti-majoritarian function so crucial to them. John Stuart Mill was at least more candid on the point. Near the end of the final chapter of his 1863 essay, *Utilitarianism*, he remarked that 'All persons are deemed to have a *right* to equality of treatment [here he might have mentioned any other condition to which we have a moral right], except when some recognized social expediency requires the reverse'.[41]

9. Conclusion

Bentham's theory brings a healthy no-nonsense approach to discussions about human rights. He says in effect: Do not deceive yourself about your rights; if they are not identified in law and protected by government, you might as well conclude that you have no such rights at all. Surely, whatever rights we claim, personal or universal, we want to have them protected by law, since the alternative is to have them at risk of violation with impunity.

However, Bentham's account of what it means to have a right and his account of the origin or source of our rights is defective. Rights are importantly (although not uniquely) anti-aggregative moral principles or anti-majoritarian moral standards; they must be able (to borrow Ronald Dworkin's now-familiar metaphor[42]) to trump aggregative aces on many occasions. Thus, their role is to limit the reach of considerations by requiring collectives and majorities to acknowledge our inherently individual interests (to borrow again from Judith Thomson). Norms derived from prior judgements about what conduces to the general welfare, as rights do on Bentham's theory, cannot then be turned around to protect conduct by a dissenting minority.

Like every theorist, Bentham implies that if one does not like the consequences of his critique of the French Declaration and his own positive alternative, the problem does not lie with belief in his theory. I have tried to suggest otherwise by examining some salient features both of his attack on the 1789 French Declaration of the Rights of Man and Citizen and of his attempt at a constructive alternative – a eudaemonist, legalist, utilitarian theory of rights. I would like to think that Bentham, were he here today, would on reflection be inclined to agree with me that we do have intelligible conceptions of moral, human, or natural rights, and that elucidating those conceptions is not most effectively done by relying on eudaemonistic, legalist, and utilitarian considerations.

Notes

* Earlier versions of this paper were presented during 1998 at the Bentham 250 conference, University of Texas, the ISSA Conference, University of Amsterdam, the University of Reykjavik, and American University. I am grateful for comments and criticisms from these audiences, and especially to Constance Putnam for her editorial counsel.

1. In the ensuing discussion, I make no distinction between the concepts of *natural* rights and *human* rights. For a discussion of the differences, see James Nickel, *Making Sense of Human Rights: Philosophical Reflections on the Universal Declaration of Human Rights* (Berkeley, CA: University of California Press, 1987), pp. 6–12.

2. 'Anarchical Fallacies; An Examination of the Declaration of Rights Issued During the French Revolution, by Jeremy Bentham', in John Bowring (ed.), *The Works of Jeremy Bentham* (London: Simpkin, Marshall & Co., 1843), vol. 2, pp. 489–534. All subsequent references to Bowring are to this work and are given to the page and column of the text. A truly scholarly text of this essay, based on the surviving manuscripts in the archives of University College London, is now being prepared at UCL's Bentham Project.

3. Bowring 501:1.

4. For recent discussions of the origin and circumstances of the drafting of the Declaration, see Lynn Hunt (ed.), *The French Revolution and Human Rights: a Brief Documentary History* (Boston, Mass.: Bedford Books, 1996); Sherman Kent, 'The Declaration of the Rights of Man and Citizen', in R. M. MacIver (ed.), *Great Expressions of Human Rights* (New York: Kennikat Press, 1950, 1969), pp. 145–81.

5. Bentham says he takes for his text 'the paper published ... by the French National Assembly of 1791'. Bowring 496:1. This 'paper' of 1791 is identical with the Declaration of 1789; where the 1789 text stood as a complete document in its own right, the 1791 version is simply the 1789 text placed as a preamble to the French Constitution of 1791. The English translation of the Declaration Bentham quotes would appear to be his own.

6. For discussion of Bentham's essay, see Jeremy Waldron, *'Nonsense Upon Stilts': Bentham, Burke, and Marx on the Rights of Man* (London: Methuen, 1987), pp. 29–45; Ross Harrison, *Bentham* (London: Routledge, 1983), pp. 77–105; William Twining, 'The Contemporary Significance of Bentham's Anarchical Fallacies', *Arkiv für Rechts- und Socialphilosophie*, 61 (1975), pp. 325–55, reprinted in Bhikhu Parekh (ed.), *Jeremy Bentham: Critical Assessments* (London: Routledge, 1993), vol. 3, pp. 700–26; and H. L. A. Hart, 'Natural Rights: Bentham and John Stuart Mill', reprinted in Hart, *Essays on Bentham* (Oxford: Clarendon Press, 1982), pp. 79–104.

7. *The Book of Fallacies: From Unfinished Papers of Jeremy Bentham*, by A Friend (London, John and H. L. Hunt, 1824). Revised and reprinted as *Bentham's Handbook of Political Fallacies*, Harold A. Larrabee (ed.) (Baltimore: Johns Hopkins University Press, 1952). Quotations in the text are from this version.

8. Bentham, *op. cit. supra* note 7, p. 3.

9. J. H. Burns speculates that the omission is owing to Bentham's change of mind (or heart?) in his later years, leading him to want to avoid provoking

his French admirers of the post-Revolutionary era. See J. H. Burns, 'Bentham's Critique of Political Fallacies', in B. Parekh (ed.), *Jeremy Bentham: Ten Critical Essays* (London: Frank Cass, 1974), pp. 154–67.

10. Bowring 496:2.

11. Bowring 500:1. Bentham would have had a stronger case for his objections had he cited the 1793 version of the Declaration; its article 11 declares that the citizen oppressed by 'arbitrary and tyrannical' government has the 'right to repel it by force'. Article 35, with which the Declaration closes, repeats the point, declaring that when government 'violates the rights of the people, insurrection is ... the most sacred of rights and the most indispensible of duties'. The full text of the 1793 Declaration will be found in MacIver (ed.), *Great Expressions of Human Rights*, pp. 262–5.

12. We might usefully think of Bentham's idea of 'imprescriptible' natural rights as an early version of what today in international law would be called 'non-derogable rights'. On the latter idea, see Paul Sieghart, *The International Law of Human Rights* (Oxford: Clarendon Press, 1983), §11.

13. For an account of the Terror in late 1793, see R. R. Palmer, *The World of the French Revolution* (New York: Harper & Row, 1971); and Simon Schama, *Citizens: a Chronicle of the French Revolution* (New York: Knopf, 1989), pp. 726–92.

14. See John Rawls, *A Theory of Justice* (Cambridge, Mass.: Harvard University Press, 1972); Eliot M. Zashin, *Civil Disobedience and Democracy* (New York: Free Press, 1972); and Burton Zweibach, *Civility and Disobedience* (New York: Cambridge University Press, 1975).

15. Despite the emphasis Simon Schama (*Citizens: a Chronicle of the French Revolution*), places on the centrality of 'violence' from the very inception of the Revolution, he nowhere tries to explain this violence as an effect of devout belief in the natural rights alleged and advertised in the 1789 Declaration. The same silence (neglect?) will be found in other recent writers, e.g. Emmet Kennedy, *A Cultural History of the French Revolution* (New Haven, Conn.: Yale University Press, 1989), and William Doyle, *The Oxford History of the French Revolution* (Oxford: Clarendon Press, 1989). See also J. H. Burns, 'Bentham and the French Revolution', *Transactions of the Royal Historical Society*, 5th series, 16 (1966), pp. 95–114.

16. No attempt is made in the following pages to give a full statement of Bentham's theory of rights; in that regard, see the works cited above in note 6. Nor do I attempt to assess the extent to which his account of rights in 'Anarchical Fallacies' is consistent with that fuller view.

17. Bowring 501:1

18. Jeremy Bentham, *De l'ontologie* (Paris: Editions du Seuil, 1996), pp. 210–15. The English text (pp. 77–193) in this bilingual edition was prepared by Philip Schofield. For more on paraphrasis, see also Jeremy Bentham, *A Fragment of Government* (Cambridge: Cambridge University Press, 1973), p. 108.

19. Bowring 500:2.

20. For the relationship between the French Declaration and the United Nations Declaration, see Stephen P. Marks, 'From the "Single Confused Page" to the "Decalogue for Six Billion Persons": the Roots of the Universal

Declaration of Human Rights in the French Revolution', *Human Rights Quarterly*, 20 (1998), pp. 459–514.
21. Bowring 502:1.
22. Thomas Hobbes, *Leviathan* (1651), Pt. I, ch. 14, paras. 1–6.
23. Bowring 502:1.
24. Bowring 503:1.
25. See, e.g. Judith Jarvis Thomson, *The Realm of Rights* (Cambridge, Mass.: Harvard University Press, 1990), pp. 41–3.
26. See Thomson, *The Realm of Rights.*
27. Bentham, *De l'ontologie*, pp. 80, 164.
28. Bowring 501:1.
29. Rudolph Carnap, *The Logical Syntax of Language* (London: Routledge, 1936), pp. 238–9. On the distinction between use and mention, see W. V. O. Quine, *Methods of Logic* (New York: Holt, 1950), pp. 37–8.
30. Jeremy Bentham, *An Introduction to the Principles of Morals and Legislation*, ed. J. H. Burns and H. L. A. Hart (London: Athlone Press, 1970), p. 294.
31. Immanuel Kant, *The Metaphysical Foundations of Morals* (1785), sections 2 and 3.
32. Bentham, *De l'ontologie*, pp. 80, 164.
33. Bowring 501:1.
34. Nickel, *Making Sense of Human Rights*, pp. 84–98.
35. Thomson, *The Realm of Rights*, pp. 214–17, 222–4, 269–70, 271.
36. Bowring 523:2.
37. Bowring 523:2.
38. J. S. Mill, *Utilitarianism* (1860), ch. 5.
39. Richard B. Brandt, *Morality, Utilitarianism, and Rights* (Cambridge: Cambridge University Press, 1993), pp. 179–95, and L. W. Sumner, *The Moral Foundation of Rights* (Oxford: Clarendon Press, 1987).
40. For an exception to this generalization, see Alan Gewirth, *Human Rights: Essays on Justification and Applications* (Chicago: University of Chicago Press, 1982), pp. 208–33. For a criticism of the doctrine of absolute rights, see Thomson, *The Realm of Rights*, pp. 82–7.
41. Mill, *Utilitarianism*, ch. 5.
42. Ronald Dworkin, *Taking Rights Seriously* (Cambridge Mass.: Harvard University Press, 1978), pp. xi, xv.

10
Pre-empting Humanitarian Interventions

Thomas Pogge

Let me define humanitarian intervention, roughly, as coercive external interference in the internal affairs of a sovereign state justified by the goal of protecting large numbers of persons within this state in the enjoyment of their human rights. In most cases, the massive human-rights problems that provide reasons for humanitarian interventions are due to those who hold, or try to gain, power in the foreign state in question. What follows will implicitly have this central case in mind, though I recognize that there are other cases, such as natural calamities or the collapse of governmental authority.

Normative discussions of humanitarian intervention often focus on the question whether some particular actual or hypothetical intervention is good or bad, whether it may or should be undertaken or not. Such discussions then give rise to a more general examination of what moral criteria might be suitable for answering questions of the first type in a principled way.

These discussions are important, but resting content with them is myopic by failing to acknowledge that *all* humanitarian interventions are bad in a sense, that it would be best if the world could get along without them. This is not to say that there is anything wrong with the existence of humanitarian intervention as an available response to serious human-rights problems. But we should want – partly through the availability of this option perhaps – to avoid situations that call for its exercise. We should want to avoid humanitarian interventions both because it is bad for there to be the kind of massive human-rights problems that furnish reasons to intervene in the first place and also because, due to their coercive nature, such interventions themselves usually cause, or at least risk, human-rights problems of their own, even when they are beneficial on the whole.

Put in so abstract a way, the point can hardly be disputed. Yes, other things equal, it is indeed a worthy goal to reduce or eliminate the situations that provide reasons for humanitarian interventions. The interesting questions are: Whose goal exactly is this supposed to be?, and: How exactly is this goal to be pursued?

Let me distinguish four approaches defined by how they respond to this pair of questions. The first is *preventive diplomacy*. It assigns the worthy goal to the foreign policy establishment of a certain noble superpower and instructs these experts to conduct its foreign policy with this goal in mind. Taking the world as it is, they are to exert the influence of the US in support of human rights abroad. There is little more that can be said in general terms by way of specifying that instruction. This is so because of the need for flexibility, which arises from the triple complexity of diplomacy. There is, first, the complexity of facts. To act effectively with regard to some particular foreign country, our experts must proceed with a rich and contextualized knowledge of the local circumstances and possibilities. They must know about the personalities, aims and values of the persons holding or plausibly seeking political or economic power, about their options and opportunities, about the major groups in the country in question as well as their histories, values and internal organization, about the relations such persons and groups have with third parties abroad and the influences they are subject to on account of such relations – and so on and so forth without limit. A foreign policy expert can never know enough details.

There is, secondly, the complexity of ends. The prevention of human-rights problems abroad is at best only one among many goals of our foreign policy. Here it may be objected that, to the contrary, foreign policy has, or should have, only one such goal: the pursuit of our national interest. There is, however, no widely accepted and clear-cut explication of this expression that would allow us, on purely empirical grounds, to identify and to weight candidate foreign policy goals by reference to their importance to the national interest.[1] Appeal to the national interest cannot then settle debates about how to balance the many candidate ends of foreign policy – for example, about whether and how much to discount the future or about how to trade off concerns about global resource depletion, human rights, the risk of nuclear war, and the US share of the global economy.

There is, thirdly, the complexity of means. These are truly endless, as becomes clear by reflecting simply on the ways one person can try to influence the conduct of another: directly, through rewards and punishments, offers and threats, providing and withholding of information and misinformation, etc., or indirectly, by influencing the ways in which third parties influence the target person. If the goal is to influence the policies of, or conditions in, a foreign country, these possibilities grow exponentially.

These rudimentary reflections on the triple complexity of diplomacy show that preventive diplomacy, like diplomacy more generally, is more of an art than a science, at least for persons with merely human brains.

These reflections also begin to reveal the main disadvantage of preventive diplomacy as a method for pursuing the goal of reducing and pre-empting human-rights problems: diplomacy deals with incipient human-rights problems in a future-oriented way and on a case-by-case basis, taking full account of the relevant context and the full panoply of US foreign policy goals. Both of these features lend it flexibility, but both of them also make it vulnerable to strategic manipulation. Regarding its contextualized future-orientation, we can appreciate this point through a simple example: suppose we see a human-rights problem emerging in a foreign country and find that its present government is largely responsible for this. We are able to weaken this government in a number of ways, thereby making it more likely that it will be displaced by another. Insofar as we are concerned to promote human rights, we will take this course if and only if we believe that the potential successor government will do better in human-rights terms than the present government. Assuming that the present government understands that this is our criterion, it has an incentive to eliminate any moderate opposition so as to ensure that the only viable alternatives to itself are ones that are even worse. In this way, our known disposition to promote human rights may in fact aggravate human-rights problems abroad – in this case by encouraging the elimination of the present government's more moderate opponents.[2]

Similar considerations hold for the second feature of diplomacy, which is that, when considering the myriad ways of exerting influence abroad, diplomacy ideally takes into account not only the human-rights effects of such exertions, but also their costs and benefits in terms of all our other foreign-policy goals as well. Our foreign policy establishment seeks to maintain and enhance US credibility abroad, to have good relations with foreign governments and other organizations, to support US economic interests, to prevent the spread of dangerous technologies, to reduce global pollution, to enhance public support for the current US administration at home and abroad, and so on and so forth. Assuming that foreigners understand that we care about all these goals, they can discourage any human-rights promoting policy on our part by increasing its relative cost in terms of our other goals. They can, for example, reward us in various ways for ignoring human-rights problems in their country: they can buy more of our products, support our interests in the UN, reinforce our policies towards third parties, or enhance our government's popularity here or abroad. Equivalently, they can attach various penalties to our attempts to promote human rights in their country. In both of these ways, then, the very flexibility and sensitivity to detail, which are the pride of the art of diplomacy, are also its Achilles heel. They make preventive diplomacy *predictable in the wrong way*, putting foreign governments on notice that they can get away with perpetuating or ignoring their human-rights problems if instead they eliminate plausible alternatives to their rule or establish a negative correlation between our human-rights goal and our other foreign-policy goals. In my view, this mutuality of manipulation in the diplomatic arena is often overlooked by popular commentators (though surely not by true professionals): our attention is always focused on how *we* are trying to influence *them* in the service of some objective, and rarely is it asked how *they* are trying to influence *us* and, in particular, are trying to influence our attempts to influence them.[3]

These difficulties in the first approach suggest a second, that of a *principled foreign policy* or *PFP*. The word 'principled' here stands in contrast to the two sources of flexibility in the *preventive-diplomacy* approach. First, rather than seeking the best response to a particular situation, PFP seeks the best rules or principles for responding to situations of a certain type and then follows these principles even when doing so is not best in a particular case. One such principle might be that we are not going to support a regime under which gross violations of human rights occur, even if its only viable alternative would be even worse, lest we encourage unscrupulous governments to eliminate their more moderate opposition. This point is familiar from many other contexts, ranging from dealing with kidnappers and hijackers to the principles of threat-fulfilling and threat-ignoring in nuclear deterrence.[4] Second, rather than view human rights as one foreign-policy goal among others, PFP views them, to some extent at least, as trumps or side constraints. Thus we might categorically refuse to support repressive governments through arms sales, no matter how much we may stand to gain in terms of our other goals. The main justification for being principled in these two ways is that this makes our foreign policy predictable in the right way: foreigners are put on notice that they will not be able to manipulate us and that it is therefore pointless for them to try to arrange things so that it would be best for us, in light of our goals, to do what they want us to do.

The main difficulties with the PFP approach are well known: it is hard for a democracy to commit itself to principles and make this commitment stick. This is so not only because the costs and opportunity costs of sticking to a principle may be high, but also because an election may bring in a different foreign-policy crew (as happened quite dramatically after Ronald Reagan's 1980 defeat of Jimmy Carter). There is the further problem of how principles can cope with the fact that foreign states differ enormously in power and geopolitical importance. Principles that ignore such differentials will demand too little from us in our relations with weak countries or will prove implausibly costly in our relations with strong ones (e.g. by demanding humanitarian intervention in China). And principles that take such power differentials into account are bound to seem hypocritical, as indeed Carter's foreign policy appeared to many (why are human rights of Chinese worth less than those of Haitians?).

In the real world, foreign policy tends to oscillate between these two poles of preventive diplomacy and PFP, though it is usually closer to the pure diplomacy than to the pure principle end of the spectrum. The reason for this may well be that the diplomacy approach allows politicians more leeway for dissimulation: almost any foreign policy towards China can be presented as one that earnestly seeks to promote human rights through constructive engagement. The announcement of a principled foreign policy guided by human rights, by contrast, imposes real constraints on what decisions can be justified as compatible with these principles.

I don't think there is any general solution to the question where foreign policy should settle on the multi-dimensional diplomacy-principle spectrum. It is easy to say, of course, that we should choose the point that makes our foreign policy most effective in terms of the goals we have assigned to it. But this point is bound to move around with shifts in personnel on the international stage and with changes in many other factors (such as technologies and the distribution of military and economic power). Moreover, this point of maximum effectiveness is impossibly hard to find as the global benefits of commitment to principle cannot be identified, let alone quantified. We cannot identify or quantify the human-rights problems that would have occurred had we taken a more or less principled stance than we did. So we cannot really know what sort of foreign policy is best – nor can we know how much worse we did than we might have done in a best-case scenario.

What we do know, in general terms, is that the human-rights situation in most countries remains rather bleak even while most of the world's powerful states claim a commitment to human rights as among their foremost foreign-policy goals. And this knowledge provides an impetus to seek and explore alternative approaches.

The two approaches discussed so far differ on how to pursue the goal of reducing or eliminating the situations that provide reasons for humanitarian interventions. But they agree on whose goal this is supposed to be. Both single out, as the main independent variable affecting the overall level of human-rights fulfilment, the ways in which the major democracies conduct their foreign policy.

One main alternative to this shared focus is to identify as the main independent variable the framework of international laws, treaties and conventions within which governments and other powerful agents interact. Once we assign the goal of promoting human rights to these international 'rules of the game', we again face two possibilities. The third approach of *local institutional reform* has recently been illustrated by the proposal of treaties through which small countries would pre-authorize military interventions against themselves for the event that a future government significantly violates democratic principles (Tom Farer) or human rights (Stanley Hoffmann).[5] The point of such treaty pre-authorizations would be not merely to make it easier for outsiders to organize a humanitarian intervention when one seems necessary, but also to hinder the emergence of such serious human-rights problems in the first place. In this respect, pre-authorizing a humanitarian intervention against oneself is akin to anti-takeover measures in the business world, such as poison pills and golden parachutes: predators are less likely to strike as the expected pay-off associated with victory is reduced. The predators whom Farer and Hoffmann are seeking to deter are persons and groups disposed towards taking power by force or towards repressive rule.

Once we begin thinking along these lines, similar anti-takeover measures readily spring to mind. I will come back to these after having introduced the fourth approach of *global institutional reform*, which seems to me to hold the most promise. I will develop this approach at some length, beginning from its roots in a particular institutional understanding of human rights. The point of doing this is to clarify the moral reasons we have to be concerned about the human rights of foreigners.

1. An institutional understanding of human rights

A conception of human rights may be factored into two main components:

1. the *concept* of a human right used by this conception, or what one might also call its *understanding* of human rights, and
2. the *substance* or content of the conception, that is, the objects or goods it singles out for protection by a set of human rights.[6]

We face then two questions: What are human rights? And: What human rights are there? Answers to the second question clearly presuppose an answer to the first. But the first question can, I believe, be answered without presupposing more than a vague and uncontroversial outline of an answer to the second. This, in any case, is what I attempt to do here, in order to clarify what those human rights are in the name of which the option of humanitarian intervention should be available and, if necessary, exercised.

The concept of human rights has six central features that any plausible understanding of human rights must incorporate. First, human rights express *ultimate moral* concerns: agents have a moral duty to respect human rights, a duty that does not derive from a more general moral duty to comply with national or international laws. (In fact, the opposite may hold: conformity with human rights is a moral requirement on any legal order, whose capacity to create moral obligations depends in part on such conformity.) Second, they express *weighty* moral concerns, which normally override other normative considerations. Third, these moral concerns are focused on *human beings*, as all of them and they alone have human rights and the special moral status associated therewith. Fourth, with respect to these moral concerns, all human beings have *equal status*: they have exactly the same human rights, and the moral significance of these rights and of their violations does not vary with whose human rights are at stake.[7] Fifth, human rights express moral concerns that are *unrestricted*, that is, they ought to be honoured by all human agents irrespective of their particular epoch, culture, religion, moral tradition or philosophy. Sixth, these moral concerns are *broadly sharable*, that is, capable of being understood and appreciated by persons from different epochs and cultures as well as by adherents of a variety of different religions, moral traditions and philosophies. The notions of unrestrictedness and broad sharability are related in that we tend to feel more confident about conceiving of a moral concern as unrestricted when this concern is not parochial to some particular epoch, culture, religion, moral tradition or philosophy.

Various understandings of human rights are consistent with these six points. The proposed institutional understanding of human rights interprets the postulate of a human right to X as the demand that every society (or comparable social system) ought to be so organized that all its participants enjoy secure access to X.[8] A human right to freedom of expression, for example, implies then that human beings have a moral claim that the institutional order of their society be maintained or reformed in such a way that they can securely exercise this freedom. To honour this claim, its citizens must ensure not merely that their government and its officials respect these freedoms, but also that limitations and violations of them on the part of other persons are effectively deterred and prevented.

On the institutional understanding I propose, your human rights are then moral claims *on* any institutional order imposed upon you and moral claims *against* those (especially: more influential and privileged) persons who contribute to its imposition. You have a moral claim that any institutional order imposed upon you be so structured that you have secure access to the objects of your human rights. And you have a correlative moral responsibility that any institutional order you help impose on others be so structured that *they* have secure access to the objects of their human rights. When a society fails to realize human rights when it could, then those of its members who do not support the requisite institutional reforms are violating a negative duty of justice: the duty not to cooperate in the imposition of an unjust institutional order without making serious efforts within their means towards initiating and supporting appropriate institutional reforms or towards protecting the victims of injustice.[9]

Though somewhat unconventional, this institutional understanding of human rights accords well with the understanding implicit in the *Universal Declaration of Human Rights*.[10] Its article 28 reads: 'Everyone is entitled to a social and international order in which the rights and freedoms set forth in this Declaration can be fully realized.' As its reference to 'the rights and freedoms set forth in this Declaration' indicates, this article does not add a further right to the list, but rather addresses the concept of a human right. It is then, on the one hand, consistent with any substantive account of the objects that a scheme of human rights ought to protect, but also affects, on the other hand, the meaning of any human rights postulated in the other Articles: they all are to be understood as claims on the institutional order of any comprehensive social system.[11]

Though meant to be a plausible explication of Article 28, this institutional understanding of human rights is somewhat novel by being both *more* and *less* demanding than the common view according to which, by postulating a human right to X, one declares that every society ought to incorporate a right to X into its basic law or constitution and ought effectively to honour this right whether or not it is so juridified. This institutional understanding is *less* demanding by not requiring that persons enjoying secure access to X must also have a legal right thereto. Having corresponding legal rights in addition is not *so* important that this additional demand would need to be incorporated into each human right. A person's human right to adequate nutrition (Article 25), for instance, should count as fulfilled when this person has secure access to adequate nutrition, even when such access is not legally guaranteed. Insistence on juridification would not only dilute our conception of human rights through the inclusion of elements that are not truly essential. It would also provoke the communitarian and East Asian criticism that human rights lead persons to view themselves as Westerners: atomized, autonomous, secular and self-interested individuals ready to insist on their rights no matter what the cost may be to others. Employment of the institutional understanding of human rights singles out the truly essential elements of human flourishing and, in particular, avoids any conceptual connection with legal rights. Even those hostile to a legal-rights culture can share the goal of establishing for all human beings secure access to certain vital goods.

My institutional understanding of human rights is in two respects *more* demanding than the common view. It is *more* demanding by requiring secure access even against private threats. To illustrate: even if there is an effective legal path that would allow domestic servants in India to defend themselves against abuse by their employers, many of them nevertheless cannot make use of this opportunity because they do not know what their legal rights are or lack either the knowledge or the economic independence necessary to initiate legal action. The existing institutional order fails to establish adequate social and economic safeguards, which might ensure that such servants are literate, know their rights and options, and have some economic security in case of job loss. This is a grave fault that a plausible understanding of the human right to freedom from inhuman and degrading treatment (Article 5), should be sensitive to.[12] So, according to the institutional understanding, an institutional order fails to fulfil human rights even if it merely fails sufficiently to protect their objects. By imposing an institutional order upon others, one takes responsibility for their human rights.[13]

The second, and here more relevant, respect in which this institutional understanding of human rights is *more* demanding than the common view has to do with its giving no special moral significance to national borders. This point, again, accords with Article 28. It entails that our international institutional order is to be assessed and reformed by reference to its relative contribution to human rights fulfilment.[14] Understood institutionally, human rights in our time have global normative reach: a person's human rights entail not merely moral claims on the institutional order of her own society, which are claims against her fellow *citizens*, but also analogous moral claims on the *global* institutional order, which are claims against her fellow human beings. We thus have the same kind of duties with regard to our international order as with regard to the institutional order of our own national society.

To appreciate how this last point brings out the tight association between the institutional understanding of human rights and the fourth approach to pre-empting humanitarian interventions, one must distinguish this point from another, more common view which also ascribes to us a responsibility for the human rights of all – demanding that we ought to defend, as best we can, the objects of the human rights of any person anywhere on earth.[15] What Article 28 is asking of the citizens and governments of the developed states is not that we assume the role of a global police force ready to intervene to aid and protect all those whose human rights are imperilled by brutal governments or civil wars, but that we support institutional reforms towards an international order that would strongly support the emergence and stability of democratic, rights-respecting, and peaceful regimes. The institutional understanding of human rights becomes international not by assessing how governments conduct their foreign policy, but by assessing how they shape international practices or institutions. It is this global institutional order that gives rise to our responsibility for the human rights of foreigners, and it is this order to which the goal of realizing human rights is most immediately assigned.

Thinking of human rights in this way makes sense only insofar as it is empirically true that the realization of human rights importantly depends on the structure of our global order and that this global order is to some extent subject to intelligent (re)design by reference to the imperative of human rights fulfilment. Returning to the examination of the fourth approach to pre-empting humanitarian intervention, let me then try to make plausible that these two empirical presuppositions hold, looking specifically at global institutional reforms that would reduce the occasions on which humanitarian intervention seems morally compelling.

2. Global institutional reform

Talk of a 'global institutional order' sounds horribly abstract and requires at least some brief explication. There is, first and foremost, the institution of the modern state. The land surface of our planet is divided into a number of clearly demarcated and non-overlapping national territories. Human beings are matched up with these territories, so that (at least for the most part) each person belongs to exactly one territory. Any person or group effectively controlling a preponderant share of the means of coercion within a territory is recognized as the legitimate government of both the territory and the persons belonging to it. This government is entitled to rule 'its' people through laws, orders and officials, to adjudicate conflicts among them, and to exercise ultimate control over all resources within the territory ('eminent domain'). It is also entitled to represent its people against the rest of the world: to bind them *vis-à-vis* outsiders through treaties and contracts, to regulate their relations with outsiders, to declare and prosecute wars in their name, and to control outsiders' access to the country's territory. In this second role, a government is considered continuous with its predecessors and successors: bound by the undertakings of the former, and capable through its own undertakings of binding the latter. There are, of course, various minor deviations[16] and also many further, less essential features of our global order. But these most basic features will suffice for now.

This global order plays a significant role in generating the endemic underfulfilment of human rights, which keeps the topic of humanitarian intervention on our agenda. So long as the international criterion for the legitimacy of governments is effective control, there are strong incentives to attain and to keep power by force: once in power, putschists can count on all the rewards of international recognition. They can, for example, control and hence profit from the sale of the country's natural resources. They can also borrow funds abroad in the name of the whole country and then spend these funds as they see fit. Foreign bankers need have no special worries about being repaid in the event that democracy returns, because any future government will be considered obligated to repay the loans of any predecessor and will have to comply on pains of being shut out of the international credit markets.

Could we modify our global order so that it contributes better to the stability of democratic governments? One might begin by incorporating into international law the option for countries to declare that they assume no responsibility for repaying loans incurred by a future government that will have ruled in violation of constitutionally prescribed democratic procedures. This principle prevents neither putschists from coming to power nor lenders from loaning money to putschists. But it does render such loans considerably more risky and thereby entails that putschists can borrow less – and this on less favourable terms. It thus reduces the staying power of undemocratic governments and the incentives for attempting a coup in the first place.

It may be said that this idea could be just as well implemented pursuant to the third approach: through *local* rather than global institutional reform. The current democratic government of Brazil, say, could unilaterally make such a declaration and could even seek to amend Brazil's constitution so as to make it unconstitutional for any future Brazilian government to repay loans incurred by undemocratic or unconstitutional predecessor regimes.

In response: unilateral strategies of this sort are indeed viable and, I think, should be explored and employed far more than they are today. Still, global institutional reform, though harder to pull off, has three important advantages. First, it provides assurance. By specifically recognizing the right of a democratically elected government to make such a declaration, all governments undertake not to put pressure on future democratic governments to repay the loans of illegitimate predecessors. This strengthens the incentive against lending money to illegitimate regimes and hence also the incentive against seeking to grab power by force.

Second, the global approach could, and should, include the instituting of a neutral council that would determine, in an internationally authoritative way, whether a particular government is constitutional or not.[17] This council might be fashioned on the model of the International Court of Justice in The Hague, but it should also have specially trained personnel for observing – and in special cases even conducting – national elections. Democratic governments could facilitate the work of the council, and thereby contribute to the stability of democracy in their country, by incorporating into their written constitutions clear legitimacy criteria that also fix precisely how these criteria can be legitimately revised.

Thirdly, the global approach can also help remove a disadvantage of the contemplated reform through which it is liable to have a destabilizing influence on existing democratic governments. Such an influence might come about as follows. If an officially illegitimate government cannot, in any case, borrow abroad in the name of the entire country, it may see no reason to service debts incurred by its democratic predecessors. Anticipating this fact, foreign lenders may then be reluctant to give loans to democratic governments perceived to be in danger of being overthrown – which would not be, of course, in the spirit of my proposal.[18] This difficulty might be neutralized through an international loan insurance fund that services the debts of democratically legitimate governments whenever illegitimate successors refuse to do so. The fund, just as the council proposed above, should be financed jointly by all democratic states. This would require some states, the enduringly stable democracies, to contribute to a fund from which they will hardly ever profit directly. Their financial contribution would, however, be small, because my proposal would render the overthrow of democratic regimes much less frequent. And their financial contribution would also be well justified in view of the gain for democratization, which would bring with it gains for the fulfilment of human rights and the avoidance of wars and civil wars, whereby it would also reduce the incidence of occasions for – often costly – humanitarian interventions.

It is more difficult to design a reform that would enable democratic governments to prevent illegitimate successors from selling the country's natural resources. In this regard a local reform pursuant to the third approach seems entirely impossible. The only thing that could work is an international agreement not to recognize property rights in natural resources that were purchased from undemocratic and unconstitutional governments (e.g. crude oil bought from Sani Abacha). The difficulty is to enforce such an agreement especially in the case of resources whose origin cannot easily be ascertained.

Even if such global reforms succeed, Farer and Hoffmann's idea of preauthorized military interventions might still be useful. But it should be employed somewhat differently from what they envision, in two respects: first, the decision about whether an intervention is called for, and presumably also the intervention itself, should be made by an international council (of the sort described before) rather than by a particular government whose decisions are bound to be influenced by partisan considerations. This modification would make the pre-authorization option more palatable to many countries and would also increase the deterrent effect of pre-authorizations by blocking the hope to avoid intervention through concessions unrelated to human-rights fulfilment. Second, pre-authorized interventions should function in combination with the other anti-takeover measures. This maximizes the deterrent effect of the proposal overall. And it offers the hope that, should deterrence fail, the illegitimate rulers can be brought down by the economic measures alone, *before* a pre-authorized intervention need be undertaken as a last resort. The consequent reduction in the incidence of pre-authorized interventions (relative to the Farer/Hoffmann proposal) is a further gain, because military interventions will, sometimes at least, themselves be costly in human-rights terms.

3. Conclusion

The moral question generally asked about humanitarian intervention is: under what conditions, to what extent, and in what form is humanitarian intervention morally permissible? This question tends to lead to arguments between those who hold that an adequate international ethic should impose somewhat weaker constraints upon humanitarian interventions than current international law and those who hold that, since military interventions will in many cases produce more harm than good and will set dangerous precedents, there sadly is little we can do about the deplorable global state of human-rights fulfilment.[19] If we truly care about the fulfilment of human rights, we must go beyond this question and think also about reforms of our global institutional order, which can greatly reduce the occasions for humanitarian intervention by providing strong incentives to national societies towards fulfilling the human rights of their members. In this regard, the wealthy democracies have a duty to intervene at the level of global institutional design. Insofar as they ignore this duty by continuing to support the existing international order, they share responsibility for the underfulfilment of human rights it engenders.

Notes

1. Felix Oppenheim has done much to develop an account of the national interest that satisfies these two conditions, i.e. that is acceptable to citizens and politicians across much of the political spectrum and also clear and specific enough to facilitate consensus on how foreign-policy outcomes should be assessed by reference to it. (Oppenheim accepts that *ex ante*

assessments of foreign-policy options by reference to the national interest so defined must remain controversial because of the other two complexities, of facts and of means.) Having had many engaging and highly productive written and oral exchanges on this issue with Professor Oppenheim over many years, I am still not convinced that his project can succeed. Irrespective of this disagreement, my claim in the text is true so long as Oppenheim's project has not in fact succeeded – specifically, so long as his conception of the national interest has not come to be widely accepted. If his project were to succeed, the second complexity of diplomacy would indeed have been overcome. Cf. Felix Oppenheim, *The Place of Morality in Foreign Policy* (Lexington, Mass.: Lexington Books, 1991), pp. 10–15, as well as his forthcoming essay 'The National Interest: a Basic Concept'. Oppenheim's project is further discussed in George Kateb's contribution to the present volume.

2. This is a general point: having a known disposition to promote a certain goal may get in the way of the promotion of this goal. Thus, your overwhelmingly powerful motive to protect your daughter may make her a preferred kidnapping target.

3. One such rare instance was the public debate over China's most-favoured nation status, during which some of the strategic aspects of the relationship were attended to in the media. We may recall here the old joke about the inmates of a zoo or asylum who view their own conduct as successfully conditioning the behaviour of the wardens, just as the wardens view themselves as successfully manipulating the behaviour of the inmates.

4. For a brief discussion, see Derek Parfit, *Reasons and Persons* (Oxford: Oxford University Press 1984), section 8.

5. Tom J. Farer, 'The United States as Guarantor of Democracy in the Caribbean Basin: Is There a Legal Way?', *Human Rights Quarterly*, 10 (1988) 12, pp. 157–76, and Tom J. Farer, 'A Paradigm of Legitimate Intervention', in Lori Fisler Damrosch (ed.), *Enforcing Restraint: Collective Intervention in Internal Conflicts* (New York: Council on Foreign Relations Press 1993), pp. 316–47; Stanley Hoffmann, 'Delusions of World Order', *New York Review of Books*, 39 (1992) 7, pp. 37–43; and Stanley Hoffmann, *The Ethics and Politics of Humanitarian Intervention* (Notre Dame: University of Notre Dame Press, 1996).

6. Here the *object* of a human right is whatever this human right is a right to – adequate nutrition, for example, or physical integrity.

7. This second component of equality is compatible with the view that the weight agents ought to give to the human rights of others varies with their relation to them – that agents have stronger moral reasons to secure human rights in their own country, for example, than abroad – so long as this is not seen as being due to a difference in the moral significance of these rights, impersonally considered. (One can consistently believe that the flourishing of all children is equally important and also that one should show special concern for the flourishing of one's own children.)

8. What matters is secure access to the objects of human rights, rather than these objects themselves, because an institutional order is not morally problematic merely because some of its participants are choosing to fast or to compete in boxing matches. Moreover, no society can make the objects of

all human rights absolutely secure. And making them as secure as possible would constitute a ludicrous drain on societal resources for what, at the margins, would be very minor benefits in security. To be plausible, any conception of human rights that uses the concept I propose must therefore incorporate an idea of reasonable security thresholds: your human rights are fulfilled when their objects are sufficiently secure – with the required degrees of security suitably adapted to the means and circumstances of the relevant social system. Thus, your human right to freedom of peaceful assembly and association is fulfilled, when it is sufficiently unlikely that your attempts to associate or assemble with others would be thwarted or punished by official or non-official agents or agencies. The task of making this idea more precise for each particular human right belongs to the second, substantive component of a conception of human rights.

9. The institutional understanding of human rights sketched in the last four paragraphs is more extensively elaborated in my 'How Should Human Rights be Conceived?', *Jahrbuch für Recht und Ethik*, 3 (1995), pp. 103–20.

10. Adopted and proclaimed by the General Assembly of the United Nations on 10 December 1948, as resolution 217A(III).

11. One can get from Article 28 to my institutional understanding of human rights by making four plausible interpretive conjectures: (1) Alternative institutional orders that do not satisfy the requirement of Article 28 can be ranked by how close they come to fully realizing human rights: social systems ought to be structured so that human rights can be realized in them as fully as possible. (2) How fully human rights can be realized in some institutional order is measured by how fully these human rights generally are, or (in the case of a hypothetical institutional order) generally would be, realized in it. (3) An institutional order realizes a human right insofar as (and fully if and only if) this human right is fulfilled for the persons upon whom this order is imposed. (4) A human right is fulfilled for some person if and only if this person enjoys secure access to its object. Taking these four conjectures together: human rights can be fully realized in some institutional order if and only if this order affords all those upon whom it is imposed secure access to the objects of their human rights.

12. Similarly, and closer to home, a plausible understanding of human rights should also be sensitive to an institutional order that does not adequately prevent and deter domestic violence.

13. And yet, an institutional order is nevertheless more unjust when it officially authorizes or even mandates avoidably insecure access to the objects of human rights than when it allows the same insecurity to result from insufficient prevention or deterrence. This differential weighting is deeply rooted in our moral thinking and shows itself, for instance, in our attitudes towards the criminal law and the penal system: harms done to innocents which are inflicted in the course of police work or through official punishments weigh more heavily than equal harms inflicted on them through 'private' crimes not sufficiently prevented and deterred by the penal system. Our institutional order and its political and legal organs should not merely serve justice, but also symbolize it. This point is important, because it undermines the plausibility of consequentialist and hypo-

thetical-contract (e.g. Rawls) conceptions of justice which assess an institutional order from the standpoint of prudent prospective participants, who, of course, have no reason to care about this distinction among sources of insecurity. Cf. Thomas W. Pogge, 'Three Problems with Contractarian-Consequentialist Ways of Assessing Social Institutions', *Social Philosophy and Policy*, 12 (1995) 2, pp. 241–66, esp. section 5. We must avoid the mistake of many consequentialist and contractualist conceptions of justice which base the moral assessment of an institutional order solely on the magnitude of the benefits and burdens it 'distributes' to persons while ignoring the nature of the relation between that order and these pay-offs. A plausible conception of human rights must then establish not only a scheme of vital goods (to be recognized as objects of human rights), but also a method for weighting shortfalls from secure access which takes account of the different kinds of connections between institutional schemes and human-rights fulfilment.

14. 'Relative', because what matters is how well an institutional scheme does in comparison to its feasible alternatives.

15. The concept of human rights is so understood, for example, by Luban: 'A human right, then, will be a right whose beneficiaries are all humans and whose obligors are all humans in a position to effect the right.' David Luban, 'Just War and Human Rights' in Charles Beitz et al. (eds), *International Ethics* (Princeton: Princeton University Press, 1985), pp. 195–216, at p. 209. This view is more radical than mine, because it does not make the global normative reach of human rights conditional upon the existence of a worldwide institutional order in whose coercive imposition we collaborate.

16. There are stateless persons, persons with multiple nationalities, and those who are citizens of one country but reside in or are visiting another. We have Antarctica, continental shelves, disputed areas, and areas that are contracted out (such as Guantanamo Bay and Hong Kong, though the latter case is also a beautiful illustration of the continuity condition). And groups are sometimes recognized as the legitimate government even though they do not control a preponderant share of the means of coercion within the relevant territory (Pol Pot's Khmer Rouge in the 1980s or Bertrand Aristide in the 1990s).

17. This council would, of course, work only in the interest of democratic constitutions. Its determinations would have consequences not only for a government's ability to borrow abroad, but also for its domestic and international standing. A government that has been officially declared illegitimate would be handicapped in myriad ways (trade, diplomacy, investments, etc.) – a fact that would contribute to the deterrent effect of the proposed institutional innovation and hence to its tendency to reduce the risk of coup attempts.

18. Thanks are due to Ronald Dworkin for seeing this difficulty and for articulating it forcefully.

19. See, for example, the exchange between Michael Walzer – defending the latter view in *Just and Unjust Wars* (New York: Basic Books, 1977), and in 'The Moral Standing of States', *Philosophy and Public Affairs*, 9 (1980), pp. 209–29 – and the critics he responds to in the latter piece: Charles Beitz,

Gerald Doppelt, David Luban and Richard Wasserstrom. Cf. also the meta-responses by two of the criticized critics – David Luban, 'The Romance of the Nation State', *Philosophy and Public Affairs*, 9 (1980), pp. 392–7, and Charles Beitz, 'Cosmopolitan Ideals and National Sentiment', *Journal of Philosophy*, 80 (1983), pp. 591–600.

11
Oppenheim's Realism and the Morality of the National Interest*

Luigi Bonanate

I am finally given the opportunity of correcting an error I made a few years ago when I claimed that Oppenheim's conception of realism was 'totally in tune with the one H. Morgenthau proposed 40 years ago in his famous "Six Principles of Political Realism", listed in the first chapter of his *Politics among Nations*'.[1] Oppenheim pointed out to me in a letter: 'I do not agree with Morgenthau. He considered the pursuit of the national interest a *moral* duty, whereas I view it as a practical necessity, hence neither morally right nor wrong, since ethics is meaningful only where there is choice'.[2] What was the nature of my mistake? Let me say right away that the target of my argument was not one or other of these authors, but political realism as such, in the context of international relations. From this perspective one can indeed say that Morgenthau and Oppenheim share the view that the defence of the national interest has and must have absolute priority over any other kind of consideration, while nevertheless admitting – as I indeed do – that whereas Morgenthau holds the defence of the national interest to be a *duty*, Oppenheim treats it simply (or at least alternatively) as a *rational requirement* of action on the part of the politician or statesman.[3] The uncompromisingly deontological position defended in my books *Ethics and International Politics* and *I doveri degli stati*[4] would not be accepted either by Morgenthau or by Oppenheim – and it was this difference that my initial claim aimed, overhastily, to capture. Oppenheim shows his awareness of this difference in the preface to the Italian edition of *The Place of Morality in Foreign Policy*[5] (the work on which I shall here concentrate almost exclusively), where he observes that 'the position he [Bonanate] defends is diametrically opposed to mine'.[6] Our positions on foreign policy certainly are rather different, as I shall now show, developing this point in two stages. First, I shall provide a concise exposition of Oppenheim's approach, highlighting the aspects I consider most important, together with some which seem to me to render unacceptable his restrictive conception of the relation between morality and foreign policy (concentrating in particular on the role he assigns to the idea of the 'national interest'). I shall then present a discussion of the problem addressed by Oppenheim, together with a conclusion that is 'diametrically opposed' to his but also, I hope, more plausible. But I'd also like to add that my project should be understood as carried out in the same calm, detached, scientific spirit in which, thirty years ago, Oppenheim concluded *Moral Principles in Political Philosophy* with an admonition of which I have always much approved:

> It may at first be frustrating to realize that there can be no objective foundation for our most basic moral and political convictions. Yet, it seems to me to be the mark of a mature person and of a mature civilization to be able to stand on one's own feet without the crutches of what I hope I have shown to be a mistaken philosophy [cognitivism] ... [Non-cognitivism] helps us to realize that it is not only impossible but also presumptuous to attempt to shape the rest of the world in our image. It helps us to uphold the values of human dignity – fervently, but with humility.[7]

1.   Oppenheim's position

The Place of Morality in Foreign Policy is divided into two more or less equally sized parts. The first three chapters set out a 'general theory about the role of morality in foreign policy',[8] while the subsequent three contain a series of applications of the theory. To begin with, it will be useful to state the fundamental theoretical proposition behind Oppenheim's whole argument: 'It is rational to aim at what is practically unavoidable, and not rational to attempt the impossible'.[9] Applying this principle to foreign policy, we find that it is rational to pursue a national interest that is practically unavoidable, and irrational to pursue a national interest that cannot be realized. (Clearly, practical necessity should here be understood as involving means–ends reasoning and not simply as consisting in moral or political prescriptions.) The environment in which a state looks after its national interest is an anarchic one that 'has no moral or ideological implications',[10] and this means that the state can only be concerned with its success in this endeavour and not with the moral judgements to which this might give rise. In an anarchic, rule-less environment, Oppenheim's conclusion seems inescapable. And given that the environment to which we are referring is that of international relations, his argument seems to hold water. This, however, will only be so as long as one fails to dispute the conception of international anarchy on which the argument rests. Certainly it cannot be denied that international relations lack rules, if these are meant in a legal or quasi-legal sense (given that there is no supranational authority); but it seems equally evident to me that states do nevertheless effectively *obey* rules – those constructed on the basis of history, the outcomes of conflicts, relative wealth, the quantity of resources they possess, the types of alliances they have made and to which they are bound, and so on. Thus, while it is plausible to say that a bank-teller would not risk his life by resisting a hold-up, it is much less plausible to suggest that anyone else who enters the bank is a potential bank-robber – that is, that every state is simultaneously a bank-teller and a bank-robber – because this would mean that every state puts itself in the position of a robber in relation to all others:[11] we should indeed also have to conclude that every state is forced to behave as a robber in order to realize its national interest, and this does not seem to me to mirror historical reality. The point I am disputing could do with further qualification, since it might be more plausibly interpreted in the light of a form of historical relativism. In this sense, we could limit ourselves to observing that this attitude has indeed for many centuries been that of all or nearly all states, and that later, especially over recent decades, the behaviour of states has *improved*, and does not normally involve recourse to bank-robbing. Thus, Iraq's attempt to 'rob' Kuwait provoked almost complete disapproval on the part of world public opinion.[12] The fact remains, however, that anarchy is not a key that opens doors for us in our attempt to interpret international history – or to put it another way, it is only a key to doors that are already open, failing as it does to account for the richness of exchanges between states which, over the centuries, has been determined exactly on the basis of the existence of an ever-increasing quantity of *rules* imposed, negotiated and observed by nearly all states. To pursue this point further would lead us outside the scope of this chapter, and I therefore limit myself to observing that the bank-teller model seems to me to be a misleading one.[13]

The anarchic clause heavily influences the structure of Oppenheim's argument, especially regarding the two central aspects of rationality and practical necessity. Let us look at the meaning of these two terms. Oppenheim's view of rationality constitutes an important presupposition of his theory and is, I would say, a major motivating force behind his ethical non-cognitivism.[14] He defines rationality as instrumental in nature, that is, as concerning 'the appropriateness of means to an agent's ends, whatever they may be, in contradistinction to the view that intrinsic ends or desires themselves can be said to be rational or not',[15] and he rejects any possible implications concerning the ends to which that instrumental rationality is applied. The nature of the link between rationality and practical necessity is spelt out a few pages on by Oppenheim – 'It is rational to aim at what is practically unavoidable, and not rational to attempt the impossible'[16] – and he further specifies that a situation of practical necessity is one in which anyone 'would find it too risky or difficult or costly to do otherwise'.[17]

What does instrumental rationality aim at when faced with a practical necessity? As far as the management of foreign policy is concerned, the answer is clear: it aims at the realization of a country's national interest. The content of the national interest is equally simple: territorial integrity, military security, economic well-being.[18] Every government that acts for its country therefore knows that it is practically necessary to act rationally and that this involves realizing the interest of the nation. To complete the picture, we need only one more step: the insertion (only to be followed by the virtual exclusion) of the moral dimension, which Oppenheim accomplishes with the claim that 'The conduct of states is not susceptible of moral assessment, *as far as such conduct consists of the pursuit of the national interest*'.[19] In other words, if the state rationally pursues its national interest, the content of its actions will be nothing more than that which is dictated by the practical necessities it faces, and cannot be subject to any moral evaluation – though the scope of its freedom will be equally inexistent.

2. Some first doubts

Oppenheim's position seems to imply that foreign policy is so constrained by the national interest and its practical necessity that its contents turn out to be completely determined. In order to challenge this view, I propose to concentrate on the idea of the national interest, with respect to which practical necessities and their rationality play an instrumental role rather than one involving the choice of ends. One could discuss the concept of the national interest at length, observing, for example, that there is no way of determining its contents comprehensibly, as David Clinton does where he groups its different possible conceptualizations under the two headings of 'ambiguity' and 'dangerousness'.[20] One might also pursue Martha Finnemore's suggestion that the national interest reflects the way in which states intersubjectively construct a collective picture of the world,[21] so that – to use an expression that is well known in academic circles – anarchy (or any other picture of international relations) is 'what states make of it'.[22] The criticism implied by these two approaches is important: if the determination of the national interest is simply a product of the picture of reality which statesmen construct for themselves, and if that interest can be manipulated at will by a country's ruling class, the requirements of rationality and practical necessity lose their attraction for the political scientist, being merely the operative instruments used by a statesman to impose his will both within and outside the state.

More generally, it might be observed that the content of the national interest (territorial integrity, military security, economic well-being) is defined so widely that it fails to identify anything in particular: is there anyone at all (a state or a person) who would not include these as minimal requirements for their own survival? Is there anyone who would give up their own physical integrity, their own security and a minimum of well-being? Giving the national interest such a content means that the national interest of all states is roughly the same: if we accept Oppenheim's condition (to which I have no objection) that our analysis must concentrate on states-as-actors without going into their different natures – their formation or the political struggles that might take place within them[23] – we shall have to conclude that the notion of national interest loses all meaning, being merely the synonym of 'that which states do'. This does not help us in the least in understanding why things are as they are – that is, why states do what they do. Thus, the whole system on which Oppenheim constructs his analysis – involving the idea that there are 'objective criteria by which to answer' the question whether a state's foreign policy choices 'fall within or outside the range of moral relevance'[24] – becomes an empty container: there are objective criteria (the container), but we have nothing to put in the container, it being imperative simply that states pursue their national interest, following the dictates of instrumental rationality in the face of practical necessity.

3.   Enter morality

My main argument for holding Oppenheim's 'morality container' to be empty derives from his assertion that there can be no moral judgements as long as it is *necessary* (in the way we have seen) for the agent to act as he does. As we all know, moral arguments can only apply where there is freedom of choice, which can only be exercised where two or more (equally pursuable) possibilities are found to conflict.[25] Outside this condition of freedom it is natural to say that morality cannot come into the picture. But Oppenheim also naturally admits that 'statesmen are sometimes faced with moral choices' and, to escape the trap he may appear to have set himself, adds that '[m]oral considerations are relevant whenever statesmen must decide whether to adopt a goal different from, but compatible with, the national interest'.[26] At this point, Oppenheim locates two possible areas of application of moral criteria. The first concerns cases in which the moral judgement is simply incidental or additional to the line implied by rational necessity: this area includes cases such as the promotion of human rights, global distributive justice, and imperialism. (While the first two might be seen as having moral *value*, the third might be seen as having moral *disvalue*.) Here, the idea that we should act in favour of or against such policies is usually irrelevant: in the case of imperialism, Oppenheim indeed concludes that '[m]oral considerations are relevant only if, from the point of view of a country's national interest, *it does not matter* whether it embarks on an anti-imperialistic course of action'.[27] The second area of application concerns cases in which genuine alternatives exist but 'none of them [is] *a priori* decidedly superior to all others'.[28] The concessions Oppenheim makes to the applicability of moral judgements in this second area seem quite substantial: he recognizes, indeed, that in many cases we find ourselves in a 'genuine moral dilemma' – for example, when the American government had to choose whether to drop the first atomic bombs for real or to limit themselves to a demonstration, dropping them on an uninhabited island. The first alternative would guarantee Japan's rapid capitulation, reducing the loss of American lives to a minimum; the second alternative would have meant a slower Japanese capitulation (and more American dead), but would also have meant avoiding the deaths of tens of thousands of innocent victims (almost all civilian). In other, less dramatic cases, a government can find itself forced to choose betwen 'expediency and truthfulness',[29] as when Truman forced the hand of public opinion in his country and announced his *doctrine* in defence of Greece and Turkey, over-emphasizing the danger of communism.[30] Although I agree with Oppenheim's proposed analyses of these examples, two questions nevertheless seem to me to remain unresolved. First, there is the question of how a government is to proceed in addressing such moral dilemmas; secondly, there is the question of whether the range of dilemmas is narrow or whether we should not instead admit that *all* foreign policy decisions fall within that range.

As far as the first question is concerned, Oppenheim notes that morality can be interpreted in deontological or consequentialist terms, but he does not appear to take a clear position in favour of one or the other.[31] However, assuming (as Oppenheim does) that a government must rationally pursue the national interest given the practical necessity of doing so, the best alternative seems to me to be to say that 'it is right' for the government to pursue integrity, security and well-being, specifying this as a deontological rule that guides all of its decisions. This can be argued in the following way. A belief in moral principles as absolute determinants of moral conduct constitutes (whatever the content of those principles) too abstract a position, not only because such principles are themselves historically determined (as I have already hinted), but also because it does not fit with our experience of moral conduct as involving choices. In the absence of such choices, our moral world would seem to be deterministic, and we would not experience that 'realm of freedom' in which we are faced with alternatives and where we have to deliberate about which of various possibilities is the right one. Moral choices exist, and they present us with dilemmas. The deontological position is based on the belief that *a priori* constraints (based on principles which in the present case would include that of the national interest) provide a more promising criterion, given this fact of choice, than those of the rival, consequentialist or teleological theories. In a world governed by the principle of the national interest, the adherent of deontological ethics will suppose there to be a duty to respect such a principle, whereas the teleologist will see the agent as constrained to select the best means to such an end (this in particular seems to be Oppenheim's preferred position). The difference lies in the procedural basis of moral choice: the deontologist chooses that which he thinks is right, whereas the teleologist or consequentialist chooses that which seems most realizable and successful. Thus, the former retains a greater degree of responsibility, the latter tending to prefer the more reassuring logic of utilitarianism.[32] It is much more difficult to make predictions and to calculate which alternative will be the most successful than it is to fix on a form of conduct and make the effort to stick to it (assuming one is convinced of its validity), and it is for this reason that I not only find the deontological position ethically superior but also see it as more realistic, in as much as it provides a rule that constrains *in each choice situation*. It does not force one to calculate in situation after situation, and it widens the range of political responsibility, making this something more than the mere responsibility for choosing adequate means to given ends.

As far as the second question is concerned, the range of possible decisions is for any state always in fact wider than Oppenheim suggests. I doubt, in other words, whether there are any cases in which there is only one way of pursuing the national interest (this is why we need a criterion of evaluation like the deontological one, which allows for a greater flexibility of choice). I doubt, moreover, whether the picture of the state (and its foreign policy) painted by Oppenheim corresponds to reality. The foreign policy of a state is something more than a straightforward manifestation of its will or a mere response to external stimuli; the international system comprises various national interests and 'changes state action, not by constraining states with a given set of preferences from acting, but by changing their preferences'.[33] International politics is a complex and continuous play of inter-relations and reciprocal influences which force every state, at all times, to weigh the pursuit of its national interest against possible changes in the general situation. This brings out the way in which the range of possible (and morally equivalent) choices is reasonably wide, requiring every state to have its own consistent, programmatic line which must, in being pursued, be adapted to changing circumstances.

4. An application to the problem of deterrence

My basic difference with Oppenheim is best clarified by means of an example. Among those mentioned by Oppenheim, a particularly useful one for present purposes is that of the morality of nuclear deterrence – the policy adopted by the United States and the Soviet Union to neutralize each other's nuclear potential and the threat of it being unleashed. We need not go into the details of this case, which will be familiar to most. What interests us here is the fact that Oppenheim tends towards a justification of this policy through an application of his theoretical principle: that it was part of the national interest to pursue that which was, in rational terms, the practical necessity of the moment. Let us see how he gets there. The theoretical assumption is clear, but is worth restating in order to apply it to this case: 'Moral judgements are relevant when a government is faced with the decision whether to adopt a foreign policy goal *compatible* with its national interest'.[34] In other words, the decision of the US government to adopt the policy of deterrence can be the object of a moral judgement if the decision, as well as being compatible with the national interest of that country (this is a necessary condition, though not a sufficient one), was only one of the possible decisions compatible with the safeguarding of the national interest. (Of course, the same kinds of considerations could be applied to the Soviet Union, but we have a better knowledge of US foreign policy and military history, and it seems sufficient to refer to the latter.) I should add that the view that the US had no realistic alternative to the policy of deterrence was an almost universally shared one: political philosophers were drawn into a discussion of the moral justifiability of a policy based on the decision to make threats one does not intend to carry out, but in spite of this discussion, they never doubted that threatening some evil act (without the intention of carrying it out) was morally preferable to carrying out that evil act directly or to simply forgoing the safeguarding of one's own national interest. (They all agreed about the immorality of abandoning the population of one's own country to nuclear blackmail on the part of another.)

What allows for differences of judgement regarding the morality of this resort to threats is the fact that in the case of nuclear deterrence the state finds itself in an exceptional situation – one of 'supreme emergency'. The nature of this situation has been explicated most clearly by Michael Walzer (in his *Just and Unjust Wars*[35]), who sees it as depending on two conditions: the danger being faced must be clear and present.[36] What needs to be ascertained is whether these conditions, typical of a 'state of necessity', were present in the case of the reciprocal deterrence of the United States and the Soviet Union – that is, whether the policy of deterrence was the only policy available (in Oppenheim's sense). My own answer is that it was not. Since Oppenheim – like the vast majority of academics who have written on the subject – takes for granted that there was indeed a clear and present danger, he simply limits himself to asking whether there were alternative ways of reacting to that danger, and takes the stakes in the contest as given: the destruction of one or the other of the nuclear powers (together with the further possibility of mutual destruction – a paradoxical outcome but for that very reason a credible one).[37] We can search for alternatives either at the level of means or at the level of ends. Oppenheim chooses to search for them at the level of means,[38] asking whether deterrence was 'the most effective *means* to a practically necessary goal',[39] because there was no question of alternatives in terms of ends. Anyone would concede that it was *right* for the United States to prevent an attack from the Soviet Union. However, the real question is, Would the Soviet Union ever have attacked? And would the United States ever have done so? In other words, were there ever really such 'extreme' situations?[40]

All that is known for certain is that for around forty years the two adversaries paralysed each other by recourse to nuclear deterrence, and that subsequently – luckily, without the launch of a single missile – one of the two contenders threw in the towel, gave up the struggle and indeed collapsed,[41] thus bringing to an end the era of reciprocal deterrence. It might be concluded from this that deterrence worked perfectly. But this can only be said if it is admitted that there were no alternatives, and that the nuclear policy was aimed at preventing an attack from the adversary. In order to prove this we should have to demonstrate that in the absence of such a policy the Soviet Union would have attacked the United States (and *vice versa*), and this hypothesis seems to me to be extremely difficult to defend on the basis of the facts. In the first place, we should not forget that for the first ten years of the Cold War the Soviet Union was a great deal weaker than the United States, and that in the following decade the Cuban crisis clearly showed that the two contenders were far from wanting to attack each other. In the 1970s the backwardness of the Soviet Union, and its difficulty in keeping up with the scientific and technological progress of its adversary (this being necessary for the continuation of deterrence) were clear to all. The sclerosis of the Soviet ruling class also provided evidence of this. The 1980s, on the other hand, saw the progressive disintegration of the Soviet threat.[42] It seems to me quite clear that the Soviet Union never hypothesized an act of aggression against the United States, and even more obvious that a similar act of aggression was never the intention of the United States either, despite the fact that the Soviet Union's preferred 'countercities' option indicated a defensive strategy whereas the 'counterforces' option adopted by the United States involved a conflictual strategy at different, successive levels (a choice based on the option's supposed greater flexibility). It might realistically be hypothesized, then, that the policy of deterrence was an instrument not of international peace, but for the construction of some sort of greater 'governing coalition' based in the first instance on the dividing up of 'votes' (that is, of the allies and of the zones of influence) and in the second instance on their control. This was reciprocally guaranteed by the two powers as a result of the extreme nature of the alternative: the fact that a breaking of the agreement might have produced the very end of history.

There is another sense, however, in which American foreign policy could be approved of from Oppenheim's point of view: it was indeed extremely rational of the United States to put the Soviet Union under enough pressure to force her to make the military investments that would in the end wear that regime out and lead to its overthrow. But this *was not* the United States' declared foreign policy. Thus, we should add that the United States government deceived the public, including both its own electorate and that of all of the allied countries, and that military spending went well beyond that which was strictly necessary. This, despite the fact that a democratic state ought surely to distinguish itself from a totalitarian one at least by rendering explicit its intentions and the motives behind its choices.

However fanciful my historical reconstruction might appear, there is a sense in which Oppenheim himself points me in this direction. Commenting on the philosophical literature on deterrence, Oppenheim says that '[c]uriously, most writers who judge nuclear deterrence by ethical criteria fail to deal with the possibility of alternative strategies, the only situation to which moral considerations seem to me relevant, and fail to apply the ethical standard that it is wrong to have a stronger (and more expensive) defense system than required for national security'.[43] Now, the point I am making is not that we should doubt whether the choice of the policy of deterrence was in the United States' national interest (I would class such a choice as rational in this sense), but that we should doubt whether the choice of deterrence was really aimed at counterbalancing the Soviet threat. I do not wish to discuss whether it was immoral to spend so much money on an operation which turned out, in a sense, to be useless (Oppenheim notes this possibility),[44] but whether the end pursued in doing so was really that which it was stated to be. Taking a different perspective from that adopted by Oppenheim, one might say – in order further to clarify my hypothesis – that on both sides the policy of deterrence was probably a mask for a form of political and ideological control exercised by both of the great powers, not in order to counter one another, but in order to obtain the unconditional compliance of their respective allies and in order to provide each other with proof of their intention to guarantee the stability of the system. The bipolar system collapsed in a way that has no precedent in the entire history of international relations (never before had a great power admitted defeat without fighting, but spontaneously 'liberating' its colonies, transforming its own political regime and finally dissolving itself), and this can be considered a proof – however indirect – of the validity of my thesis, which fits in with the idea that this course of events was anomalous in terms of international history. Thus, we might say that the United States (and the Soviet Union) could *rationally* have given up the policy of deterrence for the simple reason that their survival was not in question. What was in question was their international dominance, and if this is to be seen as part of the content of their national interest, then we ought at least to reconsider the value-judgement that the pursuit of such an interest was practically necessary. It is not even easy to understand a state *wanting* to be the main world power. (After the First World War, for example, this was not the attitude of the United States.) If the situation of clear and present danger did not really exist, but was in fact *invented*, then it is possible that our moral evaluation should be changed accordingly.

My own suggestion is different from that made by Oppenheim where he writes: 'If U.S. national security could have been protected just as well without deployment of MIRVed missiles, it is appropriate to criticize the government for having adopted immoral measures'.[45] Oppenheim is simply distinguishing here between the different degrees to which a deterrent can be developed, and all of these possible degrees of development occur within the same hypothesized world in answer to the same problem. My objection is that deterrence was itself based on a fabric of lies, propagated by both of the great powers, not in order to deceive each other, but in order to deceive world opinion as a way of guaranteeing their common supremacy. I am aware that this thesis may appear ideologically motivated, or just one among many possible interpretations of contemporary history, but I can also point to a number of particular circumstances that convince me of its truth: the first is that the United States never took advantage of its superiority; the second, that the Soviet Union always took an extremely defensive stance; the third, that each of the two powers was always in the last analysis tolerant of the other's more daring foreign policy ventures; and the fourth, that the whole story petered out of its own accord rather than coming to an end through a direct conflict (which is, as I have said, anomalous from the point of view of the history of international relations).

5.   Conclusions

My re-reading of *The Place of Morality in Foreign Policy* has convinced me that Oppenheim's arguments are more solid than I had first perceived them to be, at least in the sense that, once one accepts Oppenheim's main premises (the definition of national interest and the concepts of instrumental rationality and practical necessity) his conclusions can be deduced unequivocally. Therefore, those who remain disatisfied with Oppenheim's conclusions must concentrate on his treatment of the concept of national interest, as I have tried to here.

If one compares the results of the empirical applications contained in the last three chapters of Oppenheim's book with the principles set out in the first three, one finds that Oppenheim in fact recognizes the existence of a margin of choice in foreign policy. He recognizes that one can promote human rights, that global justice is a good end and imperialism a bad one, that there are indeed many authentic moral dilemmas (such as whether or not to bomb Hiroshima, or whether or not to lie, as in the case of the Truman doctrine or Contras–Irangate), and that the policy of deterrence could have been more limited or less expensive. All this leads me to suggest that government decisions (which are supposed to give content to the safeguarding of the national interest) are taken in the context of a range of choice that is wider than might at first appear. A great number of alternatives can in fact be placed under the heading 'The National Interest – a Practically Necessary Goal',[46] so widening the role of governmental *choice*. This is, after all, implied by what Oppenheim himself says in the final lines of his book: 'In the last analysis, we should not squander our moral energies where they can do no good (and may do some harm), but concentrate on areas of foreign policy where our moral commitments do matter, and their expression can make a difference'.[47] So strongly do I agree with Oppenheim on this point that I hold the foreign policy of the Italian govenment, which had close commercial links with Algeria, to be *immoral*: however advantageous this trade might have been for the Italian economy, there remained the option of purchasing elsewhere those raw materials supplied by Algeria, and indeed at little extra cost. Instead of doing this, the Italian government preferred to hide the seriousness of events in Algeria, and did nothing to promote the return of democracy in that country. In my view, one has the *duty* to dissociate oneself from, or to oppose, a government that systematically violates human rights. Were most countries to have united in adopting such an attitude towards Algeria, the situation in that country might well have changed as a result.

The difference between my position and Oppenheim's therefore regards the breadth of the area within which moral judgements about foreign policy are relevant: his idea is that this area only regards a fairly limited part of the content of the national interest, whereas mine is that such an area is *as wide as* that of the national interest. Although this is a difference in quantity, it also gets transformed into a difference of quality, so to speak: Oppenheim's conclusions give statesmen a role which my conclusions attribute to world public opinion; his conclusions assign almost deterministic imperatives to statesmen (so that any ruler, once in place, is almost wholly constrained in his choices), whereas mine recognize a much wider degree of freedom of action and decision in foreign policy; his *liberate* the statesman from most of his responsibilities, whereas mine *attribute* many responsibilities to the statesman. More generally, there is a basic incompatibility between our conceptions of international relations. For Oppenheim, 'given the present state system, governments have practically no choice but to aim at the promotion of the national interest, and often little choice but to enact the single most effective policy'.[48] In my view, on the other hand, in the system of international relations in which we live (and ever more so since 1989) just about any state can fill in the content of its national interest in both rational *and* moral terms: so it was for the Serbian government over the last decade, for the Iraqi government in relation to Kuwait, for the Turkish government concerning the Kurdish question, for the French government in its policy of nuclear experimentation at Mururoa, for the Italian government on the question of immigration, and so on and so forth. The claim that the behaviour of these states in each of these cases consisted in the rational pursuit, through practical necessity, of the national interest, seems to me extremely difficult to sustain. In sum, as I suggested at the outset, my central criticism of Oppenheim concerns his misunderstanding of the nature of the international political system, which for him does not in itself carry any moral or ideological implications.[49]

On the other hand, one should recognize as a merit of Oppenheim's argument the fact that it correctly opposes the tendency to retreat into a form of moralizing. This tendency is all too easy to succumb to,[50] particularly in the field of foreign policy. History is full of moralistic proclamations which masked the pursuit of mere 'interests' – not of national interests, but of egoistic or partial or ideological interests. My own view is that this work of demystification might indeed also improve the way we reflect on moral and philosophical matters, and it is with this view in mind that I should like to conclude with a counter-proposal to the central aim set out by Oppenheim in the Preface to *The Place of Morality in Foreign Policy* – 'to convince political scientists that it is useful to avail ourselves of the concepts of rationality and national interest, taken in an objective sense, and that these concepts are indispensable for determining the place of morality in foreign affairs'.[51] My counter-proposal is that one should aim to convince philosophers that it would be useful for them not to take the national interest as an objective given but as the product of a politico-ideological construction which needs unmasking, that the way in which politicians pursue their ends itself implies a commitment to rationality, so that any discussion of the rationality of their pursuing practically necessary ends is redundant, and finally, that the analysis of international political reality ought to be considered a more complex, a more complicated, and even a more refined task than philosophers have often perceived it to be.

Notes

* Translated from the Italian by Ian Carter.

1. Luigi Bonanate, *Ethics and International Politics* (Cambridge: Polity Press, 1995), p. x.
2. Letter from Felix Oppenheim to the author, 17 July 1995.
3. This point had already been clarified by Oppenheim, in relation to Morgenthau, in *Moral Principles in Political Philosophy* (New York: Random House, 1968), pp. 109–13.
4. Luigi Bonanate, *I doveri degli stati* (Rome-Bari: Laterza, 1994).
5. Felix E. Oppenheim, *The Place of Morality in Foreign Policy* (Lexington, Mass.: Lexington Books, 1991).
6. Oppenheim, *Il ruolo della moralità in politica estera* (Milan: Angeli, 1993) – Italian translation of *The Place of Morality in Foreign Policy*.
7. Oppenheim, *Moral Principles in Political Philosophy*, p. 184. As should be clear, it is not to Oppenheim's judgement about cognitivism that I refer, but to the style of academic life that he proposes.
8. Oppenheim, *Il ruolo della moralità in politica estera*, p. 9.
9. Oppenheim, *The Place of Morality in Foreign Policy*, p. 28.
10. Oppenheim, *The Place of Morality in Foreign Policy*, p. 25.
11. The references to the bank-teller–bank-robber relation occur at pp. 27–8 and p. 38 of *The Place of Morality in Foreign Policy*. The claim that every state is a robber in the eyes of every other is made at p. 28.
12. I do not, however, make the least attempt here to discuss the justifiability either of the Iraqi attack or of the American reaction.
13. I present a systematic critique of the anarchic conception of international relations in *Ethics and International Politics*, pp. 62 *et seq.*
14. In this connection, see in particular the final chapter of *Moral Principles in Political Philosophy*.
15. Oppenheim, *The Place of Morality in Foreign Policy*, p. 15.
16. Oppenheim, *The Place of Morality in Foreign Policy*, p. 28.
17. Oppenheim, *The Place of Morality in Foreign Policy*, p. 27.
18. Oppenheim, *The Place of Morality in Foreign Policy*, p. 11.

19. Oppenheim, *The Place of Morality in Foreign Policy*, p. 40 (my emphasis). A few pages on, Oppenheim is even more explicit: 'all states must pursue their national interest out of practical necessity, not out of moral choice' (p. 43).
20. See W. David Clinton, *The Two Faces of National Interest* (Baton Rouge: Louisiana State University Press, 1994), pp. 25–49.
21. See Martha Finnemore, *National Interest in International Society* (Ithaca: Cornell University Press, 1996). See also Jutta Weldes, 'Constructing National Interest', *European Journal of International Relations*, 2, 3 (1996).
22. Alexander E. Wendt, 'Anarchy is What States Make of it: the Social Construction of Power Politics', *International Organization*, 46, 2 (1992).
23. See Oppenheim, *The Place of Morality in Foreign Policy*, pp. 5 *et seq.*
24. Oppenheim, *The Place of Morality in Foreign Policy*, p. ix.
25. See Stuart Hampshire, *Morality and Conflict* (Oxford: Blackwell, 1983), p. 152.
26. Oppenheim, *The Place of Morality in Foreign Policy*, p. 41.
27. Oppenheim, *The Place of Morality in Foreign Policy*, p. 56, my emphasis.
28. Oppenheim, *The Place of Morality in Foreign Policy*, p. 66.
29. Oppenheim, *The Place of Morality in Foreign Policy*, p. 69.
30. Oppenheim, *The Place of Morality in Foreign Policy*, pp. 69–70.
31. Oppenheim, *The Place of Morality in Foreign Policy*, pp. 18 *et seq.*
32. For some introductory remarks on the notion of deontology, cf. A. Berten, 'Déontologisme', in M. Canto-Sperber (sous la direction de), *Dictionnaire d'éthique et de philosophie morale* (Paris: Presses Universitaires de France, 1996).
33. Martha Finnemore, *National Interest in International Society*, p. 6.
34. Oppenheim, *The Place of Morality in Foreign Policy*, p. 3.
35. Michael Walzer, *Just and Unjust Wars* (New York: Basic Books, 1977), ch. 16. A good introduction to the philosophical debate about deterrence can be found in Russell Hardin, John J. Mearsheimer, Gerald Dworkin and Robert E. Goodin (eds), *Nuclear Deterrence: Ethics and Strategy* (Chicago: University of Chicago Press, 1985). The case of 'clear' danger is discussed by Terry Nardin in 'Nuclear War and the Argument from Extremity', in A. Ohen and S. Lee (eds), *Nuclear Weapons and the Future of Humanity* (Totowa: Rowman and Allanheld, 1986).
36. Walzer, *Just and Unjust Wars*, p. 255.
37. It should not be forgotten, however, that many years ago, A. Rapoport called the choice of deterrence psychopathic. Cf. *Strategy and Conscience* (New York: Harper and Row, 1964).
38. This is not only his choice: did anyone ever claim during the Cold War that appearances might turn out to be deceptive?
39. Oppenheim, *The Place of Morality in Foreign Policy*, p. 94.
40. A more systematic analysis of this problem can be found in my *Ethics and International Politics*, ch. 3.
41. From the point of view strictly of nuclear strategy, the turning point came with the signing of the INF (Intermediate-range Nuclear Forces) treaty between Reagan and Gorbachev at Washington on 8 December 1987.
42. It can be demonstrated statistically that the American nuclear potential was in fact always clearly greater than – and superior to – that of the Soviets. Is it possible that the leaders of the two countries were not aware of this?

43. Oppenheim, *The Place of Morality in Foreign Policy*, p. 92.
44. Although I happen to believe that it was immoral.
45. Oppenheim, *The Place of Morality in Foreign Policy*, p. 92.
46. This is the title of chapter 3 of *The Place of Morality in Foreign Policy*.
47. Oppenheim, *The Place of Morality in Foreign Policy*, p. 100.
48. Oppenheim, *The Place of Morality in Foreign Policy*, p. 97.
49. See Oppenheim, *The Place of Morality in Foreign Policy*, p. 25.
50. I suppose Oppenheim will say that I have succumbed to it myself.
51. Oppenheim, *The Place of Morality in Foreign Policy*, p. x.

12
Oppenheim and the National Interest

George Kateb

Felix Oppenheim has devoted his scholarly life to conceptual analysis in the service of ethical and metaethical understanding. He has illuminated some of the most important political-ethical concepts, including freedom, equality and power. And though he is sympathetic to the project of achieving for the study of politics a conceptual clarity comparable to that often found in natural science, he is admirably tentative in the face of recalcitrant complexity. He has even gone so far as to end his magisterial essay, 'The Language of Political Inquiry', with four sets of 'unresolved issues' that leave his readers with a sense of Oppenheim's own inclinations but also provide some assistance in taking issue with him.[1] This open-mindedness, despite strongly held views, makes reading him especially valuable.

I would like to examine Oppenheim's latest book, *The Place of Morality in Foreign Policy* (1991), in which he extends his method of inquiry to international relations. Here, too, he shows rigour in the pursuit of clarity. But I find that the result of his effort may be to strengthen social forces that damage his own humane commitments. I believe that his earlier work, by and large, has helped humane politics, even if the ostensible aim was clarity for the sake of clarity. This most recent book, however, achieves its clarity while leaving a larger mystification untouched. It was a marvellous decision to enter the field of international relations, a field that needs as much theoretical attention as it can get. Any practitioner in it – and I am certainly not one – must benefit from the painstaking analysis of the idea of national interest that Oppenheim provides. Indeed, any political theorist will also benefit. Yet at the risk of appearing ungrateful for the abundant instruction that I have received from the book, I must, in the spirit of Oppenheim, take issue with him.

1. The public interest

Analysis of the concept of the national interest is the central aim of *The Place of Morality in Foreign Policy*. I wish to concentrate on this concept, but first attention is due Oppenheim's treatment of the domestic equivalent of this concept: the public interest.[2] His analysis of the concept of the public interest is, in some respects, a trial run, so to speak, for the later work on the national interest. As Oppenheim develops the idea of the public interest, he establishes a number of good points, but he also makes a few moves that are questionable and that portend some trouble when he takes up the national interest. Above all, he tries, even if not with a complete consistency, to purge the idea of public interest of any distributive quality. That is, Oppenheim wishes to establish the idea that the public interest is served by policies that 'promote the welfare of the public as a whole rather than the personal welfare of each, or any, of its members'.[3] The public interest is the welfare of the public as 'collectivity', not the welfare of the public as an aggregation or collection of *individuals*.

What would it mean to promote the public interest and not promote the welfare of *any* of its members? I take it that Oppenheim is saying that the public interest can be promoted while promoting *no one's* welfare. Isn't this position odd? Oppenheim's wording makes it appear as if he believes that the public is a real entity that exists apart from all persons, and has an interest not only separate from theirs but also superior to it. If that is a correct surmise, here is the disquieting portent for the later analysis of the national interest. The danger, in both cases, is to impute real existence to an abstraction, and thereby justify the sacrifice of real persons for or to an abstraction. Am I correct, then, in my initial surmise about the meaning of Oppenheim's conceptualization of the idea of public interest? Or is it possible that, despite the words that I just quoted, the overall tendency of Oppenheim's analysis isn't a potentially dangerous reification?

I think that what causes trouble for me as I try to take in Oppenheim's notion of the public interest is that he assumes that the self-interest of each person in society is wholly selfish. If we begin with such a notion we must conclude that any limitation on selfishness is, in itself, an abridgement of self-interest. Thus, any impediment to my selfishness is an interference with my self-interest. But if we are going to talk about self-interest within the frame of the public interest, we are already in society. That means that we are social creatures who have been raised, from the start, to take others into account as we strive to attain our interests. Restraint is inherent in any notion of self-interest that a socialized or civilized person, well before adulthood, acts on. In society, any society, the notion of self-interest is entwined with a basic code or morality or sense of justice. The notion of self-interest is no more primordial than a sense of moral conduct or proper conduct.

Of course, temptations in everyone to be selfish – that is, to satisfy self-interest at the expense of others, and even, sometimes, to define one's self-interest as precisely that which penalizes others – never go away. People sometimes act on these temptations, whether criminally, or within or by means of the conventions of society. To restrain certain especially destructive temptations governments exist. The principal end of government, domestically, is to make good the deficiencies of self-restraint. It would be a terrible mistake to think, however, that fear of punishment is the only consideration that keeps people from the kinds of selfishness that lead a person to rob another of life or liberty or property, or even to try in every imaginable circumstance to be a free rider, to get away without paying one's share of public costs.

Oppenheim claims that 'most people care little about the "common good" and more about their individual and group interests'.[4] That is true, but only some of the time. Social life is full of recklessness, unaltruistic self-sacrifice, excess, and extremism of all kinds. Most people, that is, often care little about their own interests, including their economic self-interest. They have many passions. To subscribe to a one-dimensional pessimism in the name of realism is to lose one's way; one substitutes a social-science reduction for a realistic picture of social life. To claim that it is rational to be selfish when one can be, and restrained only when one must be, may be all right for economists who work with models, but not suitable for political theorists who try to uncover reality.

The public interest *is* justice, the maintenance and development of justice. Only when self-interest is defined as selfishness is self-interest seen as necessarily separate from and perhaps even in contradiction to justice. Oppenheim says that 'Justice often conflicts with utility and thereby with the public interest'.[5] But none of the great utilitarian philosophers agrees with that statement. They assume that just as most people in society habitually take the interests of others into account (at least minimally), so government as the administrator of the public interest is supposed to take everyone's interest into account. The public interest reposes on the distinction between valid self-interest and illicit selfishness. To provide justice is to protect everyone's valid self-interest. And for non-utilitarian thinkers, valid self-interest is largely defined (but not exclusively) as the possession of basic individual personal and political rights. Indeed, to have one's rights recognized is to one's interest, but it is more than self-interest. It is more than an interest of any kind because one's human status is tied to rights; and the human status isn't merely one more important interest. Then, too, if the public interest is justice, it is not at stake in every policy issue; nor does it, even when justice is at stake, dictate a particular decision in many cases but rather can be so underdetermined as to permit a wide range of contending proposals, one of which may stand temporarily for the realization of the public interest. Just recall the disputes and their resolution in the courts' adjudication of claimed rights.

Oppenheim indicates that he comes closest to Rousseau on the matter of the public interest.[6] Rousseau's general will is indeed defined as the common or public interest. But the general will is essentially distributive. It is the will of the generality when that will looks to the preservation of each citizen in basic rights as well as to the preservation of the society against both systematic internal deviation from justice and externally attempted destruction of the system of justice. When the citizen votes in the assembly, he knows that justice is what he should vote for. But this is not moral altruism: justice is to his good or to his advantage in the largest sense as well as to everyone else's. Rousseau doesn't expect altruism; he even worries that selfishness may intrude in the vote and tries to check it by various social customs and practices and other structural political provisions. He wants and plans for benevolence, good will; it isn't far from Oppenheim's sense of benevolence. The point is that what Rousseau says or implies about the distributive nature of the common interest in the good political society must be true – to some important extent – of any society where it would be appropriate to posit the existence of a public interest at all.

As his discussion makes clear, Oppenheim isn't interested in all societies, only in democracies, where the notion of public interest can be plausibly postulated. In general, however, he wants to offer purely descriptive non-normative conceptual definitions that are universally applicable.[7] But I doubt that this is a tenable aspiration for either concept, public interest or national interest. Appeals to both are, in practice, invariably normative, whatever the propriety or accuracy in any given case. They are necessarily honorific because they are solely terms of justification for conduct and policy.

In sum, Oppenheim seems driven to ascribe real existence to an abstract public interest – a non-distributive interest distinct from 'the personal welfare of each, or any, of its members' – because his theoretical predisposition requires him to define self-interest as selfishness. He then has to save the concept of public interest from an imputed universal selfishness, an imputation that isn't empirically validated but is nevertheless presented as a hard-won truth about reality. A less economistic point of view would be more true to the reality while avoiding the disadvantages of reification. At the same time, to sever the public interest from justice is to make the concept unusable in political discussion and political theory.

2.   The national interest

When we come to the analysis of the national interest, the stakes are even higher than with the public interest. The national interest – grant for the moment that it exists – can be promoted only by violence or its threat. Violence and its threat are the extreme methods of domestic policy; their use often signifies failure of either government or society. In contrast, violence and its threat are the norm for promoting the (alleged) national interest in the world of international relations. Where violence and threatened violence are normal, premature violent death and other great injuries on a large scale are a regular part of the picture. The affected interests of persons are actually or potentially huge. That in turn means that – or should mean that – moral judgement becomes urgent. What is moral judgement for, if not the gravest human interests? If there is either improper reification or mistakes about the place and kind of appropriate moral judgement, then our intellectual troubles become very serious, very risky. I hope to show that Oppenheim doesn't avoid something like improper reification in his analysis of the national interest and that the place he allows moral judgement is too small. I therefore want to make some criticisms of *The Place of Morality in Foreign Policy*; but, as I have said, this book is immensely valuable. It is a sustained and integral argument that has the power to stimulate reflection and to arouse the wish to answer Oppenheim in a spirit of respectful disagreement.

From the very words, the national interest is the interest of the nation, of the nation-state. The nation-state is an armed sovereignty that exists in a world of numerous armed sovereignties. What is the interest of the nation? Minimally, to preserve itself against foreign efforts to conquer it and then use it for the purposes of the conqueror, and sometimes to occupy it and, in occupying it, sometimes expelling or despoiling or enslaving or massacring its people. In protecting its people from conquest and the often dire effects of conquest, a nation's government protects the rights or entitlements of its people against violent attack. Of course some wars or other kinds of sustained violence have other aims than conquest or resisting conquest. But let us stay, at least for the moment, with a primitive idea of the national interest as protection against conquest and its possibly dire effects.

On such a supposition, the national interest is essentially a distributive idea. The national interest, like the public interest, is the protection of a system of fundamental personal and political rights; it is the protection of justice. The national interest is only the protection of the public interest, against the outside world. To be sure, the primary method of protection is, internationally, violence and threatened violence, whereas the public interest of a settled democratic society is characterized by much less violence and its threat. But I begin with the assumption that, despite a profound difference in normal methods of protection, the national interest is the face of the public interest turned outward. And just as the public interest must be in the interest (the highest and longest-lasting interest) of all persons, so too is the national interest. The nation-state is its people organized for constitutional purposes. The government's purposes can't be different from those of its people. The government, properly understood, is only the agent or instrument of its people. In constitutional democratic theory, it has no separate interest of its own. To think that it does is to run the risk of making the nation-state something distinct, at least partly, from the collection of persons, who are bound intergenerationally by certain constitutional understandings, and according it a superior status, a kind of reality, that it does not deserve. Once the nation-state is seen as an entity in its own right, the government tends to become its embodiment and, as such, to assign itself the same superior status. The nation-state dissolves into the state, and the state into the elite of top officials. These are the risks of adopting a non-distributive notion of the national interest, the risks of reification, that are comparable to the risks of viewing the public interest as distinct from the interests of any or all persons in society.

The national interest is the protection of the fundamental rights of all the people in society against foreign destruction. I don't deny that quite a few difficulties are attached to this position. Suppose that some rights of some people in society aren't recognized and hence not protected? Suppose that some people don't have the economic or other resources to take advantage of some of their rights? Suppose that some people are called upon to die or suffer in order that the nation-state may protect the rights of others in the same society? Each of these questions – and they all point to recurrent or structural actualities – requires and has received in numerous treatises careful and lengthy theoretical discussion. I mention them here only to indicate that I am aware that even when a country is fortunate enough to possess a constitution of personal and political rights, there may only be an imperfectly public (or common) interest, to begin with. The stakes may not be sufficiently equal for all persons. Sacrifices may be disproportionate to the stakes. An imperfect public interest, a seriously imperfect constitutional equality, may call into question whether there is a truly national interest at all. There may be only a partial interest that organizes and uses (and thus exploits) the whole society to defend itself. But the point remains that without a public interest, a domestic common interest, there can be no national interest. Like the public interest, the national interest is properly distributive.

There have been and are now only a few nation-states (or earlier, city-states) to which a national interest can be properly attributed. Naturally this doesn't mean that even nation-states with a national interest have usually been guided predominantly by the national interest – protection of the constitution of personal and political rights – in the conduct of their foreign policy. Many partial interests have been powerfully present, and have sometimes acted to the detriment of fundamental rights at home, often at the cost of the rights of people abroad. (I work with the assumption that there is a great inconsistency when a country subscribes to universalist individual rights at home and then violates these rights abroad, except when some strict necessity appears to demand that these rights not to be respected. The right of life is especially liable to be violated needlessly abroad. It is the height of irrationality to be so self-inconsistent.)

If many nation-states, then, have no national interest in the proper meaning of that term, we must still see that the claim by leaders everywhere is that their nations have a national interest and that it guides their foreign policy. The term has tremendous moral prestige. I suppose that we must say that in a manner of speaking these nations have the simulacrum of a national interest, or a grossly truncated (not merely a seriously imperfect) version of one. I mean that the very right of (or to) life, which I just mentioned, may be protected by a basically unconstitutional state, even if no other right is. The right of life may be protected not only from internal but also from external danger. The more important fact, however, is that a sizeable part of the populations of many nation-states would be better off, where well-being is measured by the extent of constitutionalism, if by some chance they could be liberated from their rulers at little cost and then governed constitutionally. Protection of their lives hardly ever requires their government to deny them their other basic rights. I certainly don't advocate a regular practice of intervention: the costs in life are generally high. However, I doubt that intervention implicates any other major principle. Many nations have an actual national interest only in an attenuated sense, if that. A true national interest is for them only a future possibility.

The national interest is distributive. What does Oppenheim think? His analysis of the public interest prepares us to expect that his notion of the national interest would be non-distributive, and our expectation is confirmed by his argument in *The Place of Morality in Foreign Policy*. He maintains that Wolfram Hanrieder captures the idea when Hanrieder says that the national interest is 'based on nondistributive values, enjoyed by society as a whole'.[8] Oppenheim specifies the constituent elements ('collective welfare goals') of the national interest: 'territorial integrity (or political sovereignty), its military security, and its economic well-being'.[9] Thus, it is to the interest of the nation that it be sufficiently militarily powerful to defend its territory and secure its economic wherewithal. I would rather describe these goals as the preconditions of a society that protects the constitutional rights of all its members, and thus has a national interest, to begin with. Put that way, there seems nothing reified in the concept. One would wish for a world in which constitutionalism didn't have to be associated with violent defence. But as long as the world is as it is, the wish will not be granted. Yet at least we can see merit in the view that there are, after all, preconditions for the systemic maintenance of the personal and political rights of all persons, and that armed defence of these rights may be necessary. The question remains, why does Oppenheim describe his concept as non-distributive?

He insists, as he also does in his analysis of the public interest, that when the state acts to defend itself it may have to sacrifice some of its members. Their interests, therefore, aren't being served; yet the state must act as it does. It must protect the whole society, the collectivity. It is certainly true that the sacrifice of life for the sake of protecting life (and other rights) is an awful paradox. Some theorists who affirm the right of life of all persons nevertheless defend mandated self-sacrifice, conscription, in arguments that are only ingenious and not convincing. They aren't convincing because Hobbes and Rousseau, say, are too deeply troubled by the matter to provide very compelling arguments. But neither of them would have called the national interest non-distributive. They both have to conclude with the suggestion or implication that on balance those who are called on to sacrifice their lives or risk such sacrifice would have been even worse off if the society they are asked to die for didn't exist. That is cold comfort; no comfort at all. But the awfulness of the predicament isn't assuaged, much less removed, by positing the national interest as non-distributive. The reification covers over the terrible cost that is often paid by viewing it as a cost to one's selfishness. To shudder at the thought of risking or losing one's life isn't selfishness. How, in any case, is the sacrifice made more palatable when the people who are asked to die are told that they die for the abstract nation rather than for the protection of the constitutional rights of others? The brutal truth is that when some die for others, or when some civilians are killed in the course of a war brought home, a minority is sacrificing itself or being compelled to sacrifice itself for the rest. The truth is distributive, if appalling.

The tendency of non-distributive notions of national interest, including Oppenheim's, is to assume that every nation-state as such deserves to exist. I know that Oppenheim doesn't put it that way. But I fail to see what other theoretical outcome is possible when the national interest is defined as a concern for territorial integrity, political sovereignty, military security, and economic well-being. If that is all the national interest is, every nation, whether its polity is autocratic, oligarchic, or democratic, will have a national interest: the same in every case. There is no way left for discriminating between nation-states. The non-distributive notion of the national interest equalizes all nation-states; it gives them the same status in the eye of the detached observer, not only in the eye of standard international law. A non-distributivist doesn't even have to follow Michael Walzer in attempting to establish the equal standing of all but the worst states on the grounds that each is a separate culture, rooted in a distinct nationality or ethnicity or religion or language or some combination of these, and entitled equally to sovereign self-determination.[10]

Posit a non-distributive stake that any nation-state can adopt, and the observer can then have no way of denying to any kind of political leadership the instantaneous and scarcely detectable shift to defining the national interest in either one or the other of two related and perhaps mutually reinforcing ways. The first way is to see the national interest as the will and ability to play the game of international relations as well as possible. This game is one of the types of pure politics. By this perspective, to have enemies becomes an almost sacred obligation. The prizes are glory (for some) and psychic gratification (for some, perhaps for most people). Psychic gratification also comes from the risks and dangers, the exhilaration of action, the treasure of accumulated experiences. The reified national interest becomes entwined with abstract or imaginary aims and ambitions. The second way is to see the national interest as the power interest of the government or state. Here I have in mind the claim that the national interest is tantamount to the strength of the state. But what that really means is that anything that serves to maintain or augment the power of a leader or elite or bureaucratic apparatus, whatever the nature of the polity, is the national interest. In reality, foreign adventures serve as a method of distracting, controlling and uniting people at home as well as gaining advantages abroad. An activist foreign policy allows the state's self-importance to metastasize. It is clear from remarks that Oppenheim scatters throughout this book that he is fully aware that a state's power interest can interfere with the national interest, as he himself conceptualizes it. Nevertheless I believe that his objections must remain untheoretical because of his insistence on a non-distributive national interest, which tends strongly to the two kinds of – shall we call it usurpation? – that both he and I dread.

Fortified by a non-distributive conception of the national interest, both kinds of elitism have the effect of making the nation-state into an individual pitted against other nation-states also converted by the imagination into individuals. Both kinds see the world of international relations as made up of homogeneous units, monads, monoliths – unitary actors. And I use the word *usurpation* because both derivatives of the non-distributive national interest that I find latent in Oppenheim's theory work to convert the people – often with their cooperation, alas – into means and resources for either the game of foreign policy or for the enhancement of the state's power interest. The end for which government exists, the protection of constitutional rights from danger, is subordinated, even when it is recognized, and the glory of the nation or the power of the upper political, military, and perhaps economic strata are substituted for that end. Society becomes an organization put at the disposal of a few; a base for their action.

Nation-states are improperly figured or conceived in the image of biological individuals. Nor is the matter helped when nation-states try to take advantage of the fact that, say, teams or corporations are seen as individuals. Why should these latter be allowed the analogy, and not nation-states? Isn't the single-minded purpose of all these entities to prevail in competition? This single-minded purpose does lend plausibility to the analogy between individuals in some circumstances (on the one hand) and teams and corporations (on the other). Teams and corporations are considered unities or legal personalities for good and putatively harmless reasons. But the metaphors are terribly misleading in regard to nation-states. As I have argued, many nation-states lack a common interest; they aren't a proper unity; they lack the overall purpose that a government as such is supposed to have. And even when there is a common interest, states pursue goals that are often cloudy, ill-defined, possibly limitless, in spite of and because of the methods of violence that are employed, while contrastingly, it is obvious that teams play to win and corporations strive for profits. The conduct of teams and corporations doesn't puzzle the observer. It is a rare nation-state, especially when it is activist, that doesn't puzzle the observer who looks to explain why it acts as it does. Even if we work with the notions of the power-game mentality and elitist partial interests, foreign policy remains obdurately opaque. It is hard to talk about the fantastic when it presents itself as rock-hard reality.

The force of Oppenheim's concept of the national interest is to make the nation-state into a single entity, like an individual, despite his awareness that a process of metaphorization lies behind this move.[11] Most analysts who make the same move do so without any awareness, like Oppenheim's, of what they are doing. But he indicates some hesitation only to dismiss it. His analysis proceeds with the postulate of the nation-state as an individual in a world of other comparable individuals – that is, other competing nation-states. In the background of Oppenheim's postulate is, of course, the social contract tradition of political theory, especially as represented by Hobbes and Locke. Both of them are given to the metaphor or analogy between individuals and nation-states (political societies). But let us see that what drives them is the desire to shore up the theoretical defensibility of the idea of a social contract between individuals who emerge from the natural condition created by civil war and who go on, with right, to found a new political society. That is, Hobbes and Locke may be said to begin with the natural condition of nation-states and then move theoretically to the natural condition of individuals. In the progression of concepts, natural freedom is attributed first to nation-states and then by analogy or metaphor to individuals; and the innovative purpose is to protect individuals, and to give them equal standing.

But the matter isn't so simple. Thinking perhaps to make room for the idea of a natural right of all individuals equally to self-preservation by taking advantage of the inherited assumption that all nation-states (and other armed political entities) have a right or moral entitlement to defend themselves, Hobbes and Locke prepare the way to shift the prestige of the idea that individuals have a right to preserve themselves – a prestige they powerfully promote – back to the right of the metaphorically or analogically individualized nation-state to do the same. Both Hobbes and Locke take it for granted that all nation-states have the right of self-defence. That is in itself a tremendous favour done to elites and leaders who look on their peoples (with popular acquiescience or approval) as a heap of material resources indispensable to the competition of nation-states. I don't wish to deny, however, that Hobbes and Locke dignify individuals by investing them with the natural right of self-preservation. The irony is that they simultaneously facilitate the sacrifice of individuals and their rights by the use of the analogy of individual and nation-state.

Let it also be said, however, that these two theorists occasionally help to undermine this analogy. Now and then in *Leviathan*, Hobbes alludes to international relations as the game of kings.[12] And Locke, at one point, places rulers and princes of independent political societies into the state of nature, rather than their peoples or the whole societies.[13] But damage is done whenever an analogy is drawn between individuals and nation-states so as to make the nation-state into an individual. I have so far pointed to the effects on the imagination of the powerful few and their theoretical supporters: the transformation of the people into a base for either the game of international relations or the imposition on the many of the particular interest of one minority or another. I believe there is an even worse effect of the analogy, and it is an effect that shows itself quite prominently in Oppenheim's book. I refer to the place that the analogy gives morality in foreign policy: no place or an incidental place. In fact, to give morality only an incidental place is precisely Oppenheim's principal purpose.

3.   Morality and the national interest

He can give morality an incidental place only because he transfers back to nation-states the right of self-preservation that theorists of rights after Locke, in the eighteenth century and later, have insisted on attributing primarily to individuals. But even Hobbes (not to mention Locke) would have found it odd to claim, as Oppenheim does, that it is a major mistake for anyone to believe that moral considerations can play a central role in assessing the foreign policy of any nation-state. I have already said that the national interest is the defence of constitutional rights of persons from danger: defence of the rights of a country's citizens from external danger and, as well, abstention to the fullest degree possible from harming the rights of citizens of other countries in the course of defending the country's own citizens. In my judgement, the national interest is an essentially moral concept; the defence of the national interest is an essentially moral enterprise. However, even if *per impossible* Oppenheim would accept my proposed definition of the national interest, he still would maintain his position on the place of morality in foreign policy. If I may ascribe a view to him, he would say that although the national interest may be defined morally as I define it, its defence against external danger isn't an undertaking to which moral considerations are applicable, except in those occasional situations where the national interest isn't at stake.

Oppenheim holds that where persons, including political actors, have no choice but to act in a certain way, they are acting under necessity and hence must be exempt from moral judgement. Acting under necessity, practical necessity, is acting when confronted with only the semblance of a choice. If one doesn't act in a certain way, one will sustain injuries that are in the quoted words of Alvin Goldman, 'too *difficult*, or too *costly*, or too *painful*'.[14] The alternative action is 'practically impossible', even if, provided one is willing to suffer terrible losses or death, it is literally possible.[15] Oppenheim adopts the Humean view that the 'strict laws of justice are suspended'[16] in cases of dire threat, scarcity or emergency – that is, in cases of such strict necessity as to outweigh strict justice.

I think that Hobbes is a better guide than Hume on this matter. In the Hobbesian conceptualization, self-preservation is a *moral* right. (Hobbes calls it a right of nature.) I would add that its defence, like that of any right, is not a non-moral act but a moral act. In defending one's life, one is doing justice to oneself when no one else is able or willing to provide it. To be sure, one's right of self-preservation, as Hobbes sees it, doesn't establish a corresponding duty in anyone who is similarly threatened, either by oneself or by a common danger. All persons have the same right, but there is no agency to preserve them all. Furthermore, in injuring or killing another in order to preserve oneself one isn't administering justice to that person. He doesn't deserve what I've done to him; but I have to do it. If calling self-preservation an act of justice to oneself is to go too far – though I don't think it is – we should at least call it a morally allowable act. The upshot is that necessity must so to speak clear itself at the bar of justice or morality by securing permission to act in accordance with the imperatives of self-preservation. Necessity must really be necessity, and one retains a feeling of moral obligation to others *in foro interno*, even if one must injure or kill them. One should always feel bound by a desire that morality's obligation 'should take place', even when to follow morality would pose a terrible threat to one's self-preservation.[17]

Hobbes refuses to sever necessity and morality. In any case, how could the use of violence ever be a morally irrelevant act, no matter how implausible or supererogatory the alternative? (The law takes an interest even in 'justifiable homicide'.) A good indication that one feels obliged *in foro interno* even when one injures or kills another *in foro externo* is that if not in the midst of desperation, then afterwards, if one has prevailed, one feels regret or remorse. The moral (or morally allowable) act is totally undesirable. In the midst of desperate circumstances antagonists preserve a moral innocence or guiltlessness, but only provided that both are faced with a situation in which one or the other must die or suffer grievously, if both are not to do so.

Individuals face dire necessity when the protection of government (or some other armed entity) has lapsed, either because of civil war or foreign invasion or criminality. Individuals find themselves in the natural condition or state of nature. Each must become his own protector, and does so by moral right. Yet the normal expectation is that individuals will rarely if ever find themselves in a state of nature. Good governments will protect them in their rights, and firstly in their right of life. But the constant condition of nation-states is the natural condition. There is no authoritative power to which nation-states can appeal for protection. The condition of nation-states is 'essentially anarchical'.[18] Not only does Oppenheim claim that in a condition of anarchy, morality is irrelevant except incidentally, he also suggests that what holds for individuals in a condition of nature also holds for nation-states, just because nation-states are analogous to individuals. And since nation-states are always unable to leave the anarchy of the condition of nature, they are permanently located in the realm of necessity. Even if Oppenheim were to grant the point that necessity must face the bar of justice, he would still insist on the permanent presence of the necessity. In a world of nation-states, each one of them supposedly knows nothing but necessity, except incidentally. They can rarely afford to be moral in their specific policies abroad, even if their overall purpose is the moral one of protecting a domestic system of rights.

Is it true that necessity is the best word to describe the usual condition of nation-states? I don't think so. The alleged necessity confronting nation-states is nothing like the necessity that individuals would face in the natural condition. Individuals are more or less equal in power and are therefore equal in vulnerability. The danger to their self-preservation is equal. Individuals feel real fear, suffer real injury, and die real deaths; this tragedy can end only if individual survivors first band together as a warring group, and then initiate a settled society. But how can an analyst attribute such desperation to nation-states? Nation-states are radically unequal in power, for one thing. That point is obvious. The heart of the matter is that the analogy between individuals and nation-states does perhaps its greatest theoretical mischief when we are asked to transfer the tragic sense of necessity that individuals would face in the natural condition of anarchy to nation-states in a condition of anarchy. (I know that Oppenheim doesn't speak of tragedy but his notion of necessity, of having to act in a certain way because the alternative is too painful or costly, implicitly relies on it.) We are asked to think tragic thoughts about the fate of nation-states, and amidst the tragic situation of their necessity, we are told to exempt their specific policies from moral considerations, except incidentally. Leviathans and behemoths, and middle-sized powers, too, are accorded the standing of desperate, fragile, and necessitous equal individuals.

Closer to the truth (even if still a gross characterization) is the view that the anarchy of nation-states is not a natural condition but an artifice, which is brought into being not by prudence that arms itself to protect both the preconditions of individual rights and the rights themselves, but, as I have already mentioned, by the desire of numerous elites to secure instead the preconditions of their great games or their selfish interests. Violence and its threat aren't employed because of the serious stakes; violence and its threat make the situation of anarchy, which is intrinsically unserious internationally, a serious, mortally serious, matter. The stakes are invented to suit the capacities. The possession of the weapons of war disposes any government to find occasions to use them where possible. What self-respect would a political elite have if its arms were confined to the police power at home? The armed defence of people's fundamental rights, even where they are recognized, is secondary or incidental or even a pretext. The readiness to sacrifice individuals is steady and the actual sacrifice recurrent and inevitable, not only in the case of comparatively powerful nation-states but with lesser powers as well, whenever a tempting opportunity arises or is forced into being.

International relations are typically the realm of surplus, not necessity: surplus energy, too often deriving from the compliance of the people, and put to ambitions that impair the rights of the people by risking and wasting their lives and resources. How rarely in foreign policy do even constitutional governments aim above all to fulfil every government's obligation to protect constitutional rights or even what I have called the preconditions that Oppenheim formulates as the only goals – namely, territorial integrity, political sovereignty, military security and economic well-being.[19] There wouldn't be much foreign policy if all that nation-states ever did was pursue that aim. But leaders and elites, and ordinary persons, too, love the international anarchy that supplies the setting in which drama and struggles abound. They may be said to want war. They love their supposed necessity even when they get themselves to believe that it is necessity and not what it often is – freely chosen adventure.

The mere fact that a government exists and is armed inclines observers, including Oppenheim, to impute equal standing (and hence agency on behalf of national interest) to that government with all others, no matter how destructive of constitutional rights it is at home or abroad or both. Analysts should rather derive the national interest from the prior existence of a constitutional government.

In sum, Oppenheim's non-distributive and non-moral idea of the national interest works disquieting effects by itself, and these effects are aggravated by three further elements: the analogy of individual and nation-state; the questionable attribution of necessity to the world of nation-states; and the severance of necessity, even where genuine, from moral judgement.

Felix Oppenheim wants to substitute a hard head for a soft (and sometimes harmful) heart in our thought about international relations.[20] He wants to demystify. He wants sensible interests to rule. Yet in the sincerity of his intentions he has given countenance, in some respects, to the unbridled and self-destructive fantasy-projects of leaders, elites and people alike.

Notes

1. Felix E. Oppenheim, 'The Language of Political Inquiry: Problems of Clarification', in Fred I. Greenstein and Nelson W. Polsby (eds), *Handbook of Political Science*, vol. 1 (Reading, Mass.: Addison-Wesley, 1975), pp. 328–9.
2. Felix E. Oppenheim, *The Place of Morality in Foreign Policy* (Lexington, Mass.: Lexington Books, 1991), p. 11.
3. Felix E. Oppenheim, *Political Concepts: a Reconstruction* (Chicago: University of Chicago Press, 1981), p. 132.

4. Oppenheim, *Political Concepts*, p. 136.
5. Oppenheim, *Political Concepts*, p. 129.
6. Oppenheim, *Political Concepts*, pp. 147–9.
7. Oppenheim, *Political Concepts*, pp. 150–76.
8. Oppenheim, *The Place of Morality in Foreign Policy*, p. 13.
9. Oppenheim, *The Place of Morality in Foreign Policy*, p. 11.
10. See the article cited by Oppenheim: Michael Walzer, 'The Moral Standing of States: a Response to Four Critics', *Philosophy and Public Affairs*, 9 (1980), pp. 209–29.
11. Oppenheim, *The Place of Morality in Foreign Policy*, pp. 5–7.
12. Thomas Hobbes, *Leviathan*, ed. C. B. Macpherson (Baltimore: Penguin, 1968), ch. 11, p. 161 and ch. 29, p. 375.
13. John Locke, *Two Treatises of Government*, ed. Peter Laslett, rev. edn (New York: New American Library Mentor Books, 1963), ch. 2, sect. 14, p. 317.
14. Oppenheim, *The Place of Morality in Foreign Policy*, p. 26.
15. Oppenheim, *The Place of Morality in Foreign Policy*, p. 27.
16. David Hume, *An Enquiry Concerning the Principles of Morals*, ed. L. A. Selby-Bigge, 2nd edn (Oxford: Clarendon, 1902), p. 186.
17. Hobbes, *Leviathan*, ch. 15, p. 215.
18. Oppenheim, *The Place of Morality in Foreign Policy*, p. 23.
19. Oppenheim, *The Place of Morality in Foreign Policy*, p. 11.
20. Oppenheim, *The Place of Morality in Foreign Policy*, p. 100.

Part III
Coda

13
Oppenheim in Italy: a Memoir*
Norberto Bobbio

I first heard about Felix Oppenheim from my friend and colleague Alessandro Passerin d'Entrèves, who held the chair in 'Doctrine of the State' at Turin University and was simultaneously giving a course at Yale in the United States. As I see from the first letter in my long and continuous correspondence with Oppenheim, dated 26 October 1963, d'Entrèves had spoken to him about our Institute of Political Science, and had made him all the more keen to participate in our discussions. He looked forward to meeting me the following year in Turin, and I answered him on 6 November thanking him for choosing Turin as the first port of call in his teaching visit to Italy. I also expressed my admiration for his excellent knowledge of Italian – the more so, I added, as I had never really managed to learn English properly. Finally, I told him that I had just received his recent book on freedom,[1] which both d'Entrèves and I wished to make known in Italy, albeit for different reasons.

The organization of Oppenheim's Turin seminar took longer than expected, partly because of the so-called 'lentocracy' of the Italian public administration, and did not in fact take place until the period from March to May 1966. It turned out to be rather more than a seminar, and consisted in eight meetings with around twenty students, some of whose names Oppenheim still recalls. In the meantime, our first meeting had taken place, together with d'Entrèves, in Turin in July 1964, after which Oppenheim wrote to me, this time in French: 'Je suis encore plus enthousiasmé par l'idée de séjourner à Turin et de participer à vos travaux.'

The University of Turin, and in particular the Faculty of Law, was the first in Italy to open the way to neo-empiricist philosophy, thanks above all to the Centre for Methodological Studies, which brought together academics from such diverse disciplines as mathematics, physics, economics, law and sociology to discuss problems of common interest, initially those arising from our reading of the *Encyclopedia of Unified Science*. In this context, and thanks partly to the presence of d'Entrèves, who acted as a sort of *trait-d'union* between the Italian and English-speaking philosophical cultures, the courses I taught in jurisprudence differed from traditional courses in that discipline in as much as they concentrated on analysis of the fundamental terms of legal theory. This was especially true of the seminars restricted to around twenty students. A book like *Dimensions of Freedom* seemed almost purposely written to support and encourage us in this teaching.

During the summer vacation, which I usually spent in the Val d'Aosta mountains, I wrote a long letter to Oppenheim (dated 31 August) in which I gave him some first comments on his book. I asked some questions of clarification and he answered patiently with a letter dated 13 September, expanding on the issues on which I had raised doubts. Our difference basically turned on two points I was unconvinced about or found obscure: his distinction between negative and positive duties and his definition of power.

I see from a letter dated 14 February 1965 that the seminar, which we had first talked about two years earlier, was to start on 4 March, there being 'one seminar a week, which would take us through to 13 May'. Something I had completely forgotten is that he was also to hold a lecture course on American political science. I encouraged him in this endeavour, saying 'it seems an excellent idea'. As if this were not enough, in the same letter I referred to an invitation from the Centre for Methodological Studies to hold a lecture on a subject of his own choosing, and I introduced him to the Centre with the following words: 'For the last few years in Turin there has been a Centre for methodological studies which organizes lectures, meetings and conferences. To this centre we owe the recent introduction into Italian philosophy of a good dose of empiricism and common sense.'

Together with a letter of 5 December 1963, Oppenheim had sent me some of his earlier writings, the first of which, in chronological order, was 'Outline of a Logical Analysis of Law' (1944). This provided confirmation – if confirmation was still needed – of the affinities between our studies regarding both subject matter and method.

The Italian translation of *Dimensions of Freedom* was published by Feltrinelli as part of a distinguished book series called 'Facts and Ideas'. The volume contained a long preface by Giulio Preti,[2] which placed the author and his work 'within the philosophical and cultural context of logical empiricism'. Preti gave an account of this intellectual movement – of the difficulties it had encoutered in a country as dominated as Italy was by idealistic or spiritualistic philosophies, and of those of its supporters who applied the analytical method to the analysis of moral concepts. He provided an extensive examination of 'explicative definitions', citing Carnap and Hempel, saying that Oppenheim's book represented a deft application of this method to the definition of the concept of freedom, and emphasizing the value-neutrality of Oppenheim's definition. He suggested that the apparent aridity of the analytical style was redeemed by the beauty and elegance of the analysis presented, and that contrary to what happens in most theorizing on the subject, 'no political line emerges' from the work. Mentioning the Weberian thesis of *Wertfreiheit*, Preti reaffirmed the cognitive rather than evaluative nature of the scientific approach, and thus the lack of any intended 'persuasive effect'. In a research project like Oppenheim's, 'one does not aim to construct a political theory, but only a suitable vocabulary for a theory of this kind that aspires to be scientific, rational and empirical'.[3] He agreed with the author in his claim that a meaningful value-disagreement depends on agreement on what it is one disagrees about, and in this connection recalled Stevenson's well-known distinction between disagreement in belief and disagreement in attitude:[4] 'it is pointless to discuss the value of freedom (whether or not it should be considered a good) until we are in agreement about its actual meaning'.[5]

Preti's preface had an explicit, precise and polemical aim within the Italian philosophical community; from his point of view, the vast majority of the members of that unsocially sociable community displayed a disgracefully unscientific, humanities-oriented mentality. He was fundamentally committed to the view that a favourable disposition towards scientific research is itself based on a value – the value of science itself – and he contrasted the 'civilization of letters' with the 'civilization of science' found in more developed countries, saying that 'the only value left intact in the contemporary world crisis of values is the value of science'.[6] In the apologetic fervour of his defence of value-neutrality, Preti even went as far as to deride such 'ill-fated foolishness' as the 'religion of liberty' or the 'religion of democracy' that infest the impoverished culture of our country (and not only our country).[7]

The immoderate style of this preface, vitiated by rhetorical passages denouncing the rhetoric of others, was not such as to please our 'arid' author. In his brief preface to the second Italian edition (which came out in 1982), Oppenheim acknowledged that Preti had set out 'clearly' the main arguments of his book, but also went on to explain that his aim had been to distinguish between empirical and normative proposi- tions about social freedom and related terms, contrary to Preti's claim that the descriptive concepts he had defined 'should be used to describe facts and to state laws rather than to form valuations'.[8] He also contested Preti's classification of his research as 'positivistic', and as fitting within the tradition of neopositivism, of logical empiricism and of behaviourism – schools of thought that were by now surely too outdated to have justified republishing a work after almost twenty years. He did not deny having been influenced by some of the Vienna Circle philosophers, but he certainly did not consider himself, or at least he no longer considered himself, a behaviourist. After expressing disagreement with a few other of Preti's claims, he concluded that 'overall, the book fits in well with the contemporary thesis in the philosophy of science that there is no clear separation between ob- servational terms and theoretical terms, and that facts do not exist independently of theory'. This view was perfectly compatible with the claim on which he and Preti agreed: that there is a distinction between descriptive and normative concepts, and thus between facts and values. He called his own research a kind of 'analytic reconstructivism', which was opposed both to 'extreme conceptual relativism' and to 'positivist reductionism'.[9]

The debate over Oppenheim's book had only just begun. In a letter of 6 August 1964, Uberto Scarpelli,[10] a strong defender of the analytical method in legal philosophy and one my pupils at that first Turin seminar I mentioned earlier, told me that he had written a critical review article on *Dimensions of Freedom* and on Preti's preface, to be published in the journal *Rivista di filosofia*. Having received the manu- script, I wrote him a letter on 9 September 1964 in which I strongly and openly disagreed with him. I told him that I had been struck by his comment because I had not reacted to the book in the same way, and I believed that the content of the book left both his reaction and his critical analysis completely unjustified. Oppenheim was not, as the review made him seem, 'a cynic; a realist of the worst kind, for whom one political regime is as good as another; a sort of new Thrasymachus'. Oppenheim, I continued, had never addressed the question of the best form of government; he had simply limited himself to stating that, given a descriptive definition of social freedom, there is no regime con- taining only freedom and no regime containing only unfreedom.[11] I added that this conclusion seemed to me perfectly correct and that I did not believe Scarpelli's arguments succeeded in refuting it. I shall not dwell on the rest of my indignant, or rather, angry sermon of four densely packed pages.

Scarpelli answered me in a letter dated 18 October 1964, apologizing for the delay in replying, having had to reflect on my objections. He explained that if he had committed the crime of excessive aggression, it was a crime without malice. He had meant to be lively but had instead come across as nasty; he had meant to jab with a foil but had instead hit out with a stick. His unintentional sourness was a reaction less to Oppenheim's book than to Preti's preface, 'with its sharp sarcasm about the religion of liberty and democracy'. If he was to be condemned, he said, continuing to use the metaphor of the judge (his own profession previous to that of university lecturer), he asked that this serious provocation be considered an excuse. Scarpelli had always been worried by the accusation that logical positivism showed a lack of political commitment. He concluded with a profession of faith: 'Perhaps, living outside the world of religious symbols and emotions, I nevertheless have a religious temperament which I vent with the ambiguities and confusions of a religion of liberty, making this word my religious symbol and latching onto it with my religious emotions.'

When Scarpelli's review appeared in the *Rivista di filosofia*,[12] I informed Oppenheim in a letter of 14 February 1965, telling him that Scarpelli's criticisms seemed to me 'completely mistaken'. I became convinced that it would be useful to go public with our disagreement and to open a debate in the same journal. I invited Oppenheim to participate, and added: 'When you read Scarpelli's review you will see that unfortunately the primary cause of his irritation is Preti's preface. As you may remember, when we met in Turin we predicted that this preface would not have done the book much good, even though, personally, I didn't dislike it.'

The public debate appeared in the third 1965 issue (July–September) of the *Rivista di filosofia*, which in the same year had carried an article by Oppenheim called *Scelta razionale e fini politici* (rational choice and political ends), written when he was visiting the Institute of Political Science at Turin University. The debate was given the title 'Freedom as a Fact and as a Value', and apart from Scarpelli and myself, the participants included d'Entrèves, who completely agreed with Scarpelli. Oppenheim himself wound the debate up,[13] concentrating in particular on the criticisms of his two adversaries. He explained once more that 'an adequate empirical language is a fundamental requirement for the resolution of both empirical and normative problems',[14] and concluded by turning to an example that had proved particularly contentious: 'Instead of trumpeting that there is more freedom in Italy today than under Mussolini', he said, 'we should be more precise, and say that Italians today have more freedom of speech (with respect to their government) and less freedom to dispose of their possessions (given the higher levels of taxation and more social legislation, which are, moreover, generally considered to be a good thing)'.[15]

A few years later, Oppenheim published a new book called *Moral Principles in Political Philosophy*[16] and sent me a copy. In a letter of 29 August 1968 (the first in which we abandoned the polite form of address in favour of the familiar form), I thanked him and pointed out that the book's subject matter was particularly topical, not just for me but for Italian philosophers in general, given that on d'Entrèves' initiative we were discussing a project for the reform of the political science faculties which would introduce courses specifically on political philosophy (a discipline that was not yet formally recognized in Italy), analogous to the philosophy of law courses traditionally taught in the law faculties.

Over the last few years, d'Entrèves and I had been diligently attending the Paris meetings of the *Institut de philosophie politique*, the president of which was Professor George Davy and the general secretary our common friend Raymond Polin. Oppenheim was himself a member and occasionally participated in the Institute's meetings, one of which had indeed been devoted to the nature of *la philosophie politique*.

The first to hold a chair in political philosophy in Italy was d'Entrèves himself, at the political science faculty at Turin University, and to mark the creation of the chair, a conference was held at Bari (11–13 May, 1971) on 'Tradition and Novelty in Political Philosophy', where I gave a paper on 'Some Possible Relations between Political Philosophy and Political Science'. The paper made use of Oppenheim's above-mentioned book, which deals with this question at various points. Of the four meanings I attributed to political philosophy as it had been understood in recent debates – the theory of the good society; the problem of the justification of power and political obligation; the nature of the political; political language and the methodology of political science – the meaning attributed to it by Oppenheim in his subtle, historically documented analysis corresponded to the fourth. Oppenheim's view was that ethical and political philosophy is related to ethics and politics in the same way as the philosophy of science is related to science. One could also call the philosophy of ethics 'metaethics', in order to distinguish it from normative ethics. He explained that '[m]etaethics of politics does not itself propound moral principles but makes statements *about* them – their meaning, function, and justification'.[17] He distinguished three different kinds of metaethics – intuitionism, naturalism and noncognitivism – and illustrated these with examples taken from the history of political thought, from Plato to the present day, and he concluded by professing himself a convinced non-cognitivist in the modern tradition of Max Weber, 'perhaps the most outspoken noncognitivist among social scientists before the first World War'.[18] The last chapter was devoted to 'refuting' accusations to the effect that non-cognitivism borders on irrationalism or relativism.

The opportunity of producing an Italian translation of this second book was not to be missed, all the more since Oppenheim had in the meantime made other trips to Italy and had frequently been invited to other Italian universities. In the same letter as that mentioned above, where I thanked him for his book, I mentioned the proofs of a translation of one of his essays on equality, which was to come out in the *Rivista di filosofia*.

The translation of *Moral Principles* was published in 1971, by Il Mulino, with the title *Etica e filosofia politica*. The task of introducing the book was given to Uberto Scarpelli, who was by now making a name for himself as one of the most convinced and hard-nosed defenders of the analytical method as applied to legal philosophy.

In his long introduction, Scarpelli first set out clearly and concisely the main principles of non-cognitivism based on the 'great division', which he saw as implying that only descriptive propositions can be said to be true or false and that there is a logical gap between the descriptive and prescriptive functions of language. In a second part, which was less expositional and more critical, he claimed to share Oppenheim's position, but only on one condition: that this position itself be considered a prescriptive, ethical position, and therefore as such neither true nor false. He also made a point of distinguishing his own political position from Oppenheim's liberal-democratic individualism. It seemed to him that despite Oppenheim's continued attempts to reaffirm his value-neutrality, he nevertheless demonstrated a certain loyalty to American ideals. Scarpelli himself preferred to include 'a socialist dimension' in his own prescriptive ethic. In any case, he concluded by emphasizing the importance of this 'lucid, stimulating and provocative' book as a healthy reaction to the wave of irrationalism typical of the militant student movement of the time and adding, with a polemical reference to the promoters of an *Italia civile*[19] (an allusion to me), that we should not give up the fight.

My impression is that this book had less impact than *Dimensions of Freedom*, though I am not able to back up this impression with hard facts. In any case, Oppenheim was by now very well known in Italy, and his writings had been appropriated by an Italian cultural movement which we called the 'neo-Enlightenment', formed in the years after the war in opposition to the dominant philosophies of the time.[20] Among foreign philosophers, we considered Oppenheim one of our movement's most influential representatives. Proof of this can be found in the fact that, when Nicola Matteucci and I decided, with the help of Gianfranco Pasquino, to compile a dictionary of politics (no dictionary of this kind yet existing in Italy), the only foreign author invited to contribute (with the exception of the well-known German historian Karl D. Bracher, who was assigned the entry on 'national socialism') was Oppenheim, to whom we entrusted three fundamental entries: 'justice', 'freedom', and 'equality'.[21] In the introduction, I explained how the words used in political language come from ordinary language, that the former retains all the vagueness of the latter, and that this was one of the reasons why political science had until now failed to be rigorous enough to fix and impose the meanings of its most common terms in a univocal and universally accepted way. This first Italian dictionary of politics could indeed have appropriated the Italian motto with which Oppenheim began his book on freedom: *per metter ordine al gran disordine*.[22]

My last formal meeting with Oppenheim took place on 27 April 1993, at a seminar on the Italian translation of his latest book *The Place of Morality in Foreign Policy*, published in 1991.[23] The translation was first proposed by the Paolo Farneti Centre for Political Science, directed at the time by Luigi Bonanate, and the book was published by Franco Angeli as *Il ruolo della moralità in politica estera*. Oppenheim had sent me a copy fresh from the press, with a letter dated 7 May 1991, advising me to read only the introduction and the conclusion, and then, perhaps, chapters 3, 4 and 5. He hoped an Italian translation might be possible.

I read the book that summer, and it puzzled me somewhat. On 10 August I wrote him a long letter from Cervinia in which I expressed great surprise at finding not a single reference to the position generally known in European political philosophy as 'reason of state', at least from Machiavelli and Guicciardini onwards. I pointed out that it was true not only for Oppenheim but also for reason-of-state theorists that the state, as an agent in international law, has its reasons – its own 'rationality', understood as instrumental rationality – from which derives the often scrupulously followed principle that 'the ends justify the means'. This form of rationality cannot be subjected to moral judgements, according to reason-of-state theorists, because it is based on different criteria, the most important of these being the principle that *salus rei publicae suprema lex*, a classic formulation of which is to be found in a famous passage in Machiavelli's *Discorsi*. It seemed to me that the 'national interest' played the same role in Oppenheim's reasoning as that played by the *salus rei publicae* in the writings of the reason-of-state theorists. I asked him if his motive in not referring to the theory of reason of state was that he held it to be too obvious to be worth mentioning, or that he disagreed about the similarity I had hypothesized between the old theory and his own. He answered in a letter of 25 August, admitting that there was an affinity between the version of realism he defended and the theory of 'reason of state' and recognizing that he ought to have made the connection more explicit. At the same time, he pointed out that the reason-of-state theorists interpreted the principle of *salus rei publicae* morally, whereas his view was that moral injunctions to pursue the national interest were irrelevant because statesmen have practically no choice other than to do so. He insisted that a state's pursuit of the national interest was a practical necessity and therefore that we had no reason for judging it to be right or wrong.

As well as our seminars in Turin, I shall never forget another meeting towards the end of the 1960s, during one of the periodic trips I took to the US in those years – when I was warmly welcomed by Oppenheim and his wife Sulamite at their house in Amherst. I have a pleasant, vivid memory of a walk we took to some nearby woods on the morning of the day after my arrival. We arrived at the top of a hill, where there was a tower that served as a lookout for forest fires. We made our way up to meet the lookout guard, and Felix stopped to converse with him for a while. I have never forgotten this episode, because in a country like Italy, where fires break out every summer in its few remaining forests, I have never come across a tower like the one I saw that day. Felix has often said, both in person and in his letters, that he loves our country and that he is always very happy to return here, despite my attempts to dissuade him from an excessive degree of admiration. In one of my letters I tell him that I have just been elected Dean of Faculty – notwithstanding my efforts to the contrary – and I confess that I am rather worried, because Italy 'is the world's most disorganized country' and is thus the sort of place 'where a Dean might be forced, if necessary, to do the work of a porter'. I think he is well aware of these problems but, as all who know him will agree, he is just too polite to let it show.

Notes

* Translated from the Italian by Ian Carter.
 1. Felix E. Oppenheim, *Dimensions of Freedom: an Analysis* (New York: St. Martin's Press, 1961). First edition in Italian, *Dimensioni della libertà*, trans. Alberto Pasquinelli and Reima Rossini, with a preface by Giulio Preti (Milan: Feltrinelli, 1964). Second Italian edition, with author's preface (trans. Libero Scoto), 1982. I shall cite from the second edition.
 2. Giulio Preti (1911–72), an Italian philosopher and historian of philosophy, is best know for his books *Idealismo e positivismo* (Milan: Bompiani, 1943) and *Praxis ed empirismo* (Turin: Einaudi, 1957).
 3. Preti, Preface to Oppenheim, *Dimensioni della libertà*, p. xxvi.
 4. Charles L. Stevenson, *Ethics and Language* (New Haven: Yale University Press, 1944), pp. 1–4.
 5. Preti, Preface to Oppenheim, p. xxvii.
 6. Preti, Preface to Oppenheim, p. xxix.
 7. Preti, Preface to Oppenheim, pp. xxv–xxvii. The phrase 'religion of liberty' comes from Croce. Cf. Benedetto Croce, *History as the Story of Liberty* (London: Allen and Unwin, 1941).
 8. Oppenheim, Preface to the second edition of *Dimensioni della libertà*, p. xxxi.
 9. Oppenheim, Preface to the second edition of *Dimensioni della libertà*, p. xxxiv
10. Uberto Scarpelli (1924–93) was an Italian legal philosopher and author of *Filosofia analitica, norme e valori* (Milan: Comunità, 1962), *Che cos'è il positivismo giuridico* (Milan: Comunità, 1965) and *L'etica senza verità* (Bologna: Il Mulino, 1982).
11. This claim, which sparked Scarpelli's reaction, is defended at pp. 105–7 of *Dimensions of Freedom* (pp. 231–3 of the Italian translation).
12. Uberto Scarpelli, 'La dimensione normativa della libertà', *Rivista di filosofia*, 55 (1964), pp. 449–67.
13. The contributions by myself, Scarpelli, Passerin d'Entrèves and Oppenheim are published in a note called 'Libertà come fatto e come valore', *Rivista di filosofia*, 3 (1965), pp. 335–54.
14. Oppenheim, in 'Libertà come fatto e come valore', p. 350.
15. Oppenheim, in 'Libertà come fatto e come valore', p. 353.
16. Oppenheim, *Moral Principles in Political Philosophy* (New York: Random House, 1968); second edition author's postscript, 1975. Italian translation by Maria Carla Galavotti: *Etica e filosofia politica*, with an introduction by

Uberto Scarpelli entitled 'La "grande divisione" e la filosofia politica' (Bologna: Il Mulino, 1971).

17. Oppenheim, *Moral Principles in Political Philosophy*, p. 17.
18. Oppenheim, *Moral Principles in Political Philosophy*, p. 164.
19. *Italia civile* is the title of a collection of essays I originally published in 1964 (1986 edition, Florence: Passigli) about major anti-Fascist Italian thinkers and political activists. The phrase subsequently came to be used as a slogan for Italian liberal democratic values.
20. For an anthology of writings by members of this movement, see Mirella Pasini and Daniele Rolando (eds), *Il neoilluminismo italiano. Cronache di filosofia (1953–62)* (Milan: Il Saggiatore, 1991).
21. *Dizionario di politica*, directed by N. Bobbio and N. Matteucci and edited by G. Pasquino (Turin: Utet, 1976, second edition, 1983).
22. Domenico Cimarosa, *Il Matrimonio Segreto*, cited in *Dimensions of Freedom*, p. 3.
23. *The Place of Morality in Foreign Policy* (Lexington, Mass.: Lexington Books, 1991).

14
Afterthoughts

Felix E. Oppenheim

Having been given this space by the editors, I want first of all to thank Ian Carter and Mario Ricciardi most warmly for their idea of this volume – a total surprise for me – and for having realized it in so stimulating a way. I am also very grateful to all the contributors who have provided so much food for thought. A number of them have chosen to deal specifically with topics which have been of concern to me in my own writings and developed them in new directions. This gives me a welcome opportunity for re-examination and clarification.

1.   Conceptual reconstruction

I have attempted to reconstruct some of the basic political concepts – that is, to provide them with descriptive definitions in order to make them available for fruitful communication even among persons or groups with different normative views. This may be a reason why I have been branded a logical positivist, most explicitly by Giulio Preti and Uberto Scarpelli (as mentioned by Norberto Bobbio in his contribution to this volume). Terence Ball agrees in a milder way that 'there is a sense in which the label fits [me]' (p. 23).[1] His – flattering – reason is that logical positivists prize 'precision, conceptual clarity, and cogency of argument' (p. 23). These, however, are qualities displayed by other philosophical movements as well. Am I then a lone survivor of a movement by now of merely historical interest?

I do not find in my writings any traces of the main tenets of logical positivism, operationalism and radical empiricism. Operationalism was the reductionist view that scientific concepts, to be meaningful, must be definable in terms designating directly and intersubjectively observable conditions, in the social sciences observable human behaviour (behaviourism). None of the proposed defining expressions of basic political concepts do meet such conditions, nor could they. They are made up of terms which are themselves theoretical, such as 'influencing', 'preventing', 'causing', 'rational', 'collective welfare'. It is now generally agreed that there are no 'brute facts', hence no 'observation terms', but that every term is a 'theory laden' linguistic construction.

Similarly, empiricism in the positivist sense held that theoretical statements are meaningful only if they are directly, or at least indirectly, derivable from 'observation statements' about sense experience, so that 'truth would mirror reality'. Again, the 'correspondence theory of truth' has long been abandoned, since even assertions closest to experience must use theoretical terms and are therefore themselves theoretical constructions. Strict empiricism would have to rule out as meaningless most, if not all, scientific theories, and also all moral judgements, as the early logical positivists in fact did. I surely do not consider sentences expressing moral convictions devoid of meaning. I merely deny that intrinsic moral principles have *cognitive* meaning, but agree with the metaethical non-cognitivists that their meaning is *expressive* of moral attitudes. Ethical cognitivists sometimes consider this metaethical view as positivistic (mistakenly so, since logical positivists discarded all morality as devoid of any meaning).

There is one idea I did take over from the logical positivists: the separability of 'facts' and 'values' on the *conceptual* level. I have proposed to define concepts such as power, freedom, equality, public and national interest, not operationally, but descriptively, without the use of valuational notions – unlike, for example, George Kateb, who defines the notion of national interest in terms of justice (to be discussed later). I have also tried to disconnect the concepts themselves from their valuational connotations, unlike, for example, the advocates of 'freedom from want'. To that effect, such key concepts must be *reconstructed*, that is, provided with explicative definitions which might diverge from ordinary language. Reconstructions, like all definitions, are not true or false, since they are linguistic stipulations. They are nevertheless objective, in the sense that they can be assessed by objective standards of suitability for both empirical and normative inquiry.

Ball denies that 'the critical reconstruction of political concepts [can] be purely descriptive and normatively neutral' (p. 31). I agree that the very purpose of reconstructing political concepts is to '*change* the way we think about some concepts [like] "power" or "equality" or "freedom"' (p. 30; my italics). To take the example to which Ball refers: I propose to use the concept of freedom only in Berlin's sense of negative liberty (non-interference by other agents) and to avoid the expression 'positive freedom' altogether, because it means something different, or rather because it has many different meanings such as *acting* in certain ways (e.g. rendering service to the community) or making certain things (e.g. a minimum standard of living) available to all equally. This linguistic proposal about how to *think* about freedom seems to me valuationally neutral. It puts me 'squarely in the camp of [the] "negative" libertarian' (p. 30) only in the sense that I adopt the *terminology* of negative freedom. I do not provide the reader with any clue (not even between the lines) as to whether I am an *advocate* of *laissez-faire* liberalism or of welfare state socialism or of communitarianism. 'To bring about changes in the meaning of freedom and equality is to alter how we think about ... these concepts' (p. 31), yes, but not how we 'act' with them (p. 31).

This does not entail aloofness from political conflict. Interest in conceptual analysis is perfectly compatible with being politically committed. I happen to be in favour of governmental limitation of certain personal freedoms for the sake of egalitarian welfare, hence to oppose the *politics* of 'negative libertarianism', but also of communitarianism – as Ball correctly *guesses*. These merely biographical facts are of no importance in connection with the topic of conceptual analysis.

Nor does reconstruction have anything to do with *de*construction, accurately denounced by Ball as 'trendy' (p. 22). I agree with Ball that 'politics is, in important and ineliminable ways, a linguistically or conceptually constituted activity' (p. 21); but the language of politics is, like all language, an *instrument* for the purpose of communicating and gaining knowledge of the extra-linguistic world. For the deconstructionists, language is the only reality. There are only 'texts', 'narratives', and subjective 'language games', offering limitless possibilities and eschewing the categories of truth and falsity.

I agree with Ball that almost all political concepts have been and will continue to be in fact *contested*. This means that persons and groups with different normative convictions are likely to use them in different senses, because they have, in everyday usage and in the context of political rhetoric, valuational connotations – positive in the case of freedom, negative in the case of power. This enables *political actors* to use this vocabulary to extoll their political preferences and to disparage those of their adversaries – for example, to recommend social welfare policies under the label of 'freedom from want'. However, as Ball points out, 'essentially contested' does not entail 'essentially contestable'. *Political scientists* are not tied to the language of political rhetoric, and political actors sometimes make some effort at 'resolving those differences through argument and persuasion' (p. 34). Ball continues: 'This requires, as a precondition, a shared language or lexicon.' But this requires, in turn, that such a lexicon be uncontestable, in the sense that its vocabulary be made up of definitions that are not valuationally tinted. But does this not contradict Ball's own contention (quoted earlier) that reconstruction cannot be 'purely descriptive and valuationally neutral'? If political concepts were 'essentially', that is unavoidably, contestable, such an endeavour would be impossible. I therefore agree with Mario Ricciardi's criticism of the essential contestability thesis in his contribution to this volume.

Commitment to a programme of conceptual reconstruction does not, of course, eliminate controversies about the fruitfulness of alternative descriptive definitions.

2.   Social freedom

2.1.   Social freedom and bivalence

Hillel Steiner's essay made me aware of an ambiguity in my original analysis of the concept of social freedom – probably not his intention. I have come to realize that the expression he quotes from *Dimensions of Freedom* – 'with respect to Y, X is free do x' (p. 58) – is misleading when taken as the *definiendum* of interpersonal or social freedom. As Steiner points out, this would indeed lead to the conclusion that, in certain situations, 'X is *both* not free to do x *and* not unfree to do so' (p. 59). It now seems to me that 'free to do x' should not be used at all in the defining expression, and, as it happens, I have not done so in subsequent writings on this topic. As I pointed out in *Political Concepts* (p. 64), while social unfreedom refers to a three-term relation between two actors X and Y and X's possible action x, social freedom 'pertains to two or more alternative actions open to [X], doing x or not doing x, or doing either x or z. I am unfree to do this; I am free to do this or that'. Hence, the expression to be defined should be: 'With respect to Y, X is free to do x *or not to do x*', and the definition: 'if, with respect to Y, X is neither unfree to do x nor unfree not to do x (i.e. not unfree to abstain from doing x)'. This language is incompatible with Steiner's 'conception of freedom that is bivalent: a conception such that ... "unfree to abstain from doing x" *implies* "free to do x"' (p. 65).

Having *freedom with respect to another agent* (social freedom) must nevertheless be distinguished from *freedom of choice* or of action – a two-term relation between one actor X and his possible action x. I lack freedom of choice as to playing the violin, lacking the ability; but I am (socially) free to play or not to play the violin – with respect to everyone (nobody prevents me from playing that instrument). I am (socially) unfree to disregard a red traffic light, but I have freedom of choice of doing so.

As I see it, Belgians are *not* 'appropriately described as not free *to* vote' (p. 60), nor as 'not free to abstain from voting' (p. 60). Rather, Belgians are *unfree* to abstain from voting, in the sense that filling out a ballot is compulsory. But they are free to cast their vote for any party on the ballot or to vote 'blanc'.[2] (Marking a ballot in any way and voting for a party are two different kinds of action.) In the latter sense, the Belgian constitution has vested its citizens 'with the freedom to vote' (p. 65). Unlike Belgians, Americans are free to vote or to abstain, as well as free to cast their vote for the Democratic or the Republican party.

I cannot see any relevant difference between a Belgian being required to vote and someone being bounced out of a night club. Both are unfree to abstain from doing something (i.e. filling out a ballot / leaving the club 'under [one's] own steam' (p. 64)). On the other hand, I agree with Steiner and (the later) Isaiah Berlin that social freedom and unfreedom should be defined independently of what the agent wants or might want to do.

I do not think that Steiner's notion of bivalent freedom is necessary to describe his example of the prisoners. Expressed in my language, they remain unfree to spread error, but have gained a new freedom, namely either to propagate the truth *or to remain silent* (i.e. not to avail themselves of the opportunity given to them.)

'On Oppenheim's analysis, then, I am unfree both to enter and to abstain from entering' the power station (p. 66). Yes, indeed; but there are two different kinds of action involved. Y makes me unfree to enter, since he would punish me if I did, and Z makes me unfree not to enter (i.e. compels me to do so), since he would punish me if I did not. This seems to me a plausible description of such tragic conflicts.

I need not deny that there are 'actions which we're *neither free nor unfree*' to do (p. 59), namely actions not involving any Y who could make it impossible or punishable to perform them. An extreme example: If I am stranded in a hot desert, I may be able to walk and unable to run, but I am neither free to walk or to run, nor unfree to walk, nor unfree to run (with respect to whom?). Such actions are 'not *freedom-relevant*' (p. 59).

Nor does social freedom (in my sense) 'logically commit us to denying that people are free to do things which they actually do' (p. 66) – free to do *or not to do* them. Americans who actually vote Democratic are free to vote Democratic or Republican.

Finally, I cannot find in Steiner's paper any argument incompatible with my thesis that relations of social freedom and unfreedom 'can be empirically identified without recourse to evaluative judgments' (p. 60).

2.2. Social freedom and practical impossibility

Ian Carter agrees with me that one way in which P (a power holder) can make R (a respondent) unfree to do X (an action of R) is by preventing R from doing X. I hold that P can do so by making it either physically or practically impossible for R to do X. It is practically impossible to do X if it is too costly or too difficult or too painful to do so, not just for R, but for any normal agent in a similar situation. (Carter accepts this definition I took over from Alvin Goldman, but proposes to use 'too costly' to cover the two other instances and to add: with a low probability of success (p. 83).) However, Carter considers 'too costly' (in the large sense) a normative expression, and this would make 'practical impossibility' in turn normative; and if 'practical impossibility' were one of the defining conditions of 'social unfreedom', the concepts of social freedom and unfreedom would fail to be descriptive.

It seems to me that 'too costly' is a descriptive notion, and 'doing x is too costly' an empirical statement, but of a particular kind: appraising or estimating or grading in terms of a given standard. Some other examples: appraising a painting by its market value, comparing cars in terms of their performance, giving a student a 'passing grade'. Often the standard of appraisal is not spelled out but tacitly assumed, as in the case of the normal or average agent. I agree that 'the question of which costs render an action practically impossible will only be an empirical one after we have first fixed the confines of the group of individuals from which we are to construct the normal or average agent' (p. 87). Doesn't it follow that the question *does* become empirical once these confines have been circumscribed? They are in general assumed to be the agent's own social group or society at a specified time. I therefore maintain that the concept of practical (as well as that of physical) impossibility is descriptive, and so are those of social freedom and unfreedom. So, it turns out that we both regard social freedom a descriptive concept, but for different reasons. For Carter, 'practical impossibility' is a normative expression, but not an instance of social unfreedom. For me, it is an instance of social freedom; but 'too costly' is a descriptive notion.

Carter states: 'One way in which P can render X practically impossible for R is by rendering X punishable for R' (p. 84). I believe that punishability had better be considered, not a subcategory of prevention, but as a second instance of social unfreedom. Crimes are made punishable because it is practically possible for criminals to commit them; yet, they are, with respect to the authorities, unfree to do so. However, prevention and punishability are overlapping categories. A high probability of severe punishment amounts to practical impossibility, like the captured spy in Carter's example compelled to reveal secrets under threat of torture. On the other hand, poorly enforced laws leave people free to act illegally; for example, drivers are free to violate certain local speed limits.

That R has freedom of choice or of action with respect to X means that R is physically able to do X (although R might be practically incapable of doing so). I therefore agree 'that we would do well to exclude the concept of practical impossibility from our explication of freedom to act' (p. 92), because 'one *is* free *to do* that which is practically impossible' (p. 88). Thus, even if P has made R unfree to do X, R has freedom of action with respect to X, provided he is physically able to do so. As I just indicated, some have freedom (of action) to commit crimes, but are unfree to do so to the extent that they would be punished. The captured spy is physically able to remain silent, hence has freedom of action in that respect, but is unfree to do so with respect to his captors.

Nor is there any connection between practical possibility or impossibility on the one hand, and acting freely or unfreely on the other. I define acting freely or a free action as an action not motivated by fear of punishment. Carter denies that 'acting freely' can be defined empirically (p. 88). It seems to me that the determination of an actor's motives is a matter of empirical investigation. For example, one may pay taxes or abstain from criminal actions freely or unfreely. US citizens are unfree to travel to Cuba; yet, many stay away freely.

2.3.   Social freedom and nomic freedom

Turning now to Amedeo Conte's 'nomic impossibility' as an instance of unfreedom, I wonder whether this is the best expression to describe what he has in mind. His example of the illegality of driving through a red light indicates that he deals with legal prohibitions. Now one's unfreedom to act illegally is not an instance of *impossibility*; that one is unfree to act illegally does not mean that it is *impossible* to do so, but that such actions are *punishable*, hence possible (except in case of high probability of severe punishment). On the other hand (as mentioned before), drivers are free to disregard traffic rules which tend not to be enforced.

Conte's legalistic conception of freedom disregards equally important unfreedom relations involving punishment (and, again, not 'deontic impossibility'). For example, some employers make their employees unfree to criticize them by firing them if they did, and the former are unfree to keep salaries low if the latter would otherwise go on strike.

I agree with Conte that 'anankastic constitutive rules' limit freedom by making certain actions legally impossible. In a state without legal provisions for divorce, couples cannot divorce and are, with respect to the authorities, unfree to do so. It is difficult, on the other hand, to reconcile Conte's 'eidetic-possibility' with my conception of interpersonal or social freedom as a relationship of interaction. One is enabled and, hence, 'made free' to play chess by the *rules* of chess, not by some other *actor* P (unless one could point to the inventor of the game – a rather far-fetched idea). I would simply say that someone who does not 'play by the rules' of chess, doesn't play chess. This is not an instance of a limitation of *freedom*.

3. The national interest

3.1. The national interest as a descriptive concept

The national interest is surely one of the most 'value-laden', and therefore most contested political concepts, used to characterize whatever foreign policy anyone considers strategically or morally justified. Many writers are doubtful about its usefulness for political research. Luigi Bonanate advises philosophers 'not to take the national interest as an objective given' (p. 185), because 'there is no way of determining its content comprehensibly' (p. 174). Similarly, Thomas Pogge holds that there is 'no clear-cut explication of this expression' (p. 154). I have proposed a fairly precise definition of 'the national interest' in terms of certain collective goods at which a government might aim at the foreign policy level: a given foreign policy is in the national interest if it secures the state's independence, territorial integrity, military security, and the population's collective economic well-being. I must admit to Pogge that '[my] conception of the national interest has not come to be widely accepted'. Even so, he envisages the possibility that a consensus might emerge and concedes that, if so, the question of how foreign policy outcomes should be assessed 'would indeed have been overcome' (p. 167).

Kateb provides a definition of 'national interest', and of 'public interest' as well – in terms of justice. Here I would refer to my general objection against normative definitions of political concepts. Whether a policy promotes military security can, at least in principle, be determined by objective criteria; but people with different moral views are bound to disagree as to whether a policy is just. But even if we take as our basis the general principles of Western liberal justice, there are some further objections.

'The public interest is justice' (p. 190). True, both are collective benefits; but unlike justice, the public interest, as I define it, refers to collective *material* well-being. That is why I maintain that 'justice often conflicts with utility and thereby with the public interest' (quoted, p. 190). For example, hiring the best qualified applicants tends to increase productivity, a public interest goal, but may be considered unjust to the educationally disadvantaged. According to Kateb, 'to sever the public interest from justice is to make the concept unusable for political discourse and political theory' (p. 192). But to distinguish them *definitionally* seems to me indispensable for a fruitful discussion about how to balance these two different social goals.

According to Kateb, 'the national interest, like the public interest, is protection ... of justice' (p. 193). Again, I disagree, and for the same reason. Territorial independence and military security are, unlike justice, material goods. There is an additional reason. If the national interest is defined in terms of justice (in the liberal-democratic sense), there are indeed 'only a few nation-states ... to which a national interest can be properly attributed' (p. 194). A national interest could then not be assigned, for example, to Iraq, and none of its foreign policies could be judged conducive or contrary to its national interest. My proposed definition is universally applicable, so that, indeed, 'every nation, whether its polity is autocratic, oligarchic, or democratic, will have a national interest' (p. 196). This seems to me an advantage. It surely makes sense to ask whether Hitler's and Stalin's conclusion of the non-aggression pact in 1940 served the military security of Nazi Germany or Soviet Russia.

Kateb also criticizes me for offering non-distributive definitions of public and national interest. He is correct in disagreeing with my statement that public interest policies 'promote the welfare of the public as a whole rather than the personal welfare of each, or any, of its members' (quoted, p. 189). I should have said: to serve the public interest is to secure the *long-range* material well-being of the public as a whole rather than the *short-term* self-interest of each. This formulation brings out more clearly that 'the public interest' cannot be defined reductively as the aggregate of individual interests. The public interest consists essentially in the production of public goods such as free public education, public safety, clean air. Public goods are non-excludable; that is, those who fail to contribute cannot be excluded from their consumption. It is therefore in the short-term self-interest of each to free ride; but the public good will not be created unless many, if not all, cooperate. This is why I consider the public interest a non-distributive, collective concept. It is not the case that 'any limitation on selfishness is itself an abridgment of self-interest' (p. 189). Limiting self-interest may be required to promote the public interest which in turn may benefit all in the long run. However, I am not elevating the public interest into some kind of general will, which would 'justify the sacrifice of real persons for or to an abstraction' (p. 189). The *concept* of the public interest is an abstraction; but so is the concept of a person. Both designate something which has 'real existence' (p. 189), just as forests exist in reality no less than trees.

I also agree with Kateb's criticism of my generalization that 'most people care little about the "common good" and more about their individual and group interests' (quoted, p. 190). People often do act in the public interest, motivated either by utilitarian estimates of long-range benefits, or by moral considerations, or to avoid governmental sanctions. I share Kateb's view that the latter is only one of the possible grounds for social cooperation.

The national interest, as I define it, is, like the public interest, a non-distributive concept. It, too, refers to public goods such as territorial independence or collective well-being (here there is an overlap between public interest and national interest policies). In democratic societies, all or most citizens tend to care about the various components of the national interest; not so in autocratic regimes where many persons or groups might be alienated from government or even country.

I do not deny that *politicians* use the expression 'national interest' rhetorically 'to impose [their] will both within and outside the state' (Bonanate, p. 175); the more reason for *political scientists* to apply the concept only to policies meeting the objective criteria specified in the definition. If the national interest were 'merely the synonym of "that which states do"' (p. 175), it would be impossible to ascertain whether or not, for example, America's military intervention in Vietnam or Iraq or Kosovo was in its national interest.

3.2.   The national interest and rationality

Contrary to Kateb, I do not think there is any contradiction between wanting 'to offer purely descriptive non-normative conceptual *definitions*' of such concepts as public and national interest and claiming that '*appeals* to both are, in practice, invariably normative' (p. 191; my italics). As I indicated, the concepts of practical impossibility and of national interest are *definable* in descriptive terms; but statements such as 'you ought not to do what is practically impossible (but physically possible)'; or 'statesmen ought to pursue the national interest' are, of course, normative appeals. The question remains: are these norms of rationality or of morality?

I used to think that moral norms did not apply to practical impossibility or necessity. This would mean, to take Carter's example, that if it is practically unavoidable for a captured spy to reveal his secrets under threat of torture, it would not be relevant to consider him under a moral obligation to remain silent nevertheless. Carter, in his contribution, has shown that it is to the point to judge that he ought to have resisted or that it was morally permissible to give in. Supererogatory and excusable actions are within the purview of morality. While 'ought' implies 'strict possibility' is a metaethical principle to the effect that moral judgements are inapplicable to physically unavailable actions, I now agree that '"ought" implies "practical possibility"' is a moral norm (but of a 'higher order') stating that there is no moral duty to do what one practically cannot do, as opposed to the ethics of supererogation. (However, the statement '"ought" implies "practical possibility"' is a moral norm' is itself a metaethical statement, about the area of relevance of moral judgements.) Similarly, after the attack on Pearl Harbor, it was practically necessary for the United States to defend its national security by going to war against Japan. Yet, an extreme pacifist might have argued that, from a moral point of view the government should have placed pacifist principles above national interest, and not have taken up arms – a theoretical if not practical possibility.

While practical necessity and impossibility are part of the defining expression of social freedom, I now avoid these concepts in connection with the question of why governments ought to adopt national interest policies. In a recent paper 'The National Interest: A Basic Concept' I answer this question in terms of instrumental rationality. It is rational for governments to pursue their national interest, and to do so by the best available foreign policies. If it is rational to do so, it is redundant to claim that they ought to act that way on moral grounds.

The adequacy of means to given ends is, at least in theory, a matter of empirical, not moral judgement.

How can I claim that it is *instrumentally* rational for government to pursue its national interest? Isn't the national interest an aim in itself rather than a means to more ultimate goals? I did not make it sufficiently clear that the national interest should be considered a primary good in Rawls's sense, in turn a necessary means to the attainment of whatever may be the government's final ends. Thus, if after Pearl Harbor, war was the only rational way to safeguard America's national interest, and this intermediary goal in turn necessary to preserve its 'way of life', then it is redundant to justify this course of action by moral arguments.

I explicitly deny that the national interest 'can be promoted only by violence or its threat' (Kateb, p. 192). Nor am I bound to give 'countenance, in some respects, to the unbridled and self-destructive fantasy-projects of leaders, elites, and people alike' (p. 203). Self-destructive projects are, by definition, not rational from the point of view of the national interest of any state. That some dictator adopts such self-destructive policies may be to our advantage. If a democratic regime fails to secure its national interest in a rational way, we must deplore it.

Pursuing foreign policy goals different from those of the national interest, such as the protection of human rights abroad, will meet the standards of rationality, provided they are compatible with the primary goal. As Pogge points out, 'the prevention of human rights problems abroad is at best only one among many goals of our foreign policy' (p. 154). Governments must take into account the cost of such policies in terms 'of all our other foreign-policy goals as well' (p. 155), and especially in terms of the national interest. Thus, it would not be rational to adopt a human rights policy incompatible with the national interest. For example, some claim that the national interest of the United States requires its foreign policy towards China to be guided by a different principle: non-interference in the domestic matters of other states. To protect human rights at home and not to do so abroad is not – contrary to Kateb – 'self-inconsistent', let alone 'the height of irrationality' (p. 194), but may be, on the contrary, rational in view of the national interest.

On the other hand, it may yet be rational to adopt human rights policies involving a small sacrifice in terms of the national interest. Thomas Pogge has convinced me that Herbert Simon's notion of *satisficing* is applicable here: with respect to the national interest, it is sometimes rational to choose 'the next best solution' for the sake of some different principle, such as the promotion of human rights. Even so, Pogge himself points to some obstacles: 'The international criterion for the legitimacy of governments is effective control' (p. 163). Hence, governments violating basic rights, once in control, 'can count on all the rewards of international recognition' (p. 163), including their right to be immune from interference by governments committed to the protection of human rights.

Military intervention for human rights purposes 'will in many cases produce more harm than good' (p. 166), and all non-military 'humanitarian interventions are bad in a sense' (p. 153). This leaves only one alternative: 'reforms of global institutions, which ought to provide strong incentives to national societies toward fulfilling the human rights of their members' (p. 166). But incentives would not be sufficient. To be effective, such international institutions would have to include some enforceable limitations of national sovereignty. Even some of the most powerful democracies are unlikely to give their assent, not to speak of the many non-democratic regimes.

Pogge's more specific recommendations, too, seem to me unrealistic for reasons additional to those he himself provides. Refusing arms sales to repressive governments, 'no matter how much we may stand to gain in terms of our other goals' (p. 156)? Experience shows that such measures, to be without loopholes, would require agreement among all arms exporting governments, including all repressive ones – an unlikely prospect.

Is a would-be dictator, out to suppress human rights, likely to be deterred from overthrowing a democratic government because the latter had previously signed a treaty 'pre-authorizing a humanitarian intervention against [itself]' (p. 158) by other states in such a case? Would a democratic government feeling itself in danger of being overthrown conclude such a treaty, thereby implicitly acknowledging its own weakness?

For the same reason, I am sceptical about Pogge's proposal that international laws permit democratic governments to decline responsibility 'for repaying loans incurred by a future government that will have ruled in violation of ... democratic procedures' (p. 164).

3.3. The national interest and morality

Bonanate wonders 'whether we should not ... admit that *all* foreign policy decisions fall within [the range of morality]' (p. 177), whereas my view must lead to the conclusion that a national interest policy 'cannot be subject to any moral evaluation' (p. 174). Similarly, Kateb makes me claim that 'in a condition of [international] anarchy, morality is irrelevant except incidentally' (p. 201). I do claim, on the contrary, that morality has its place in foreign policy making. Moral judgements are relevant whenever there is a choice between alternative policies conducive to the national interest or a choice of goals different from, but compatible with, the national interest. To take Bonanate's example: was it wrong for the Italian government to have close economic relations with Algeria's authoritarian regime instead of acquiring raw materials elsewhere, even at a higher price. The moral question is relevant, if the latter policy would still at least have satisfied Italy's national interest. Otherwise, that policy would not have been rational, and moral condemnation would have been redundant. (Incidentally, it is doubtful whether such a policy would have contributed to the development of democratic institutions in Algeria.) At other places in his chapter, Bonanate seems to accept these criteria and concludes that the difference between our positions 'regards the breadth of the area within which moral judgments about foreign policy are relevant' (p. 183). On the one hand, he considers the range I assign to this area 'fairly limited' (p. 183), but at another place, he judges it 'quite substantial' (p. 176).

Kateb, while denying that I leave any place to morality in foreign policy, nevertheless ascribes to me a specific moral view, namely 'that every nation-state as such *deserves* to exist' (p. 196), and has the '*right* of self-preservation' (p. 199, my italics). Similarly, Bobbio tends to subsume my view under the morality of reason of state (pp. 214–15), the *right* of the state (every state? '*my* country, right or wrong'?) to pursue its national interest, even by immoral means. That it is rational for every government to pursue its national interest (as a means to its ultimate purposes) does not imply that to do so is morally right (or wrong). It is not a plea for nationalism. I myself would prefer a world without national borders. As this is, for the time being, a utopian dream, I can only hope that democratic governments pursue their long-range national interests more rationally than autocratic ones – a necessary condition for the survival of democratic values.

Bonanate believes that there is a single standard of morality by which to judge the rightness or wrongness of any country's foreign policies, namely 'world public opinion' (p. 184). I would deny that there is such a thing. Throughout history, different moral standards have been adopted by and within different societies, and economic globalization has not given rise to a global morality. The same military action tends to be condemned as aggression (usually by the victim) and justified as self-defence (usually by the attacker). Iraq's invasion of Kuwait has not met with 'almost complete disapproval on the part of world public opinion' (p. 173), and it is doubtful whether the United States would have 'punished the aggressor' were there no oil underground. Similarly, according to Pogge, 'most of the world's powerful states claim a commitment to human rights' (p. 158), including those who do not practice what they preach. That 'all human beings ... have exactly the same human rights' (p. 159) expresses essentially the moral view of Western liberal societies. In Saudi Arabia (to take a single example), the unequal status of men and women is generally accepted as just even by women. Powerful Eastern governments like China or Iran accuse the West of cultural imperialism, using the idea of universal human rights to justify their economic domination over less developed countries. Of course, these governments in turn invoke cultural relativism to legitimize suppression of their own subject's basic rights.

The question is rather: is a given foreign policy to which moral standards are applicable right or wrong according to *our own* principles of liberal-democratic morality? 'That every society ... ought to be so organized that all its participants enjoy secure access to [human rights]' (p. 160) expresses the conviction prevalent in our Western culture.

In spite of my scepticism, shared to some extent by Pogge, it cannot be denied that there has lately been some progress in the area of international protection of human rights, among countries securing them to a large extent within their own borders. Perhaps the most radical example is the European Court of Human Rights in Strasbourg. Citizens of member countries can petition the Court against their own governments, and its decisions are binding on member governments, and generally carried out, including awards of compensation. By contrast, the United States has been reluctant to adhere to binding human rights conventions. The US government did not back the project of an international criminal court, and has not ratified a number of international treaties, including a convention banning land mines.

Perhaps non-governmental organizations such as Amnesty International provide more hope for progress on a worldwide scale. There is no doubt that at least some prisoners of conscience all over the world owe their freedom, or at least some improvement of their conditions, to individual or group pressure of this kind. Claims that 'all human beings have equal status' with respect to human rights

(p. 159) made by intellectuals without political power are bound to have little impact on a desperate human predicament.

I am digressing, taken by a topic which worries me greatly; those of my writings that are critically examined by the contributors to this volume do not deal with substantive moral issues of domestic or foreign policy. Even so, Bonanate wonders why, in the book he discusses, 'the question of how a government is to proceed in addressing such moral dilemmas' remains unsolved (pp. 176–7). My answer: it did not fall within my topic to make moral judgements but only to delimit their area of relevance. Nor did I deal with the rightness or wrongness of any government's ultimate purposes with respect to which the pursuit of the national interest is the necessary means.

Metaethical issues, too, are outside the purview of the book under discussion. Yet, Bonanate identifies me, at least in principle, with ethical non-cognitivism. It is true that I have defended this metaethical theory in some of my other writings. The controversy between cognitivists and non-cognitivists concerns the logical status of *intrinsic* moral judgements. Here I had to deal only with judgements of instrumental rationality and morality. There is no disagreement between the two metaethical schools about judgements of means to given ends. These are, at least in principle, to be assessed on the basis of empirical criteria.

For the same reason, I have not sided with either deontological or consequentialist ethics (p. 177). Whether morality should be judged on the basis of principles (e.g. rightness) or consequences (e.g. promoting happiness) pertains, again, only to intrinsic norms, such as the ultimate ends of governments. I have taken these ends as given. To determine the adequacy of means to ends is, of course, to determine consequences.

All the writings discussed here deal with the analysis of basic political concepts and the logic of normative political discourse. These are preliminary questions. To clarify them seems to me nevertheless indispensable for fruitful discussions of concrete political issues.[3]

Notes

1. Page numbers in the text refer to the essays in the present volume.
2. In terms of my proposed language, of the six propositions Steiner examines (p. 60), I consider 3 true, 6 false, and 1, 2, 4 and 5 not meaningful.
3. This essay greatly benefited from Ian Carter's numerous comments.

Bibliography of the Publications of Felix E. Oppenheim

1. Books

[1961] *Dimensions of Freedom: an Analysis* (New York: St. Martin's Press). Italian trans. *Dimensioni della libertà* (Milano: Feltrinelli, 1964; 2nd edn, 1984).

[1968] *Moral Principles in Political Philosophy* (New York: Random House). 2nd edn with a postscript 1975 (New York: Random House). Italian trans. of the 1st edn *Etica e filosofia politica* (Bologna: Il Mulino, 1971). Spanish trans. of the 1st edn *Etica y filosofia politica* (Mexico D.F.: Fondo de cultura economica, 1975).

[1981] *Political Concepts: a Reconstruction* (Chicago: University of Chicago Press). Italian trans. *Concetti Politici. Una Ricostruzione* (Bologna: Il Mulino, 1985). Spanish trans. *Conceptos Politicos. Una reconstruction* (Madrid: Editorial Tecnos, 1987).

[1991] *The Role of Morality in Foreign Policy* (Lexington, Mass.: Lexington Books). Italian trans. *Il ruolo della moralità in politica estera* (Milano: Franco Angeli, 1993).

2. Articles

[1944] 'Outline of a Logical Analysis of Law', *Philosophy of Science*, 11, pp. 142–60. Spanish trans. 'Lineamientos de un analisis logico del derecho' (Valencia: Oficina latinoamericana de investigaciones juridicas y sociales, 1980). Italian trans. 'Lineamenti di analisi logica del diritto', in U. Scarpelli and P. Di Lucia (eds), *Il linguaggio del diritto* (Milano: LED, 1994), pp. 59–85.

[1947–48] 'The Prospects of Italian Democracy', *Public Opinion Quarterly*, 11, pp. 572–80.

[1948] 'Good Will – Our Investment in Europe', *Current History*, 14, pp. 141–5.

[1950a] 'Belgian Political Parties Since Liberation', *The Review of Politics*, 12, pp. 99–119.

[1950b] 'Relativism, Absolutism and Democracy', *The American Political Science Review*, 44, pp. 951–60.

[1953] 'Rational Choice', *The Journal of Philosophy*, 50, pp. 341–50.

[1955a] 'Interpersonal Freedom and Freedom of Action', *The American Political Science Review*, 49, pp. 353–63.

[1955b] 'Control and Unfreedom', *Philosophy of Science*, 22, pp. 280–8.

[1955c] 'In Defence of Relativism', *The Western Political Quarterly*, 8, pp. 411–17.

[1955d] 'Belgium: Party Cleavage and Compromise', in S. Neumann (ed.), *Modern Political Parties. Approaches to Comparative Politics* (Chicago: University of Chicago Press) pp. 155–68.

[1957a] 'The Natural Law Thesis: Affirmation or Denial?', *The American Political Science Review*, 51, pp. 41–53, with a comment by Harry J. Jaffa, 'In Defence of "The Natural Law Thesis"', *The American Political Science Review*, 51, pp. 54–66.

Italian trans. 'La tesi del diritto naturale: affermazione o negazione?', in U. Scarpelli (ed.), *Diritto e analisi del linguaggio* (Milano: Edizioni Comunità, 1976), pp. 95–119.

[1957b] 'Non-Cognitivist Rebuttal', *The American Political Science Review*, 51, pp. 65–6.

[1958] 'An Analysis of Political Control: Actual and Potential', *The Journal of Politics*, 20, pp. 515–34.

[1960a] 'Degrees of Power and Freedom', *The American Political Science Review*, 54, pp. 437–46.

[1960b] 'Evaluating Interpersonal Freedoms', *The Journal of Philosophy*, 57, pp. 373–83.

[1962a] 'Instrumental Values and Ultimate Goals', *The American Political Science Review*, 66, pp. 975–6.

[1962b] 'Freedom – An Empirical Interpretation', *Nomos*, 4, pp. 274–88.

[1964a] 'Rationalism and Liberalism', *World Politics*, 16, pp. 341–61.

[1964b] 'The Metaethics of Natural Law', in S. Hook (ed.), *Law and Philosophy* (New York: New York University Press), pp. 241–6.

[1964c] 'Rational Decisions and Intrinsic Valuations', *Nomos*, 7, pp. 217–20.

[1965a] 'Scelta razionale e fini politici', *Rivista di Filosofia*, 56, pp. 138–49.

[1965b] 'Libertà come fatto e come valore' (a symposium with Norberto Bobbio, Alessandro Passerin d'Entreves and Uberto Scarpelli), *Rivista di Filosofia*, 56, pp. 350–4.

[1968a] 'Eguaglianza come concetto descrittivo', *Rivista di Filosofia*, 59, pp. 255–75.

[1968b] 'Equality' and 'Freedom' entries in *International Encyclopedia of the Social Sciences* (New York: Free Press), pp. 102–8 and 554–9 respectively.

[1970] 'Egalitarianism as a Descriptive Concept', *American Philosophical Quarterly*, 7, pp. 143–52.

[1971a] 'Democracy – Characteristics Included and Excluded', *The Monist*, 55, pp. 29–50.

[1971b] 'Defence of Noncognitivism Defended', *The American Political Science Review*, 65, pp. 1115–16. This is a reply to Donald Van De Veer, 'Oppenheim's Defence of Noncognitivism', *The American Political Science Review*, 65, pp. 1105–14. In the same issue of the journal there is also a 'Rejoinder to Oppenheim's "Comment"' by Donald Van De Veer, pp. 1117–18.

[1971c] 'Noncognitivism Reaffirmed', *The Philosophy Forum*, 10.

[1971d] 'Comments', in R. H. Grimm and A. F. Mackay (eds), *Society – Revolution and Reform* (Cleveland and London: The Press of Western Reserve University), pp. 53–8.

[1972] 'Egalitarianism and Moral Judgements', *Ethics*, 82, pp. 171–2. This is a reply to Virginia Held, 'Egalitarianism and Relevance', *Ethics*, 81 (1971).

[1973a] '"Facts" and "Values" in Politics: Are They Separable?', *Political Theory*, 1, pp. 54–68.

[1973b] 'Descriptive Terms of Political Discourse: A Rejoinder to Virginia Held', *Political Theory*, 1, pp. 76–8.

[1975a] 'Self-interest and Public Interest', *Political Theory*, 3, pp. 259–76.

[1975b] 'The Language of Political Enquiry: Problems of Clarification', in N. Polsby and F. Greenstein (eds), *Handbook of Political Science*, vol. I (Reading, Mass.: Addison-Wesley), pp. 283–335.

[1975c] 'Power and Causality', in B. Barry (ed.), *Power and Political Theory* (London: Wiley), pp. 103–16.

[1976] 'Giustizia', 'Libertà' and 'Eguaglianza', entries in *Dizionario di Politica*, ed. N. Bobbio and N. Matteucci (Torino: Utet), pp. 437–42; 548–53 and 1060–8 respectively.

[1977a] 'Rationality and Egalitarianism', *Nomos*, 17, pp. 280–5.

[1977b] 'Equality, Groups and Quotas', *American Journal of Political Science*, 21, pp. 65–9.

[1978] '"Power" Revisited', *The Journal of Politics*, 40, pp. 589–608. Italian trans. 'Il concetto di potere revisitato', *Rivista Italiana di Scienza Politica*, 8, 1978, pp. 57–76.

[1979] 'Justifications récentes de l'idéologie politique', *Revue Européenne des Sciences Sociales*, 17, pp. 147–58.

[1980a] 'Ideology and Objectivity', in M. Cranston and P. Mair (eds), *Ideology and Politics* (Firenze: Le Monnier), pp. 143–6

[1980b] 'Egalitarian Rules of Distribution', *Ethics*, 90, pp. 164–79.

[1984] 'Fallacies and Dangers of "Inconsequence"', *Polity*, 17, pp. 161–3.

[1985] '"Constraints on Freedom" as a Descriptive Concept', *Ethics*, 95, pp. 305–30.

[1986] 'Justification in Ethics: Its Limitations', *Nomos*, 28, pp. 28–32.

[1987a] 'Non-cognitivismo, razionalità e relativismo', *Rivista di Filosofia*, 78, pp. 17–29.

[1987b] 'National Interest, Rationality and Morality', *Political Theory*, 15, pp. 369–89. Italian trans. 'Interesse nazionale, razionalità e moralità', *Teoria Politica*, 3, pp. 3–25.

[1995a] 'Social Freedom and Its Parameters', *Journal of Theoretical Politics*, 7, pp. 403–20.

[1995b] 'La libertà sociale e i suoi parametri', *Sociologia del diritto*, 22, pp. 5–37.

[1995c] 'Si può misurare la libertà complessiva? Nota critica agli scritti di Ian Carter', *Quaderni di Scienza politica*, 2, pp. 455–61.

[1995d] 'The Judge as Legislator', in L. Gianformaggio and S. P. Paulson (eds), *Cognition and Interpretation of Law* (Torino: Giappichelli), pp. 289–94.

[1998a] 'Esistono criteri oggettivi di moralità politica?', *Sociologia del diritto*, 25, pp. 5–22.

[1998b] 'The Subjectivity of Moral Judgements: a Defence', *Critical Review of International Social and Political Philosophy*, 1, pp. 42–61.

[2001] 'Social Freedom: Definition, Measurability, Valuation', in P. Pattanaik, M. Salles and K. Suzumura (eds), *Non-Welfarist Issues in Normative Economics*, special issue of *Social Choice and Welfare*.

Index